'Counsellor ... for Segal's
lightly wor ... r steadfast
honesty an ...

... ert member
... & 2017 and
... HS England

'Julia Segal has brought to our shelves one of the most important books
of this decade and it will be of considerable value to those whose work
or life brings them into contact with illness or disability.'

– *Dr Anita Rose, Consultant Clinical Neuropsychologist*

'A really sensitive and straightforward yet comprehensive book. A great
achievement on a really needed, under-acknowledged, yet massive and
ever-present subject.'

– *Lionel Roth, husband and carer*

The Trouble with Illness

How Illness and Disability
Affect Relationships

Julia Segal

Jessica Kingsley *Publishers*
London and Philadelphia

First published in 2017
by Jessica Kingsley Publishers
73 Collier Street
London N1 9BE, UK
and
400 Market Street, Suite 400
Philadelphia, PA 19106, USA

www.jkp.com

Library of Congress Cataloging in Publication Data
A CIP catalog record for this book is available from the Library of Congress

British Library Cataloguing in Publication Data
A CIP catalogue record for this book is available from the British Library

ISBN 978 1 78592 332 6
eISBN 978 1 78450 651 3

Printed and bound in Great Britain

To all those who have shared their stories with me and contributed to my understanding of the world, in gratitude.

Contents

Introduction

Illness and disability 'wrong-foot' not only those who have them, but also anyone who comes into contact with them. Family and professionals, children and adults, friends and neighbours all find themselves thinking uncomfortable thoughts, and having uncomfortable feelings, saying the wrong thing or awkwardly avoiding saying anything – which feels just as bad – as a result of the discomfort caused by an illness. This discomfort may not be named. Children and young people with ill parents may not recognise it for what it is for many years and may misattribute the 'wrongness' actually caused by the illness or disabling condition to themselves, their own 'failings'. These feelings can be buried – they do not make up the whole of life. Meanwhile, life can be enjoyed, and there may be plenty of pleasures to distract and to contribute to a good life. But free, open communication can be inhibited – and this can interfere with long-term relationships. Relationships with sexual partners, with employers (who can take the place of a parent) and with friends, and between professionals and their clients, can all be affected by the way shameful feelings arising originally in connection with an illness interrupt communication. It is easier to cut off uncomfortable feelings than to admit their presence, but this may mean cutting off communication with some part of the self. A distance is set up: lovers feel they are excluded in some way; relations with other people can become strained; there is a sense of being uncomfortable in one's own skin. Worse, other people can be made to feel guilty, ashamed or bad as a means of getting rid of one's own such feelings into them.

If people recognise this situation and allow themselves to own the conflicting feelings which the illness or disability arouses, if they can share the shame or the guilt, they can reduce the enormity of their feelings towards this 'bad' self, so it no longer has to be denied ('I'm not like that! That's not me!'). No longer having to cut off awareness of this bad self, they may also find it easier to remain in touch with the ill person – and with a carer partner too, perhaps. Professionals find it easier to go back to an ill client who makes them feel reproached and alienated if they recognise that the client also probably feels just as reproached and alienated, and that it might be possible to share such feelings and even laugh about them. Family members may be able to share and clear up guilty thoughts or feelings, face up to the anger aroused by the illness, rather than avoiding a more real emotional contact and leaving the ill person isolated, perhaps with an equally isolated carer partner. Adolescents generally hate to recognise conflicting feelings; they want the world to be clearly 'good' or 'bad'. But age can bring more tolerance for the fact that goodness and badness cannot be fully separated, and that good people have bad thoughts and feelings when someone is ill.

WHAT PEOPLE SAY ABOUT ILLNESS

Family

> 'My mother was in pain a lot when I was a child. I didn't realise it was affecting me until my primary school headmistress met me in the street and asked me how my mother was, and I burst into tears. I was as shocked as she was.'

> 'Everything was fine until – oh, three years ago. What was going on then? Oh, I suppose, that must have been when I was in hospital. They thought I was going to die.'

> 'He was wonderful while I was ill; he was there at the hospital every day, he looked after me and took care of everything. But I came home yesterday and he had gone. He'd taken everything.'

'My [seven-year-old] daughter doesn't care about my illness. She never asks anything. She doesn't seem bothered at all. Actually, she behaves as if she was much younger than she is. It drives me mad sometimes.'

'You're on your own with it. Nobody really understands.'

'People always ask "How is she?" but they never ask how I am.'

'When I got ill again, my sister said about my husband, "Oh, poor John!" As if it was him that was ill! She always liked him better than she liked me. He couldn't bear me being ill; he always had to say "I'm ill too!" when there was nothing wrong with him really.'

Families' feelings about professionals

'I used to think, you know, you get ill, you go to the doctor, he gives you a pill and you get better. I got really angry with one doctor when I saw him six years ago, I wanted some answers and I thought he was just patronising me. But I now realise he actually didn't have any answers.'

'My GP says he will give me anything I want [to help my husband who is seriously ill and disabled with a long-term chronic disease] but I don't know what I want; I want him to tell me what to do, not ask me! How can I know? I'm not a doctor!'

'The nurses come in and they know everything and they won't listen when we tell them, "You have to do it this way." I can see she's hurting him when she moves him like that, but she won't take any notice of what I say.'

Professionals' feelings about families

'It's difficult going to see Mrs X. You never know if she will be friendly and grateful for what you do, or if she is going to bite your head off.'

'I'm finding it really hard to let go of Mrs Y. There's nothing more we can do for her, but she's always so pleased to see us, and she is so sad, she looks so forlorn when we talk about stopping coming. She's so alone.'

'The family are furious that we are not offering any more treatment. They think it means we've given up on him getting better. He might still improve, but it will be such a small improvement and will take so long and would require much more capacity for exercise than we think he has. They just want us in every day and we haven't got the staff. I feel terrible about it, but there's no more we can do. They don't want to accept he will not get back to what he was, and they are taking it out on us.'

'I love my job. I love working with Z. She picks up whatever you offer her and when you come back the next week she's worked with it, something has changed. It's a wonderful feeling. She has so much to cope with, her life is so hard, she's in so much pain, but she has this incredible determination and capacity to think and to learn. I'm not sure I'd be as resilient as she is, in her circumstances.'

ABOUT THIS BOOK

This is a book about the effects of living with illness and changing disability on the mind, on thoughts, on feelings and on the way people live their lives. It is about caring and being cared for, and about not caring and resisting dependency. It is a book for those who are interested in the way a changing health condition can affect relationships: through the understanding, assumptions, thoughts, beliefs, feelings and behaviour, not only of the person with the condition themselves, but also family, friends and professionals. It is about loving and being loved; about wanting to make someone better. It is also about hating illness and disability, about feeling useless and impotent and furious and frustrated, and about cutting off all feelings connected with illness or bodies. It is about recovering as well as about getting worse. It is about depending on 'the kindness of strangers'; about fighting to maintain independence and normality; about the realities of losing aspects of your body and your mind, or those of someone you love or once loved. It is also about being professional in the face of illness, and the difficulties people can have in coping with professionals.

This book is not about physical and practical aspects of illness except insofar as they affect people emotionally. There are other books and websites which offer practical support and advice for particular conditions.

Primarily the book is intended to contribute to the understanding of how people feel and react in the context of illness or damage to the body, both short-term and long-term. Illnesses can insert a wedge between people; create different experiences where previously they were similar. Lack of understanding, resentment and isolation can push people apart. However, understanding can transform a situation or a relationship: it can reduce anxiety; enable change to take place with less damage; allow people to grieve, to let go and move on without having to do violence to memories of the past, or to the self or to others. It can make a significant difference to the way people feel about each other and about themselves. Better understanding makes it harder to judge harshly; it can prevent unwitting cruelty.

Based on 35 years of my work as a psychoanalytically informed counsellor, lecturer and trainer, this book draws together some of the insights I have gained from working with clients who either have a serious health condition themselves, or who live with or care for someone who has one. With Karl Marx, I believe that the point is not simply to understand the world, but also to change it; with Sigmund Freud, we know that understanding can be a potent force for change. Over a lifetime of helping people to sort out their thoughts and beliefs I have seen lives transformed by the development of a new understanding of the mechanisms at work in relationships when an illness is involved. My own understanding comes from several sources, of which the most important derives from the people who have talked to me and worked with me – people with multiple sclerosis or other illnesses, 'carers' and professionals. They have shown me the effects of illness (and of attempts at cure, including both prescribed and illegal drugs) on themselves and their families. My theoretical base was the work of Melanie Klein and other psychoanalysts, in particular Hanna Segal, but I have also been influenced by Carl Rogers and other theorists of counselling and psychotherapy, including CBT practitioners. The more recent work of neuropsychologists such as Damasio has also been both stimulating and enlightening; the attachment theorists have, I think, provided a neurological view of the insights of psychoanalysts. Working with clients in counselling and with members of multidisciplinary teams, as well as teaching medical students, doctors, nurses, counsellors, carers (both professional and informal), physiotherapists, occupational therapists and the general public, has helped me to develop those ideas which seem of most practical value in helping people to understand – and often to change – both professional and personal relationships.

I am very grateful to all those who have trusted me enough to talk about their own or others' illnesses – this includes friends and family as well as clients. I am particularly grateful to those who have explicitly allowed me to use their testimony; also to those whose testimony has stayed in my mind and has coloured my experience. I have sometimes used words which derive from work with clients or conversations with family or friends who have not been asked for permission: I have disguised these, but the clients, family or friends themselves may think they recognise them, rightly or wrongly, through the disguise. I am very grateful to these people, and I sincerely hope they will not be offended or distressed. I have assumed, I hope correctly, that they will understand the motives for using their words, and will be glad that their insights, even if distorted through my lens and for this book, may help others. If not, I am truly sorry. If they would like personal thanks, or to disagree with the construction I appear to have put upon their words, please contact me. I have not used information from people who have asked me not to include them. The days when professionals could write with impunity (and sometimes insultingly) about clients have gone: we are still seeking ways of passing on professional insights for the common good, while recognising and respecting the contributions and the rights of clients. This, alongside my website, www.thetroublewithillness.com, is one of my attempts.

I have also used my own personal experience. In writing this book over many years I have gradually become aware that I am the child of parents who were both ill for a while when I was a child, and that this has had lasting effects. I am grateful to both my parents for the ways they brought me up, and particularly because they both survived to an old age, giving us the opportunity to deal with many of the issues which arose between us.

Because it is based mostly on work I did some years ago, there is little mention of the effects of the internet on living with illness and disability. I mostly came across it in terms of people seeking information, and I refer to this. However, gaming, Skype, texting and various forms of photo-messaging create and maintain relationships in new ways, as do social media, for better or worse. I am not sure if the increased chances of regularly seeing other people at their best, having fun, in fact increases people's happiness: there is some evidence that it makes them feel worse. However, I have to confess ignorance in this field and leave it to others to discuss the effect of these changes on people who are ill or disabled and those who care for them.

A NOTE ABOUT THEORY

I tried initially to write this book without recourse to anything which might be called 'theory'. I wanted to write in a way which was accessible to a lay reader and to professionals outside the psychotherapy or counselling world. However, the ideas of Melanie Klein and her colleagues, unfashionable as they are in some circles, have in fact made sense to me and to my clients over a period of many years, and they are integral to the way I think. My first book, *Phantasy in Everyday Life* (Segal 1985), was written at a time when few people knew anything of Klein, and described Kleinian ideas with very little jargon. This time I wanted to include the technical terms because there will be more readers for whom the links are useful and for whom they make sense. I have mostly limited the theory explanations to Chapter 2, and retained more 'lay' language throughout the other chapters of the book.

Klein's concept of 'projective identification' has achieved world-wide recognition. I use this concept, and clients have found it helpful when I have used it, and also when I have explained it to them (rather to the disapproval of my psychodynamic supervisors, who considered explanations as distracting from the real work of understanding the client), so I have tried to explain it in this book. There are several other psychoanalytic concepts which I feel I have only begun to understand after many years; these include not only the concepts of grief and mourning themselves, but also the idea of the 'Good Object'. I dislike the name 'Good Object', but I have not found a better one, except, sometimes, the 'mother-in-the-head', although this does not convey the full meaning at all.

What I have understood for a very long time is that people are not just concerned about themselves and their own lives. In a sense I learnt this in Sunday School, as a teenager – that happiness depends on other people in one's life being happy, too. In working with clients it was obvious very quickly that their concerns when they were ill were not just for themselves, but for the people they loved or cared for. Klein's emphasis on the relation with their Objects, the 'not-me' people in their internal worlds, completely fitted with this.

There were other ideas I found less obvious. When I began working as a counsellor, I told Hanna Segal (one of Klein's favourite pupils, from whom I learnt most of my Kleinian theory) that I sometimes worried that I might say something that caused trouble: that I might put ideas into their heads. She said, rather drily, that if I thought of it when I was with a client, they would already have thought of it without me. Once I overcame my momentary humiliation, I tried this, and found it was indeed true. Thoughts which came into my own mind, which I hesitated to say, turned out to be thoughts which had troubled clients for a long time and which absolutely needed to be discussed.

'Idealisation is a defence against persecutory phantasies, not reality' is one of my favourite Kleinian ideas. This draws attention to the fact that it is not reality which clients fear when they deny something about their illness or its significance, but something which is clearly *worse than* reality. Once people could be persuaded to talk about the things they found most frightening about their illness, some at least of the fears melted away. I sometimes translated it into 'There may be lots of bad or frightening thoughts you've hidden under the carpet; after we've looked at them you can put them back, but I think you'll find that the lump they make is smaller and less likely to trip you up.' We were left sometimes with grief, but this is different. Grief was something many clients seemed to know even less about than I did, but over the years I learnt, from them, mostly, how it worked. Freud's *Mourning and Melancholia* (1917) and Melanie Klein's *Mourning and its Relation to Manic-Depressive States* (1940) also helped.

There was another lesson I learnt from Hanna Segal, which was how to give an interpretation outside the analytic consulting room without being insulting. (She always maintained that she only interpreted when paid for it; never in a social context. Klein had been very insistent, in particular, that her pupils should not analyse their own children, on the grounds that it was too intrusive and the child needed its privacy.) When I first joined her family and had a mild flu, I told Segal cheerfully that I often got ill around February. She asked me when my little brother's birthday was (February), and then said, carefully, 'Sometimes people get ill around the time of their next youngest sibling's birthday.' This was all she said and, to me, it came as a revelation (and I have never been ill in February since, as far as I remember). She had given me a new idea. It did not require an answer, nor did it feel like an invasion of privacy or an intrusion. Rather, it was simply something I could think about. This is often how I worked with clients; we played with ideas triggered by Klein's work. Sometimes I would add, as I had understood from her, 'though this may not apply to you of course...', leaving it to them to respond or not, as they wished. This is my model when I tell parents, 'Children often feel they are responsible when a parent goes into hospital. I don't know if yours did?', and this is the model which many of my parent-clients have used, successfully, to reduce guilt or anxieties in their children.

In writing this book, I have, I think, understood a little more about the concept of the Good Object; about how and why children need their parents; about the way a parent's illness can shake up a child's whole world; and the way adults depend on their relationships for security, as a child's Good Object transforms into an adult's. The concept of grieving, which involves losing and regaining a Good Object in the internal world, also makes more sense to me now, though this is partly to do with having experienced bereavements myself. I hope I have conveyed some of this to the reader. However, I also hope that the book makes sense without the theory; that those readers who are not interested will not be troubled if they leave out Chapter 2, where I describe it. To facilitate this, I have kept in the non-jargon descriptions, sometimes alongside more technical ones.

THE STRUCTURE OF THE BOOK

Initial reactions to illness or new disabilities and to the changes they bring often include a sense of disbelief – a heroic intention to 'carry on as before', to shut eyes and minds to a new 'reality', believed to be totally unbearable, unthinkable, horrifying. This 'don't move', 'while I don't see it, it isn't happening', can hold people for a while, but after a time the discrepancies between how things *should be* and how they *are*, or how they are *in the mind* and how they are *in the external world*, may become too much. It takes a lot of effort to maintain any kind of fiction, particularly if what is being avoided seems terrifying. As I have observed in many counselling sessions, while it is being fought off, what is believed to be 'reality' is generally much worse than actual reality could ever be.

Unfortunately, illnesses often bring repeated losses and constant change, either for better or for worse, and these bring with them new struggles aimed at resisting yet another upheaval. Even a promise of a cure can sometimes seem just one more effort too many. Worse, an actual cure, if it brings someone back from the brink, does not return things to just the way they were. I look in Chapter 1 at some of the many ways people try to avoid change.

One of the ideas I have found most useful is that of the 'person-in-your-head'. When I was growing up, people used to speak of the 'policeman-in-your-head' – someone in your mind who kept you from breaking the rules. Throughout the book I use the idea of the 'partner-in-your-head', the 'sister-in-your-head', the 'mother-in-your-head' to draw attention to the fact that we do not relate simply to people as they actually are, but also to ideas of them which we carry around with us. These images are created, not only from our relationships with the people they represent, but also from associations to other people in our minds. More than just a picture, this view of other people has emotions attached to it; the image lives and moves and changes over time, both in response to changes in the world 'out there' and to changes in the ways we feel 'inside'. Derived from Klein's 'Internal Objects' and her concept of phantasies, this simplified form of these ideas made enough sense to my clients to help them to think about the distinction between their ideas about their partner and the one 'out there' in ways which sometimes transformed relationships; fuller explanation was not needed.

One problem with the 'mother-in-your-head' shorthand is that these figures are felt more as *in your body* than in your mind, and they feel very real indeed. Melanie Klein called them 'phantasies', unconscious fantasies, because they are closer to a character in a story or a dream than a flat picture.

When a parent changes in the real world, as a result of an illness, their image in their child's mind must also change. However, the 'parent-in-the-head' may change much more slowly than the real one; it may also change differently. *Deafness* may be forgotten, for example, and the parent simply be perceived as *more irritating*. The fact that a parent is *grieving for a loss* may be overlooked, and their child simply sees them as *bad-tempered*; even grown-up children may attribute this change to something they have done wrong themselves. I look at some of these ideas in more detail, including the concept of the Good Object, in Chapter 2.

People often talk of feeling isolated as a result of illness, and this isolation can be related to the sense that it is impossible for anyone else to understand how it feels to be ill or physically changed in this particular way, today, now. There may be considerable comfort in talking to others with the same condition – if such can be found – but in Chapter 3 I focus on day-to-day interactions with people who do not have the same experience. Even without illness, people find it hard enough to understand each other. An illness adds not only heightened emotions but also a new set of expectations. The differences between the way things *should be* and the way they *are* can cause rifts, both within the family and between family and professionals. 'How can they do that!' 'If it were me, I would offer to help, why don't they?' There are many ways in which *illness can make people feel bad*: about themselves and about those they love and care for – and about those who fail to show they care. This is a refrain which appears throughout the book. Understanding can help reduce the bad feelings – or at least make them less disturbing, more forgivable.

In Chapters 4 and 5 I look at some of the specific threats to relationships which arise from illness, including threats to sexual relations. Some of these threats can be diminished by awareness. For example, professionals may need to be reminded that replacing a family double bed with a 'hospital bed' may have serious consequences for the long-term health of the relationship, particularly if the couple are young. Not only may a sexual partner be excluded from the bed unnecessarily, but children too may lose 'cuddle time'. Pressure from care agencies to change the bed may be resistible, but many people find it hard or embarrassing to push for their conjugal rights to be respected, particularly if fit, healthy young professionals do not recognise that sexual desire can exist (or may return) in people who are neither fit nor healthy. This can be particularly important if there are young girls in the family who may be at greater risk of sexual abuse if their mother's availability for sexual contact with her partner are reduced.

It may not be until they become able to think about what they have lost and to grieve for it that people have a chance of finding that reality is not quite so dark and full of despair as they feared. There may be a new choice between fighting reality and fighting realistically. In Chapter 7 I look at the grieving process: at the painful work of reorganising the internal world and learning to live with a new reality – this generally takes place during the period of two years or more following a loss of any kind.

The effect of pain on relationships is looked at as a separate topic in Chapter 6, and in Chapter 8 I look at some of the difficulties related to changes in the capacity to think and to feel which can be caused by brain damage. It can be difficult to distinguish between problems which are caused by *not wanting to see*, and those which are caused by being *physiologically unable to see*. Superficially there may be little difference in terms of how the patient will be treated by the family and by professionals; however, there may in fact be important changes. Thinking the person you love *cannot* remember because of their deteriorating neurological condition has quite different implications from thinking they *cannot be bothered to* remember because they do not love you any more. (For a while, it may not be clear which it *is*; it may also be quite unclear which is *preferable*.)

Much has been written elsewhere about living with diagnosed dementia, so my focus is not on the dementing illnesses such as Alzheimer's, but on other neurological conditions such as stroke or multiple sclerosis which can cause less recognised forms of damage to thinking or feeling. These affect not only relationships with others, but also the relationship with the self. In particular, cognitive problems affect the capacity to grieve for what is lost, to remain in touch both with the current physical world and with one's own feelings, and to hold onto a sense of a good 'internal parent/partner' which affects feelings of security and the capacity to be alone.

Chapter 9 focuses on parents. Parents who have long-term chronic illnesses sometimes complain that their doctors do not take into account their responsibilities as parents, and their families don't take into account their illnesses. A parent is supposed to be strong and supportive, a patient is supposed to be looked after; these two roles do not fit well together. How people feel and how they manage the complexities of their relationships in this situation is the subject of this chapter.

Children's points of view are discussed in Chapter 10. Having a parent who is ill, particularly for a small child, can be devastating, but there is little literature on the subject apart from my own co-authored books, *My Mum Needs Me* (Segal and Simkins 1993) and *Helping Children with Ill or Disabled Parents* (Segal and Simkins 1996), perhaps because adults find it painful to think about.

Professional health workers of all kinds may be involved when someone develops an illness or new disability. In Chapter 11 I discuss relationships between the families of people who are ill and the professionals who care for them. At times of heightened emotions, where serious illness is involved, relationships may be experienced in extreme ways, as wonderfully rewarding or very destructive – and never forgotten. Professionals' own work life is bound up with those they care for, and when a relationship goes sour this can affect both the way they feel about themselves and the way they approach the next person. For both professionals and those in their care, thinking about these relationships may be an important way of working through otherwise bruising (or more seriously damaging) interactions.

THIS BOOK IS IMPORTANT...

Although this book is primarily about relationships where people get along in an ordinary sort of way, it also has implications for more troubled relationships.

According to the Crime Survey for England and Wales 2013/14 (Flatley 2015), most people in the UK (71% of women and 85% of men) have not experienced domestic abuse since the age of 16. However, long-term illness or disability more than doubled the chances of suffering domestic abuse: 15.7 per cent of women and 8.4 per cent of men *with*, as against

7.1 per cent and 4.0 per cent *without*, a long-term illness or disability suffered domestic abuse in 2009/10. In particular, 11.3 per cent of women with a long-term illness or disability were estimated to be a victim of partner abuse, compared with 4.9 per cent of women without a long-term illness or disability. (In the USA, the Bureau of Justice in 2008 also estimated that 'the age-adjusted rates of all crimes measured were at least twice as high for persons with disabilities'. In Canada the situation seems to be roughly the same: for example, 'Self-rated poor or fair health status, as well as sleep disorders and use of antidepressants or sedatives, were associated with rates of violent victimization 50% to 90% higher than the average' (Perreault 2009, p.6).) The authors of an earlier British report (Walby and Allen 2001) believed that: 'It is more likely that this [ill-]health status is either an outcome of the violence, or that health status and interpersonal violence are associated through complex pathways, than it is for poor health to be a cause of violence' (p.101). I disagree. My work has led me to think it *highly* likely that the simplest explanation is true: that as well as ill-health being a possible result of violence, ill-health may actually increase the chances of violence occurring. More recent Canadian and US reports remark on the vulnerability of people with disabilities to crime, and the United Nations Convention on the Rights of Persons with Disabilities 2006 recognises the greater risk to disabled women and girls 'both within and outside the home of violence, injury or abuse, neglect or negligent treatment, maltreatment or exploitation'. (I do not understand why men with disabilities are omitted from this statement.)

Whatever causes these correlations, the fact is that, for many people, ill-health and domestic violence go together. (Being young, female, poor and a lone parent also increase the likelihood of suffering from domestic violence of all kinds. These are also the people who find it hardest to access any kind of professional help, partly because they cannot find time to keep an appointment.)

My suspicion is that in the context of partnerships where violence is a possibility, ill-health may mean that a woman appears (or believes herself to be) 'lazy', 'useless' or insufficiently thoughtful of her partner ('selfish'); that ill-health may stop her standing up for herself or getting out of a relationship ('I don't deserve any better – who would love me anyway?');

and may also add to the ordinary difficulties of making a marriage (or a divorce) work in the interests of either party or the children. Rather than evoking a protective response, weakness itself or other signs of damage to the woman's body, particularly if caused (in reality or in imagination) by a partner's previous violence, may in some situations actually provoke an attack. Illness may also make her unwilling or unable to enjoy sexual activities which could otherwise defuse potentially dangerous situations; refusing sex can itself also be experienced as provocative. Illness can also make people feel *controlled*, and thereby provoke powerful impulses to control others. In addition, even apparently minor brain damage can increase violence and irritability in susceptible people.

These figures suggest, at the very least, that young, poor people with children who have problems with their health, especially women, are particularly at risk, as are their children. Understanding some of the ways illness itself can make people feel bad (not only themselves, perhaps, but also their abuser) may help such women. There are also an increasing number of frail elderly couples in which at least one partner is ill, and these couples too are at risk of physical abuse, from younger people as well as from each other.

CONCLUSION

This book is aimed primarily at those whose work or life brings them into contact with people who are ill or newly disabled in one way or another. Counsellors, psychologists, psychotherapists, professional carers and nurses are the main professional audience, but many other healthcare professionals find themselves having to deal with the emotional and relational impact of these conditions on themselves as well as on their clients. And, of course, anyone who themselves has a health condition, or belongs to a family in which someone else does, or as a child was concerned about a parent's health, may recognise their own experience and, I hope, see it in a new light.

CHAPTER 1

Why Does Anything Have to Change?

'I'm ill, you're ill – but everything will go on as before!'

'My mum said when I came out of hospital after my diagnosis we shouldn't let [my daughter] know anything had happened.'

'I don't see why anything should change, you're still you.'

'I don't want it to make any difference to us.'

'I suddenly realised I would never be the same again, that my body had changed and it would never look like it did before. It was a shock really. Took me a bit of time to get used to it.' (After the birth of a first child.)

'I hated him: his body hadn't been torn to pieces, ripped up; his life hadn't been destroyed; mine had.'

'After I had been attacked I just collapsed; my arm healed but I felt I was worthless, I couldn't protect myself or my family... It wasn't a bereavement but...I tried to kill myself.'

'For me, getting MS was a kind of relief. I'd always expected it to happen, and now it has. My mother had it, and her mother and they were both ok, it doesn't affect them much, so I knew I'd be ok.'

INTRODUCTION

Ill-health or a new disability often comes as a shock, as a disruption which throws life into confusion. Not only do visits to the doctor, hospital appointments or periods in hospital all interrupt normal life, but changes to the body cause a break in the normal flow of expectation of the body itself. Even if the illness does not last long, people can be surprised by their own and other people's reactions.

> 'When my husband had an upset stomach and I was struggling to cope with an eight-month-old baby I gave him a cup of tea in the morning, then ignored him all day. The doctor gave me a real telling-off. I was shocked. I'd assumed that he'd be all right left on his own. But I'd seen myself as good at looking after people, at nursing, and here I was being a terribly thoughtless wife.'

Not only everyday activities but also beliefs, sense of self, thinking and feeling may be threatened. It shakes people out of their 'comfort zones'. It sets up conflicts, both within the self and, often, between the self and others.

Anxieties about the future can be intense, and involve not just yourself but lovers, partners, children, parents.

> 'She couldn't cope with me.' 'They'd make me eat meat.' (Small boys talking about who would look after them if their parents couldn't.)

> 'I don't think life would feel worth living if you were a vegetable. I'd look after you, though. I'd rather have you a vegetable than not at all.'

> 'You could find someone else!' 'I don't think I'd want anyone else. One wife is enough!'

> 'We're going to have to move flat – we can't manage here.'

Pre-existing anxieties are ready and waiting.

'I can't look after the children on my own! What about my work? I don't get enough time for it already! I'm going to lose my job!'

'We're going to have to ask your parents for help – again. And your sister will be cross. And they're getting older.'

'I'm supposed to be the one who looks after other people!'

Frustration arises when tasks which previously could be done without thought now require new, concentrated effort. Worse, the attempt to carry on as normal may bring with it the realisation that some kinds of normal behaviour are no longer possible, and perhaps will never be possible again. Frustration can lead to anger, which may be 'taken out' on someone else – or on oneself. Withdrawal may be a tempting option, but children as well as adults can provoke fights in order to 'bring back' an adult who has turned their face to the wall and cut themselves off.

When there is a long-term change in health, the realisation that something is irrevocably changed typically 'hits' people at some point, though not immediately. People often talk of the experience in bodily terms: it feels like a 'blow', a 'jolt'; it can 'knock you sideways'. It ushers in the awareness that considerable amounts of work will need to be done to reorganise states of mind, attitudes, thoughts and beliefs, as well as, possibly, practical living arrangements. This work may already have been begun.

For some people an illness or disability has been expected all their lives. But if it happens it can still be a shock.

FIGHTING OFF AWARENESS OF CHANGE

There are many ways of protecting oneself from recognising a massive change.

'I just lay there. I didn't move. I didn't want to know how bad it was. While I lay there I didn't have to know.'

'He just smokes weed all the time. He won't do anything. It makes me angry to see him like that. I can't have a decent discussion with him about anything. I end up joining him and then nothing gets done.'

'I didn't go out for about seven years. I didn't want people to see me in a wheelchair.'

'She won't talk about incontinence. She probably can't smell it herself. She just pretends nothing is wrong. It's really embarrassing, but she just ignores it. I'm worried what it is doing to her skin.'

'I don't want to think about the future. What is the point?'

'Not doing anything' can be a tempting option. Why try, when it will just cause frustration? Why do exercises? They just show up what you *cannot* do. A fight on the lines of 'You're always trying to control me!' or an irritated withdrawal, 'Leave me alone!', may feel preferable to an admission that doing something confronts someone both with their present level of disability and with huge anxieties about their future. Equally, someone who 'just likes a smoke, it makes me feel relaxed' is not likely to say, 'I don't want to address any of the aggravating and painful issues you want to raise, but I don't want an argument about it either, so I will send my own feelings to sleep and let it go...', ignoring the fact that it actually means 'You can deal with it without me.'

'I don't want to think about the future' may be a cover-up for 'I don't want to think about losing everything, being unable to look after myself, being unloved and abandoned by everyone.' A new loss evokes old fears – the nightmares of small children in a frightening world. It is not surprising that people want to avoid thinking about 'the future' if this is what they think, or 'know', it would be. Unfortunately, 'not thinking' cuts these fears off from the clear light of day. They remain in their primitive state, generally totally unrealistic but believed to be an unspeakable reality.

The conviction that this is a no-go area for discussion can easily be shared. It is very hard to force a conversation which would actually address and, in fact, relieve the anxieties. There may be solutions which one or another knows, but the time and opportunity to pass this information on is never there. The sense of isolation is increased by being unable to share significant thoughts.

'I was so scared of being cared for by a professional carer that it's taken me years to get to the point where I could think about it at all. But now I've been forced to. Now I have discovered that everyone else I know has been getting Direct Payments for years [to buy their own care] and using it to pay their families and friends – I could have been doing that! I thought I'd get someone from social services and I wouldn't have any choice over who it was; that if I complained, I wouldn't get any help at all. I remember seeing carers with disabled children, throwing them around like sacks of potatoes, I thought it would be like that... Yes, I know there were good carers too, but I just knew I'd get one of the bad ones.' (Her counsellor had tried for many months to help her to think about getting carers; she had blocked every time.)

At the same time, in my experience there is sometimes a clue in the form of the cover-up. For example, 'there is *no point*' is often a hint, particularly for men, that there is loss of sexual function, and with it, loss of a sense that life is worth living. 'I didn't want people to see me...' contains a hint that difficulties lie in the direction of seeing and being seen: in appearance, whatever that means for the individual concerned; perhaps a kind of narcissism or vanity or the loss of an earlier pleasure in being looked at; or memories of being looked at in a 'wrong', bad or lascivious way. Smoking often seems to be linked to suppression of intolerable anger; over-eating too may suggest problems around 'stuffing down feelings', perhaps of hunger for affection, possibly stemming from loss. Drinking a lot of alcohol seems to link with phantasies in which care-giving itself is under attack – there may be a sense that somebody who should care, currently or in the past, does not or did not.

Equally, someone who angrily insists it is 'definitely *not* just in my mind!' may be 'protesting too much' against fears that this is precisely where it is. Most people with demonstrable neurological illnesses often think momentarily (hopefully, perhaps) that some at least of their symptoms are 'in the mind' rather than the body; but people who *think* or 'know' they are ill but have no physical sign of illness at all may deny ever thinking such a thing. They may not take kindly to attempts to challenge this conviction – it is as if, for these people, physical illness is strongly preferable to any thought of mental involvement, whatever this might mean. This particular cover-up can be difficult to shift. Strictly speaking, it is not usually a defence against awareness of change brought on by physical illness, but is directed against other, even more unthinkable, phantasies, such as 'I [or they] think I'm going mad.'

Avoiding diagnosis is a common strategy for putting off the evil moment. Seeking a diagnosis can also be a way of seeking reassurance that nothing has changed.

> *'I know the doctor will tell me there isn't a problem: I'm only going because my husband made the appointment for me. I would have left it.'*

CHOICE OR NO CHOICE

There may be *no choice* about lying in a hospital bed, swinging between crutches with a leg in plaster, or finding a way to cook with one hand. In some ways this makes the mental work involved relatively simple. Some people find they can just 'get on with it' and after a while 'get used to' whatever it is they have to deal with. Giving up aspects of life, of the self, capacities and beliefs, is painful and still may take two years or more, but there can be a fairly clear point at which it should begin, and normal kinds of resistance or denial may fairly easily be recognised as such.

On the other hand, many illnesses bring more subtle or slow changes which seem to *allow some choices* to be made. Having to decide every day, 'Can I walk today or not?', 'Can I get out of bed this morning?', can be exhausting. It requires thought of a difficult kind, which is not required when waking to the certain knowledge that the answer is 'no'. After a while, if the answer is always 'no', one stops asking. Until that point – and with some neurological diseases, for example, the period of not-knowing may be long and drawn-out – there may be much heart-searching.

'Am I just being lazy?'

'If I tried just a bit harder...'

'Perhaps if I prayed to Allah/took up yoga/Pilates/a gluten-free diet...'

'God is obviously punishing me...'

'I feel I have a constant battle between a "good" me and a "bad" me. The good one says I can do things, but the bad one tells me not to bother, to let my husband bring me a cup of tea, when I could do it really. It's just that, if I fetched the cup of tea myself, I feel I wouldn't be able to do something else later...but then I feel, if I did more I'd be able to do more, you know, use it or lose it...'

'I could walk if my husband gave me back my crutches. I don't know why he took them away, it makes me really angry, he just likes to control me. I'm sure I could walk if I had them.' 'Have you fallen?' 'Oh, yes, I fall all the time, I broke my pelvis last year, but that's just because I'm out of practice.'

'I was all right yesterday, I think I must have worn myself out; I shouldn't have tried to clean the oven, I won't do that again...or perhaps cleaning the oven is good exercise and I'm just having a temporary need for rest; when I do get up I will be better for having done it... But perhaps I shouldn't have gone shopping too...or it might have been the pills I started taking last week... or my sister coming over, she always makes me feel ill, perhaps I should ask my husband to stop her coming.'

These ruminations remind me of some distressing experiments with half-starved pigeons in the 1940s. Fed strictly rationed pellets of food at regular intervals, they were observed repeating any behaviours which they happened to be doing at the moment the food appeared, as if they were trying to work out what they did which caused the pellet to arrive (Skinner 1948). We are very convinced by beliefs that we control our own body and its vicissitudes.

PRE-EXISTING EXPECTATIONS

To begin with, people generally *try to fit their ideas about their ill-health into their pre-existing expectations.* They may expect it to go away by itself, perhaps with rest, Vitamin C or D, eating more fruit or taking exercise – or they expect it to be cured by a doctor. Some immediately think they are dying, however minor their illness; others firmly think of something else and constantly reassure themselves that it is nothing serious. Everyone has their own explanation for their ills, and everyone has their own set of beliefs about what will cure it. In the 1930s, smoking was likely to be prescribed by doctors as well as by the patient – today, giving up smoking may be on the prescription.

The idea that we should only have to cope with one serious illness in life can be very powerful, so there can be a sense too that one diagnosis will *prevent* any other, perhaps worse, conditions. More than one diagnosis really turns ideas of fairness upside down and leaves people struggling to make sense of what has happened to them. Some people spend their lives expecting an illness or disability, and for these there may be a sense almost of relief: at last, something really bad has happened – perhaps they can now relax?

About to go for a scan for headaches, Ann suddenly discovered her symptoms were those of a brain tumour. This had not occurred to her: she was expecting signs of a stroke, which was what her mother had. (The tests showed she had neither, and the symptoms disappeared.)

For others, the shock is all the worse for challenging a belief or illusion that life will go on as it always has done; that bad things happen to others, not to them.

Pre-existing expectations can be very strong. They can easily overrule the facts of life. I was mortified to realise once that I had forgotten that a client had told me at the beginning of our session that she could not see. Involved in her story, I had reverted to assuming she was as she appeared, able to see like anyone else. Family members and friends, too, can forget a new disability or illness; it can take a long time for a difference to register fully. This is a common source of conflict, as people are forced to register that their own existence and their own problems play a different part in others' lives, sometimes more significant than they realised, sometimes less. A child may not register their father's weakness because they so much want a strong father; a friend may thoughtlessly book a restaurant without disability access. The friend probably wants the relationship to stay the same and doesn't want to deal with the fact that things have changed – worse, they may actually be secretly angry that their friend can no longer play the same part in their lives as before. 'Forgetting' a change is one way this anger can be expressed without admitting it.

Resistance to the changes brought by illness can also be strong. It can take many months before someone with a seriously disabling disease admits that there are things they can no longer do. Every single loss may be fought. Every single loss may mean 'one step down the ladder' towards, perhaps, certain death, or long-term chronic disability of one kind or another. These fights take place not only within the mind of the individual, they may also spill over into relationships.

FIGHTING THE ILLNESS, FIGHTING THE PARTNER, FIGHTING THE SELF

'I'm going to climb Snowdon – well, I will be in a wheelchair, I'm going to be carried by a team from the army. I like the idea of all those young men... I won't let the MS beat me! I'm not going to just sit on my backside just because I've got MS.'

'She wants to take my keys away; she says I'm not safe to drive! But she's just nervous, it's her problem, she's always been like that. I'm fine...'

'He wants to stop me eating sweets, when it's the only happiness I have left. I can't do anything else, I haven't any other pleasures. I know I'm fat, I don't care, what's the point in caring? I just wish I would die soon. When you're diabetic you shouldn't eat sweets, well, I hope it will finish me off sooner...'

'My legs make me really angry. I sometimes hit them, they make me so cross.' 'Does it help?' 'No, it just hurts.' 'You don't feel they are doing their best in difficult circumstances?' 'No, I hadn't thought of it like that. I suppose they are, really.'

Heroic battles can be inspiring and can demonstrate how much can be achieved. In the public sphere this can be important for those who can, with the right support, continue to 'do things'. However, others who lack the drive or resources may have mixed feelings about an implication that they should be equally energetic and competent, however different their own circumstances. People can feel blamed for not being heroic – their illness no longer seen as a valid social reason for not doing things but as an excuse. Within the family, heroic battles do not always make for good relations. Energetic determination may demand exhausting physical work from someone else, who may or may not be willing and able.

(There are many ways in which illness makes people feel bad. While writing this I am aware that I could be making 'heroic' people feel bad – for setting the challenge – as I try to help the less heroic bear their own inertia. This book does not tell people what to do; mostly it concludes that whatever you do will upset someone if there is an illness involved.)

In order to achieve great feats (such as walking to the letter box on a 'bad' day), a certain amount of splitting off of anxieties may be necessary. This may result in them being palmed off on another person. One person insisting 'I can do it!' (or 'You can do it!') may set up in the other a worried 'No you can't!' (or 'No I can't!'). In fact, both wildly optimistic assessments of capacity *at the same time as* deeply pessimistic ones generally coexist in both partners. Two aspects of the self are in conflict, and both partners can be very frightened of either winning. If 'can' wins out, there may be real risks; but so there are if 'can't' wins. What is needed is a realistic consideration of both risks and hopes, but this requires a complex level of tolerance and thought hard to find in the rough and tumble of daily struggles with a new disability.

There is security in *somebody* keeping in mind the risks; but holding two thoughts in mind at once may be asking too much. However, neither position can be properly modified while they cannot be thought about without a fight. With contradictory positions and feelings divided between partners, each somewhere knows they are relying on the other to hold the balance. By refusing to acknowledge that they share the fears, the battle may make both feel undermined, resentful and, importantly, lonely – while each actually *does* understand and *does* know just what it is they are fighting against, though they will not admit it.

Splitting ideas or feelings or thoughts like this between two partners happens particularly when people are afraid for their lives and unable to talk about serious fears such as suicidal depression or abandonment.

'If I let her find out she really cannot get up those stairs, it will kill her!'

'He's keeping me in cotton wool! I hate it! He never takes me seriously!'

'She will leave me if I'm no good in bed any more.'

'I don't ask for help unless I absolutely have to, then I apologise all the time [because I'm afraid he really wants to leave me – unspoken]. He gets angry and says I should ask sooner.'

And so the battle commences. Better, goes the phantasy, to fight than to face suicidal despair. Unfortunately, some of these battles can actually increase the despair.

Sexual anxieties are often addressed by means of a fight. Fighting can be a prelude to sexual relations, but it can also be a means of avoiding sexual relations, in order to prevent awareness of change and possible disappointment in sexual functioning. Unfortunately, the fight and the lack of sexual relations can both contribute to increased anxieties and resentments. Lack of sexual activity can be interpreted as lack of love; and there are physical and emotional benefits in both erotic and loving touch for both partners. Only once anxieties have reduced enough to be bearable can difficulties be discussed. At this point alternative or modified forms of sexual or other physical contact may be discovered, and the disappointment is mitigated by being able to hold on to some aspects of the relationship.

INTERPRETATIONS

Interpreting other people's behaviour is what we do. We never just take things at face value. When an illness or bodily change is involved we continue to interpret. We interpret our own symptoms, very often as 'meaning' we are 'bad' in some way. 'A healthy mind in a healthy body' is not very comforting for those with unhealthy bodies.

'Spots: they're your badness coming out! – my mother used to say.'

Jesus is reported to have said to a man sick of the palsy: 'your sins are forgiven' to mean 'you are healed' (Matthew 9, 2).

The association between guilt and illness was obviously evident 2000 years ago.

We also interpret other people's behaviour, and friendships can founder on interpretations. When a friend or family member is asked for something and refuses, there are many possible interpretations to be made. Is it true that she has to do something for someone else? Who is it? Are they more important than me? Does she like them more than me? Does she find it an imposition, to be asked? What can I ask for, and what can't I? If I were in her position I would... Why doesn't she...? Surely a friend should... Surely your own family would be expected to...

In some cultures these accusations may flow. Mostly, however, I suspect they remain unspoken, partly because we do not want to find out, because we may be wrong, or because we may be right and while we do not know we can hope we are wrong (or right).

We also interpret throw-away remarks:

'It's all right for you, you have a husband!'

'I'm sure you could do it if you really tried!'

'I can't bear to see dried-up, dying leaves on a plant; they suck the goodness from it.' (In the context of talking about caring for a dying husband.)

When people hear about someone with a long-term illness, they can react with many uncomfortable feelings, whether they are close or more distant friends. There may be envy of someone who 'no longer has to work' or 'can now be looked after', or 'has no responsibilities any more'.

Some will be jealous: 'Now my dad will look after my mum, he won't notice me at all.' Or angry: 'How can you have let things change like this! They were bad enough before!' Or sorry: 'I would have liked to have been a better daughter, but it's too late now.' There can be dislike/phobia of hospitals: 'I can't go in a hospital, I don't know why but it makes me want to vomit.' Or dislike of illness of any kind, discomfort at talking to someone who speaks slowly and has lost touch with the world, irritation with deafness, contempt towards addictions or obesity, horror at the sight of an emaciated body, disgust at the sight of clumsy eating – all of these and many more affect people.

Mostly people hesitate to spell out their reactions, but their behaviour (such as 'being too busy to visit', or 'unable to come over just now') can be interpreted. Worse, the person doing the interpreting may themselves have had such a reaction (which they may not want to express or even allow themselves to recognise). They may interpret another person's behaviour through knowledge of their own feelings, perhaps quite wrongly.

If people do manage to talk about these things, they may see that the initial reaction is not the whole truth. The woman who wanted to get rid of the dead leaves looked after her husband devotedly: she was afraid of life being sucked out of her, but she also wanted to care for him to the best of her ability. Disgust is difficult to overcome but not impossible in the right circumstances – time and habituation can help. Envy and jealousy are problematical but can be worked on in various ways. How lucky to be able to play tennis during the day, but would I really want to be lifting my husband 24 times before lunch? My father will be paying more attention to my mother – but perhaps I can find a partner who will outlive him. Ugliness is in the eye of the beholder – deformed bodies may hide interesting and lovable minds (as in the 1980 film *The Elephant Man*).

Guilt and shame about having bad thoughts towards an illness, deformity or disability can lead people to avoid each other. If, however, there is some tolerance towards these thoughts, they can be recognised and put in their place; they can also be allowed to develop and change over time. Joking can defuse their sting. Just knowing that people have bad thoughts, that illness and deformity evoke them, that nobody's perfect but that we can live with imperfection, can help.

DEPENDENCE AND CONTROL

Issues with dependence and control are common causes of fights. People struggle over questions of help needed, wanted, not wanted, offered, declined, available or unavailable; they may both want and not want help; need and resist it; expect it to be offered and hate it when it is. Internal conflicts about dependence are reflected in conflicts between people. Many people idealise independence, priding themselves on not needing help, believing that accepting help would be totally humiliating, an admission of failure, loss of autonomy and loss of control. Ideas of dependence are often related to childhood, when unpredictable (and possibly unfriendly) adults were in charge. As such, they can be unrealistic and exaggerated: young children are proud and feel grown-up when they can say 'I can do it all by myself!' but this may also become a defence against recognising that there was no-one there to help them. As they grow up they have to learn how dependent adults actually are on one another and how adults' autonomy is restricted by other people.

Help has implications for power relations, with the giver generally perceived to be better than, or more capable than, the receiver. (I sometimes discuss a mythical Prince Charming, who, I suggest, may not know where his socks are kept, and may expect someone to put them on his feet, in order to challenge the idea that the person being offered a service is *beneath* the person offering; that social superiors *give* and social inferiors *receive*. Someone whose disability makes them feel like a small child – which was probably the last time someone else put their socks on – may feel better if they imagine themselves as more like this Prince Charming.) People offering help often express their frustration when it is refused and are distressed watching the person 'struggling' to cope in their own way – which may or may not feel like a struggle to the person themselves.

Attempts to prevent *awareness* of dependence threaten relationships, just as, if not more than, dependence itself can.

> *'I wouldn't mind if he just asked for a cup of tea and said thank you, but he always makes out it doesn't really cost me anything, I was making one for myself anyway, even if I wasn't, so he doesn't need to feel grateful.*

I can understand it's a pain to feel grateful all the time, but it gets me down sometimes.'

Many losses connected with disabilities or illness have a powerful symbolic meaning connected with loss of control and consequent reliance on others.

'Incontinence is the worst thing. That's what lost me my job really. I hate it. It makes me feel like a smelly child, like the poor children in my school.'

'My hands aren't working. I couldn't get out of bed this morning. I'm really terrified. If they go completely I will need a full-time carer and I couldn't bear that.'

'What I'd hate most [about the future with MS] is the wheelchair.' 'What is the problem you see with the wheelchair?' 'It's what my partner would have to do; the responsibility, he'd have to take responsibility for me, for everything.' 'You mean, if you were in a wheelchair you feel you wouldn't be able to take responsibility for yourself any more? Are we talking about your legs or your brain here?' 'Oh. I suppose people in wheelchairs can take responsibility for themselves. I was thinking it would all come together.' 'There might be a time when you couldn't take responsibility for yourself, but people usually have many years using a wheelchair before that point.'

'What does having MS mean to you?' 'I don't have any children [to take care of me in my old age/if I become disabled].'

Angry attacks on others' 'uselessness' are sometimes fuelled by an anger with the self for needing help.

'I told him [a fellow employee] he was useless and he should leave.' 'Do you sometimes think you are useless?' 'Yes, of course!'

This man, like many others with minor or major disabilities, secretly considered himself 'impotent', 'nothing', 'a waste of space', 'unwanted' and to be 'thrown on the scrap-heap' – all the while holding down a good job. Many people have such fears lurking inside their minds all their lives, and an illness (or retiring or ageing) can awaken and appear to confirm them. For others, with better experiences in childhood and more (learnt or inborn) trust in others, needing help is less of a problem.

Anxieties about loss of control of the environment are less if those around are trusted to be capable of taking care both of themselves and of others. Discussing these issues in groups of professionals, I have often found that men express less fear of dependence than women, perhaps partly because many women dismiss men's capacity to do 'caring' housework tasks, while most men assume women can do them. The reality of who can and will take care of whom is by no means so simple, and I suspect that gender plays a lesser part than many other factors.

Mature Adult Dependence can be a useful concept. Once named, it can be recognised and clearly differentiated from childhood dependence. Discussing what makes dependence satisfying, 'mature' and 'adult' to the people concerned can be illuminating. It probably requires both parties to admit and respect their differences, and some form of negotiation over issues of control. Fears of carers 'taking over' or confusing the other with themselves may be involved, as well as of carers 'not caring' or 'only thinking of themselves'. When teaching, I often ask groups whether, if asked, their mothers would make them the kind of tea *they* like, or the kind *she* would like. Many daughters seem to think their mothers are not very good at distinguishing their own tastes from their daughter's, or would not comply with their daughter's wishes for other reasons. This kind of situation may underlie very real anxieties about dependence. It does make a difference if carers are sufficiently aware to know they need to *ask* what the client wants rather than rely on their own wishes, preferences and assumptions. Whether this can be achieved or not clearly depends on many factors, but an adult client may not be totally helpless to influence the outcome, whether it is a good cup of tea or something more substantial.

Issues of when and how to accept or to refuse help, when and how to offer or to wait until asked, and an understanding of the point of view both of the person offering and the person being offered, may sometimes only be addressed openly after a period of conflict involving mutual misunderstanding and offence. If help can be accepted graciously, the fight against dependence becomes less necessary and attention can be paid to other aspects of life.

Health professionals sometimes speak as if their job was solely to foster 'independence' even where a more mature, adult recognition of realistic dependency needs would be more helpful. Enabling someone with severe cognitive or physical problems to live 'independently' is not possible; helping them and their carers to recognise the reality of their relationships, including the need to tolerate, put in place and understand the effects of realistic, mutually satisfying forms of dependency and interdependence, could be more useful.

RECOGNISING CHANGE

Clearly, many illnesses and health conditions have significant or even devastating implications for the future, for ways people see themselves, for what they can and cannot do, for their role in the world, and for their relationships. There may be changes in perception of the self, of the body, from 'healthy' to 'unhealthy', 'ill' or 'sick'; from 'normal' to 'disabled', 'different' or even 'odd' or 'strange' – all of which have slightly different connotations. Others' perceptions may or may not change too. Families may resist change for longer than the ill person themselves, or may be quicker to respond to the implications. Roles and relationships may have to change: 'How can I be a good mother/father/partner/daughter/son when I am in pain/am disabled/am physically deteriorating/cannot look after myself?' There are answers to these questions, but at the time when people ask them, they may not realise there are. Hopes, assumptions and beliefs about the future may all have to be modified. Aspects of life previously taken for granted may suddenly be under threat.

As well as practical changes, illness or new disability may bring with it a loss of more unrealistic beliefs: 'Those things don't happen to me', 'I thought I was invincible', 'He was my rock!' An image of the body as 'whole' may change to one of being damaged, spoiled, crippled or broken, with 'bits missing' and implications of lost attractiveness or loss of place in an important social hierarchy. Uncertainty is a characteristic of many of these losses, as it may not be clear at the outset exactly what will and must be lost and what can be saved; and uncertainty means insecurity, a loss of control of the future, having to 'wait and see'.

These losses can be extremely painful, and grieving for them may be avoided for as long as possible. Once it has taken place, however, a grieving process can also bring benefits. There may be new insights into the importance of different aspects of life; new capacities or a new discovery of capacities of the self or of others which previously were neither recognised nor valued. There may be a sense of the mind 'opening up', and new areas, closed for some reason *before* the loss as well as those closed *because of* the loss, becoming available for use. Even knowing this, we resist the process because it hurts.

NEED FOR A GRIEVING PROCESS

Grieving is the process by which the mind adjusts to a loss. It is work. It has a beginning, a middle and (in some sense) an end. By the end there has been some kind of transformation in expectations, attitudes, behaviour and feelings. People may feel they are 'quite a different person from the person I was two years ago, before it all happened'. At this point there can be mixed feelings about whether the process has been a good one or, on balance, not worth the pain. In spite of the transformation, some of the painful feelings never go away – although they may become familiar, 'lived with' and, in this sense, different and more bearable.

Without a grieving process, the mind remains stuck in the past – old assumptions, beliefs and ways of seeing the world and the people in it may be maintained in the teeth of a contradictory reality. Resisting awareness of the passage of time and of the changes which time has brought is both common and possible, but it leaves the person, like Miss Havisham in Dickens' *Great Expectations*, with a part of themselves which does not grow up and which remains out of touch with current reality.

I look at grieving in more detail in Chapter 7.

DENIAL CAN DELAY GRIEVING

Refusing to engage with change delays grieving. Thoughts and feelings which are not allowed into consciousness but are kept hidden from the self cannot be challenged and changed. They are not allowed to develop and be tested by reality.

It is as if a certain number of tears is required for each loss; if these are blocked, the thoughts and the feelings attached to them will keep trying to emerge, and effort has to be put into keeping them at bay. Once the source of the tears has been recognised and acknowledged, and the tears have been allowed to be shed, their force is spent. New thoughts and feelings can emerge and take their place.

It is perfectly understandable that there should be a resistance to difficult new thoughts, or the thought of a new, changed life. Old ways of seeing the world can work for a while, even if the world has changed: there may be other aspects of life which need more urgent attention.

Unfortunately, delaying grieving too long may mean that people in later life, like James in Chapter 2, who was in his seventies, may still be haunted by the losses sustained in childhood. If children and young adults never find themselves in a situation where grieving becomes both possible and preferable to denial, they may enter their final years with unresolved grief and a real risk of depression perhaps compounded by self-neglect.

The roots of problems in current relationships are often discovered in delayed grieving. Feelings which more properly belonged to an earlier period, and which would make sense if understood as linked to an earlier loss (sometimes from childhood, though not always), may be experienced later when their link with the loss has been cut. Anger towards a wife for coming home late, for example, may be exaggerated as a result of feelings which arose when a mother failed to come home at all. Relationship counselling often involves locating the source of exaggerated or misdirected feelings in earlier losses. In particular, an adult may find themselves having to deal with emotions which plausibly could have arisen when the adult was of the age which their eldest child has now reached.

Ali left his wife when his eldest son was seven. In counselling it emerged that he believed she had stopped loving him two years earlier and had begun an affair then. When he was five himself his own father became ill and died. He had had several relationships before his marriage which had each lasted about five years; clearly he 'knew' in phantasy that this was the time a relationship lasted. The affair was a way of preparing himself for the time when he knew his wife would leave. He did not accept that he was 'passing on' the feelings of being left to his son; he thought his son would be fine and his leaving would not affect him.

SUMMARY

Although illness threatens to change everything, people generally struggle to delay or put off the moment when it does. Unwelcome thoughts can be dealt with in various ways, helped along by alcohol, diverting work, fighting, withdrawing from company, or avoiding anything which triggers them, for example. After a time this may become too restrictive and the work of grieving may begin. Eventually (often, though not always, after two years) people have become used to their situation and have developed a 'new normal'. Within that two years, and after it too, there are many opportunities for illness to make people feel 'bad' in one way or another. When grieving does not take place, some of the phantasies created at a time of loss can cause disruptions in relationships many years later.

CHAPTER 2

Inner World/Outer World

INTRODUCTION

Illness threatens to disturb the way we see the world, and in this chapter I look at ways we do see it. Conscious beliefs and understanding play a part, but in counselling or psychotherapy it becomes clear how much else, forgotten, at the back of our minds, is affecting the way we see the world. Both perception and understanding depend upon what we already have in our minds. In my book *Phantasy in Everyday Life* (Segal 1985) I described what Melanie Klein and colleagues called 'phantasies' about the world, ourselves and the people in it. Here I summarise some of what I described there and link these ideas with the issues in this book.

As I said in the introduction, readers who are not interested in anything which could be called 'theory' may omit this chapter; the rest of the book should make sense without it.

PHANTASIES: *INNER WORLD/OUTER WORLD; WHAT IS MY BODY DOING?*

We do all sorts of improbable things in our minds. We are really not very clear about what is real, what is fantasy, what is inside and what is outside. We could not look around the world and take in every detail every time we move, so we create short-cuts. Like an internet search engine, we predict what it is we will want to know and we prepare templates ready to pull together perceptions. We know what chairs are like, so we are free to notice (or not) what this particular one is made of, or we can just use it without thinking. It is easy to demonstrate our capacity to be misled when we 'read' our environment; any optical illusion depends on this.

We also know what it is to be able to walk, to stand, to balance while cooking; to move our hands in order to pick something up. Paralysis and other illnesses challenge the patterns we have ready which allow us to do these things without thinking. We revert to our ready-made templates easily: it is these which have to be changed over time, during the mourning period. This is why someone can say:

'It took me a year before I stopped stepping into a boat on my bad leg.'

We can call these templates, after Melanie Klein, 'Unconscious Phantasies'. They provide us with sufficient information to move around the world, relate to other people and understand our own emotional reactions. She used the word 'phantasies' because they are close to fantasies: they are more like stories than photographs, they change and develop over time, as we grow. They are unconscious because we do not need to think about them; they provide the basic assumptions we use every day – they are our 'default setting'. This is why it takes time for them to adjust when the world or our body changes. We have to bring them into consciousness before we can modify them, and the change may not 'stick' the first time. Phantasies about stepping into boats take time to become automatic.

We also have alternative phantasies. We have ready-made phantasies which include wobbly legs, paralysis, a distorted face. These may not be benign; they may have been formed under the influence of childhood ideas about good and bad people, toys which wobbled, a parent who fell down and was taken away. These phantasies may not have been used since they were created, but an illness may mean they are suddenly required: wobbly legs? – *I know what that means! I had a 'wobbly man',* *he was fat and ugly and a bit scary.* When, of course, it does not mean that wobbly people will be 'fat and ugly' – nor scary. And what are we doing, assuming that these characteristics go together? Fat people can be beautiful. Is 'ugly' scary? We have to take a look at these unconscious, evoked childhood phantasies before we can change them.

The phantasies we use to understand other people move and change – with age, with the time of day, with emotions. We use aspects of ourselves to create the phantasies we apply to others; we put ourselves in their shoes and use our own reactions to understand what it means to them. Of course, if they have a neurological condition and we do not, this information will be misleading. We can be seriously thrown by the discovery that our world is not the same as another's. It can cause all kinds of distress and problems.

Taking all the phantasies we have, about ourselves and our world, we can call it our 'inner world'. This world is full of the phantasy versions of the people in our lives and of ourselves. Mostly they move and change through interacting with each other, though we can also to some extent 'freeze' them. In dreams we can see this process, but it goes on below consciousness all the time as we sort out and make new sense of impressions received during the day. Death does not remove these people – the phantasies we have about them remain. They may continue to play a part: we may 'hear their voices' inside, telling us what to do or how to do it. The mourning process involves disentangling the phantasies from their connection with actions in the external world; for a long time after they have gone we may automatically reach for the phone to contact an ageing parent or lay the table for a partner who will not be coming.

Phantasies involve emotion and symbolism. Phantasies about dancing may include the pleasure of dancing with a friend as a child; of seeing a mother smile; of listening to grand music and getting lost in it. To lose dancing may threaten the loss of these evoked memories; again, the mourning process involves disentangling these memories, deciding which to hold, which to let go, and how to hold them if dancing itself is now lost.

GOOD OBJECT: *AM I IN A WORLD WHICH WILL HOLD ME SAFELY?*

One of the first phantasies we develop involves being held, loved and fed by a mother-figure. Too small to see her as a whole person, we may be mainly aware of her skin, her voice, her holding and her breast, and the feelings, both good and bad, which accompany them. These experiences, we think, link with inborn predispositions which prepare us for the world, and create our basic sense of being in the world.

When babies 'seek' the nipple immediately after birth, they in some sense 'know' what they are looking for and how to get it: they focus their eyes at the right distance and move towards a dark circle, their legs pushing them vigorously up the mother's body. We can say a baby is responding to an inborn phantasy of a breast. When it finds it, the baby has some sense of what to do – it may have to struggle for a while to match up the reality with the phantasy, to get the nipple in the mouth and move the jaw so the milk comes, but eventually the milk flows, the baby is relieved, it relaxes and, eventually, can begin to look around. It makes sense that for many people phantasies formed at this time become the basis for ideas about God: goodness 'known' to exist from birth, sought both inside and outside at the same time, beyond reason, wonderful and scary, life-giving and life-threatening, all at the same time.

Melanie Klein used the concept of the 'Good Object' to stand for this very early phantasy and ones that derive from it. The Good Object includes within it a sense of being held, fed and cared for by someone who is 'not me'; in fact 'more than me', and 'my whole life depends on them'. This is something like the feeling which can be experienced within a good relationship. A partner can be felt to keep us alive, held, to provide that sense of being able to relax in security, knowing we will be safe, for a while at least, and often, in both unconscious and conscious fantasy, in our internal world as well as our external one, 'for ever'. We use phantasies derived from our 'objects', the 'not me' aspects of people in our inner world, to understand others too.

A Good Object also provides the basis for understanding places and buildings; the structure and construction of the external world which holds us together and provides a place to be. Any fundamental change or loss, such as losing a partner, may represent losing this 'good object' that takes care of us and loves us and makes up 'our whole world'. This is why it can feel as if the world has fallen apart, a home has been destroyed. Through mourning we rebuild this world.

This is not easy. (As one old lady, with several children and grandchildren, said to me, sadly, about the loss of her rather cantankerous husband: 'There's no-one for whom I come first now.')

The loss of certain aspects of a partner (for example, their ability to walk) may not challenge the way they fill the need for a Good Object. Other aspects such as their mind and their memory, or their ability to comfort or to hold or to speak, may resonate more closely and be more important. For some people a sense of goodness and being cared for can survive even powerful challenges; for others, with a weaker sense of a Good Object inside them, the world may more easily crack apart, leaving them vulnerable to internal and external furies. The fear of this disaster may not be easily separated from reality. (Is he lying in bed with his face to the wall to prevent the world collapsing, or is he afraid it has already collapsed? And lying in bed has consequences in the real world which might lead to aspects of his body and his life really collapsing – is he trying to externalise a frightening internal phantasy? Does he want someone to pull him back from the brink? Can we?)

Separating oneself from a partner who has lost significant capacities can be very difficult, partly because of the emotional difficulties of separating from someone who represents (or is felt to actually *be*) the Good Object. There is a 'one-and-only' aspect to a Good Object, which underlies, I think, anxieties about betrayal and the difficulties of replacing a partner while they are alive. We find it hard to divide our Good Object into two, one for sex and one for love, for example, without in our internal world feeling we are stripping something from both. Realising that we probably have ready-made phantasies of sharing a mother's love with someone (another parent, step-parent or siblings, for example) makes it immediately obvious this is not the same as having someone entirely for oneself: different phantasies are involved, they involve far more uncomfortable emotions (such as jealousy) and have different implications for our sense of security. Interestingly, of course, siblings in adulthood can contribute to a sense of security, of being safe in the world; and sometimes a partner's lover may in reality help a partner to continue to care.

In later life, younger people can carry something of the older person's Good Object. Just as a child sometimes refers to a teacher as 'Mum', or to mother using the teacher's name, so a common confusion in elderly people in hospital is between daughters and mothers: 'My mum came to see me today' when it was the daughter. The presence of an adult who knows and cares for an older, frail person can be very reassuring – and he or she can become controlling and anxious when the carer goes out. This can be irritating or suffocating for a carer, particularly if they are not comfortable standing in for the mother or father of someone old enough to be their grandparent. The emotional need for control of a Good Object is much greater than any practical needs; the younger carer may sense this with frustration.

'He could help himself on the toilet, I know, but he always wants me to do it!'

SENSE OF SECURITY

The concepts of the Good Object and the inner world help in understanding the sense of security, and the importance of the parents in the child's mind. When parents undermine each other, they undermine the child's inner world. If a parent tells lies, this translates into an inner world where the child cannot rely on them to know what is true and what is not, where terrifying or otherwise anxiety-provoking phantasies are less easily disposed of by solid knowledge of reality.

Returning from holiday in a train when aged six, Claire said to her mother that she hoped her cat wasn't shut in a drawer, unable to get out. Guiltily and apologetically, her mother confessed that she had had him put down before they went away; she had not been able to cope with a baby and a toddler and a cat that got under her feet. She hadn't dared tell Claire and had hoped she would forget. Claire was very upset and shocked, but as an adult she believed that her mother did not lie to her after this: she could always trust what her mother said. She was lastingly grateful that she too had learnt a lesson: she did not have to lie to her mother either, though in many ways it would have been easier at times.

We search the external world for evidence of which of our phantasies have come true. Anger or jealousy, particularly in the early years, can be accompanied by very destructive phantasies in which parents or siblings or the world are attacked and destroyed. (Think of a small baby's scream – as if all the devils in hell were after it – or a furious tantrum by a two year-old, trying to blot out a world which will *not* do what the child wants.) These phantasies persist, overlaid by reassuring ones as the child realises they have not actually blasted their little brother or their mother to smithereens.

Unfortunately, something wrong with a parent can be taken as evidence that the child has indeed done just that. It is the confirmation of these terrifying phantasies which undermines a child's sense of security, which is why trying to reduce the child's sense of responsibility rather than adding to it can help the child feel more secure.

If this happens early on, it can feel as if the whole world, including the ground, the buildings and structures of the internal world, is under threat. If a parent is out of action, children can feel they have to repair this internal world single-handedly, while being very aware of being too small and powerless. Unfortunately, if the parent regains their capacities, the child may not adjust their phantasies immediately, or at all. New phantasies will be formed, belonging to the age the child is, but if they have lost touch with earlier ones, then the ones formed earlier may not be changed.

A child who decides they have to take over responsibility for the family at the age of eight may not change their mind, however competent their parents show themselves to be later.

Actually helping in the real world may help the child to feel they can do something about their damaged inner world, that they are not 'useless', but the strongest need is for an adult to share the burden – which may be entirely in the child's mind. An adult who understands is a blessing indeed: a parent who understands is even more of a blessing, since they may be more able to modify Good Object phantasies directly.

It follows from this that respect and understanding for parents is of vital importance when talking with a child, particularly about a parent's illness. Maintaining or restoring a truthful, good picture of parents in the mind (alongside less flattering and sometimes rationally critical ones) is one of the results of successful counselling, for adults and for children. Through understanding the effects of their parent's illness on their childhood, adult children can regain a sense of security as they begin to distinguish being ordinarily angry with their parents and with the illness from a fear of the world being subject to a nuclear holocaust as a result of unconscious, furious anger with their Good Object. Being able both to criticise parents and to recognise and hold on to good aspects of them and their parenting is important for a good life, in which one is allowed both to make mistakes and to enjoy pleasures.

SEPARATION

When a mother goes into hospital and a small boy hurts himself, he wants her, and in his mind his mother is instantly there to cuddle him – but then she isn't; he becomes aware she is not there and he furiously hits out at her *for not being there*. In his mind he is hitting his mother; in fact he may be hitting the person who is trying to comfort him who is not his mother. In his mind, too, it is the phantasy mother who responds, perhaps hitting back or looking reproachful herself – and the child becomes afraid of a witch looking at him accusingly or chasing him with a stick. Nice mummy has gone and nasty witch mummy is there instead. When the mother returns from hospital the child may be very unsure if 'nice mummy' has come back, or if it is the witch: he hides his head, looks out of the corner of his eyes, clings to the person holding him.

Later, the child may be unsure if the 'nasty mummy' was *created* by his furious attacks: was it that which made his nice mummy go away?

As a child (boy or girl) rebuilds their relation with the returned mother, there is a question about whether or not the new picture fully connects with the previous 'nice mummy' phantasies. An older child will have less difficulty recognising the connection, particularly if adults help keep her alive in the child's mind while she is away. Reminding the child how they felt when she was away may not 'connect' if the feelings have been too far buried, but there may be opportunities to make connections, for example during play.

The connection may also be held better if someone else who loves the child can help to hold 'good mummy' phantasies by taking her place while she is away. This is much easier if the child already knows and loves them and knows they have a good relation with the mother. When comforting the child they can talk sympathetically about the mother being away, and about how cross the child is, 'of course', but how they are still being looked after and loved. In this way they can keep the mother 'alive' in the child's mind. Not understanding that it works like this, mothers sometimes find it difficult to allow their child to attach to anyone else: they are afraid that the child will prefer the new person to them. In fact, attachment to other people 'feeds' the good mother phantasy; love merges them all into one. And the 'good mother' phantasy is vital in supporting beliefs about a 'good child', or 'good self', who can and does love a 'good mother'.

An illness can, itself, seem like a bereavement or a separation to a small child. Even if she does not go to hospital, 'nice mummy' may have been replaced with someone different, 'ill mummy', and the child may lose the connection between them.

ENVY OF GOODNESS, ENVY OF THE GOOD OBJECT

We can be angry with our mothers in many different ways, at different ages. Particularly as children we have many phantasies involving attacking the Good Object in our minds. Mothers stop children doing so much, and they are bound to get angry with each other at times, for good reason. But life itself prevents children having it all their own way too, and sometimes children feel their mothers have 'everything' and they have 'nothing'. Envy of her goodness, her ability to love and be loved by others, to feed, to make new life, cuddle up with our father or our siblings, make decisions and choices – there are so many things a mother can do which a child cannot or is not allowed to do. In phantasy, envy, as an attack on the Good Object *because it is good*, is felt to be the most dangerous, the most 'sinful', of faults. Clearly, it spoils life for everyone, including the self. In an envious phantasy we can 'throw shit' at good ideas, at people, at valuable things, destroying their potential to help us because we cannot bear to see they have something we would like for ourselves. We can also despise ourselves for wanting what someone else has; we become 'full of shit' ourselves. Children's phantasies involve basic bodily functions which are reflected in adulthood in our forms of swearing, for example. In 'Mother, sex and envy in a children's story' (Segal 1979) I take Roald Dahl's *Danny the Champion of the World* (1975), and show how in the story faeces are thrown, in subtle symbolic ways but also literally (pheasants drop all over a big, fancy rich man's car), at symbols of adult masculine power and at mothers.

One of our fears is that we have spoiled our Good Object by such envy; that our inner world is to be poorer because we cannot bear to see the riches around us which do not belong to us. If we want to *become* mothers or sexual women or good men, we have to be able to see them as desirable rather than denigrated.

Envy can come into play when a carer feels their patient is getting better care than the carer themselves. Isabel Menzies-Lyth, in a study of nurses (Menzies-Lyth 1960), detected a tendency amongst some nurses to envy the care their patients were given, and at times even to sabotage it. When staff are well supported they are less at risk of envy and are more likely to support those in their care: this applies across all professions (and for parenting too).

When I began working with people with physical disabilities I assumed that envy would be a big problem; that someone who could not walk would envy those who could. It turned out that this was not a problem for most of the 500 or so people I met: I did observe it, but seldom. In literature it arises far more often, perhaps because we know it so well and fear it so much. In real life, vicarious enjoyment seems to be a bulwark against envy, as are love, hope and a capacity to enjoy life, whatever its characteristics. 'Counting your blessings' helps. (My grandfather used this phrase every day, as he collected the unused cutlery from the dining table.)

CAN AN OUTSIDER HELP?

Other people can play a part in building up the internal Good Object, which is anyway a composite of many different aspects of both parents and other care-givers. Someone who understands can change the structure of the internal world to some extent, though the earliest phantasies are in general the hardest to change. Changes made in childhood allow development to take place differently. Aspects of the personality which were cut off or avoided can be brought back into play, affecting how the child grows.

Someone who is less afraid of talking about disturbing ideas, or who knows about grieving, or who can see the goodness in a bad parent or the flaws in a good one, may have a powerful effect on the growth and development of a child or adult for whom these are new ideas. As much as the content of ideas, it is the modelling of a different way of looking which may be helpful.

People outside the family can help to hold ideas which are unthinkable for those most closely affected by them. They may be able to bring sense and memory to people who are in a state of panic and functioning in a more paranoid-schizoid way (see below). Ill or carer parents can be reminded that they have supportive internal parents and can once again become such parents themselves.

Outsiders can also find themselves in the role of 'bad object'; suddenly standing for all the bad aspects of a parent, for example. Idealisations in particular can 'turn' in this way; so someone who was idealised as an angel may 'change' into a devil. (Reducing the idealisation by drawing attention to flaws in the 'angel' view may help to prevent this process.)

After or during a loss, someone outside the family may be very helpful – or they may find their attempts to share grief painfully rejected. With the internal world in turmoil, the place of other people within it can fluctuate unpredictably. Unrealistic phantasies of others may show themselves, and it may suddenly be surprising and perhaps shocking to find that people seem to live in different worlds and do not understand each other at all. (The idea that it might be a relief to lose a very ill relative, for example, is often cited as something outrageously insensitive which people say. Feelings of relief may eventually come, or they may have been expected, but in the immediate aftermath of a death, the most present feeling may be the opposite of relief.) It is not always clear if an outsider is being rejected because they have said something painful (and which possibly, at another time, would have been helpful or true), or if they are being rejected because of what they represent (a painful contrast to the grieving person's situation, perhaps; or feelings which are at the time unbearable), or for some other reason. It is not easy to know how to be 'sensitive' to someone else's grief. At times of grief and mourning people often hurt each other: sadly, the effects can be lasting.

PARTNER-IN-THE-HEAD: *IS IT YOU, OR IS IT MY CONSTRUCTION OF YOU?*

'My mother warned me: "Look at his mother: that's what he'll expect you to become; and look at his father: that's what he may become."'

The internal parents, both 'good' and 'bad' mothers, and 'good' and 'bad' fathers, form part of the basic phantasies which people use to understand their life partners. Siblings also contribute to these phantasies, as do aspects of the self: we make assumptions about our partners based on our knowledge of all of these people, including ourselves. As we grow together and get to know them better, we gradually disentangle which of these phantasies were true and which were not entirely accurate.

In *Phantasy in Everyday Life* (Segal 1985) I described phantasies in which people put parts of themselves into each other: not just their 'hearts' are exchanged, but also different capacities and abilities. 'You take charge of finances and I'll do the arty things', for example, or 'You do the things our fathers did, and I'll do the things our mothers did', even though both could actually do either. When one gets ill, there is a question about what will happen to those aspects of the self which were 'handed over'. Will they be 'taken back' or are they now lost for ever? Someone has to look after the finances – will the other person do it as well, or better, perhaps? Or will there be financial disaster? Will I be so boring without my arty partner that nobody wants to visit me? When we recognise that unconscious phantasies are involved, it becomes clear that these are not simply practical issues but may involve deeply held beliefs and anxieties. Money and finances can represent life – in particular, life left to live. It is no simple task to suddenly take full responsibility for something like this which previously was shared or 'handed over' completely. On the other hand, if the partner was not dealing well with their part (allowing tax bills to build up, for example), there can eventually be a relief in being able to take it back without having to openly challenge them. 'You can't do it any more because you are ill', painful as it is, may be easier to say than 'You are incompetent, and always have been.' However, there is still some anxiety attached to 'Now it's my turn to find out if I'm the same.'

It is clear that loss of cognitive or emotional capacities can leave people struggling. For a long time, pre-existing phantasies about capacities will carry on functioning, so both the person themselves and their partner can remain apparently oblivious to the depth of the problem. (If one knows what the other would say, they may be able to carry on without them actually saying it.) But there may come a point when a response is actually needed, and if it is not forthcoming something will have to change. At this point people begin to struggle – they may still 'know' what their partner wants or would say, but with new situations this becomes less clear. Other family members also 'know' the person, and their phantasies may be different. Partners may have knowledge of opinions or facts which were never shared with the children, whose own constructions may depend on conversations with one parent when the other was not present. Different siblings remember their parents at different ages, and the parents might have changed their opinions. Each may feel they have a 'secret' relationship – and may be jealous of the others'. In addition, people do not realise how much their knowledge of the other is based on their knowledge of themselves, and may only realise when it is brought into question. Fights over funerals are often caused by different, passionately held, views of the same person coming into conflict.

PHANTASIES OF TAKING OVER THE PARENT

Children who become 'parentified', who take over parenting their parents, create phantasies in which their own childish dependence is put into their parents, to be 'looked after' there, while they take over adult, parental responsibilities. (Dahl's *Danny the Champion of the World* (1975) involves an exciting version of this: it relates a manic defence against some of the anxieties involved.) For a while this may seem to work. A child can 'step up' for a time, but in the long term, if people are asked to take on more responsibilities than their job description, they begin to complain and make demands. Both in reality and, even more, in phantasy, children do not get either the information or the power they need to look after an adult. Their own needs for parental guidance and support are not being met, at least partly because the child is resisting them. A child new at a support group for Young Carers said 'I don't do babyish things like that' and wanted to be a helper rather than allow herself to play. When a child does this, they can lose touch with their own child-self: pretending to be an adult, they try to behave as a child imagines an adult to be, which is very different from how adults actually are. This leaves them unsafe inside and they can develop a 'false self' which is uncomfortable for them and for others. Even parents may not feel warm towards children who are constantly trying to be something they are not and are terrified of being found out; such children can be irritating, perhaps because their view of the world is so different from the parent's and neither can relax, never quite knowing what to expect of the other. The parent may feel suffocated by the child's desire to control them, and by the child's 'mothering' phantasies, in which the parent is treated as if they were a child.

PHANTASIES ABOUT ILLNESS: *ILLNESS MAKES YOU FEEL BAD IN SO MANY WAYS*

As I have already said, when we were hungry or angry as very small children, we hit out: we hit our actual mothers or fathers in the real world, and the internal mother or Good Object in our minds or body. In phantasy, then, the Good Object, inside as well as outside, can turn bad or be lost for ever. At first it does not leave a gap but is replaced by a Bad Object – often many Bad Objects, as the good one is felt to be broken into bits, all of which come back to haunt or attack, through stomach aches or headaches for example. As we get older and can hold onto the idea of an absence, we remember these attacks and are afraid of their consequences; afraid that our anger caused the absence and the pain, though in reality it may have been a response to it. Later, as we get old enough to remember our angry attacks, we are afraid that we hurt our mother, our Good Object, and we may not be sure if she will forgive or if she will punish us or if, indeed, she will survive the attack.

Becoming ill ourselves may be 'read' as a sign that we are being punished; if she becomes ill we may 'read' this as a sign that we caused her illness. If we get better, we may feel forgiven. As adults, all these unconscious phantasies are ready and waiting to be applied to the illness of those around us.

Sharp pains may be 'read' as a Bad Object digging sharply at our bodies or our consciences, hurting us, preventing our limbs working;

dull pains as a sense of hopeless misery and accusation or blame for casting ourselves and others out of paradise. We may try to protect parts of our bodies which have become associated with an ill parent – where we 'feel' them, where they are being 'held'. (Feelings and phantasies about mothers are sometimes 'held' in the back, evoked in response to back pain and a sense of burden.) To other phantasies of illness are added those of being unloved or punished by God/our Good Object, and we have more phantasies to tell us what will happen next. Milton showed us his version in *Paradise Lost*.

On the other hand, if someone has a strong sense of a Good Object inside them, they may be able to withstand many knocks. Someone with a strong faith in their religion may for a time lose this faith when it fails to live up to their beliefs, but be able to restore it after modifying their understanding of what it means. People who feel more secure in their parents' love may be better able to tolerate illness than those who were never sure if they were loved or not. This feels most unfair to those who were not so well loved, but is a reason to be grateful for good parenting.

Phantasies which associate illness or deformity with badness can make it hard for parents to talk to children about illness or deformities. In the parents' minds, the children may be wanting to know 'Are you a bad person?' for example, and in unconscious phantasy the parent 'knows' they are; after all, the illness or their 'failure' as a carer (because the cared-for person is not better yet) tells them so. Phantasies are powerful – they act as knowledge, and they are often completely wrong. This is, I think, partly why parents are so relieved when they do manage to find out what is troubling the children. Consciously at any rate, they do not ask existential questions, though there might at some point be questions about life after death and the role of religious beliefs. Mostly it is questions which are utterly basic and obvious for the adult to answer: 'No, it was not you hitting mummy while playing tag which sent her to hospital two years ago', 'No, of course you don't have to go to boarding school; where did you get that idea from?'

Questions about fault are also disturbing. Again, in phantasy, love can keep someone alive (as in *Beauty and the Beast*), and a parent can be dying because the other parent does not love them enough. It can take a huge effort to challenge this phantasy and recognise the role the illness itself plays. In phantasy it is somehow always people who do things, not an abstract idea. In some families illness itself is personified; this can help to distinguish it from the person who has it and make it easier to think about the role of the illness itself. (A 2009 workbook by Jo Johnson described multiple sclerosis as a monster, suggested naming it and played at some length with this fantasy.)

CURES: *MAKING THINGS BETTER*

Just as we have ready-made phantasies of illness, so too do we have ready-made phantasies of cures. The moment someone announces they are ill, they are likely to be greeted with 'Have you tried...?' After many such offers such 'cures' may be declined less politely than they are at first. It seems we all want to make other people better – children as well as adults. Children can interpret things their parents say as implying causes and therefore cures, as did the man who sent his children to boarding school when he was diagnosed with MS because as a teenager he heard his mother's death being attributed to her having too many boys at home. This will not have been a new thought, invented because of what he overheard. He will *already* have been afraid he and his brothers were, as another child put it, 'too much for her'. The comment will simply have confirmed it.

Klein thought that the phantasies underlying any kind of creative work in adult life involved repairing damage done to the Good Object. She used the word 'reparation' to refer to this, and saw it as a basic, significant need for normal life. We want to be able to repair the damage we have done, not only to the people we love and loved in phantasy, but also to ourselves. (When we attack our mothers we become 'bad children' and temporarily lose touch with the 'good' self: it is disturbing later to find we did bad things without having any memory of them. Symbolically making up for these attacks involves recognising and bringing together both 'good' and 'bad' selves too.) This has a huge effect on our relations with the world and our job satisfaction: it influences our choice of work and the pleasure we have in doing it. To simplify, a mother-world damaged or attacked in early infancy might leave phantasies connected with the land, or with large buildings, and increase the pleasure to be obtained by working to restore them, for example. Early feeding problems might lead to a special interest in food – or an avoidance of thinking about it.

Reparation is fuelled by anxieties, so phantasies created because parents were ill or sick can push people towards working in the medical or allied professions, where anxieties about making people better can be tested. Evidence from the external world can reassure us that our efforts to restore people to health have been successful, and that therefore we are not 'bad' but 'good' ourselves.

When people talk about 'feeling bad today' or 'feeling good today', 'good' here may include not only physical feelings of lack of pain or discomfort, but also moral and social 'goodness'. The hope to be in some way 'better' in the future arises from this primitive sense of guilt. We want to be better people, able to do away with our faults; some of the distress of being ill is that this self-improvement programme may come to an end. The aim of such improvement is not only to improve the self, but also to mend damaged relationships.

Illness may bring reconciliation amongst opposing members of a family. Awareness that 'time is short' can help to mend old animosities, perhaps by bringing them into the open where they can be challenged and changed. Failure to sort out old quarrels can leave people frustrated after an unexpected death and encourage them to move more quickly to end quarrels which remain. Hope is often connected with the possibility of moving towards creating internal peace, with internal people restored to goodness, friendly towards ourselves and others, restoring at the same time a friendly, more loving self. We suspect too, I think, that our internal demons may come back to haunt us at the end of life, if not before, and that sorting them out would allow us to live at peace with ourselves to the end. 'Loss of hope' can mean loss of this hope.

We want to 'cure' our internal world at the same time as the external one. Other people's illnesses can upset our internal economy, even if we do not know them very well. These people may represent something for us, such as an ideal professional woman, or part of an ideal couple, standing for the hope that such people exist; or for the possibility of living well alone. Illness then threatens such phantasies, and we want to put them back as they were.

Illness can also set people against each other, dashing hopes of peace in our world. Sometimes it feels safer to cut 'goodness' off from 'badness', located somewhere else – this can lie behind estrangements. Unfortunately this cuts off aspects of the self too and does not feel as comfortable as living in a world where everyone loves each other. On a wider stage, 'seeing' or locating all one's own aggression in one's neighbour, while allowing oneself to feel more virtuous perhaps, does not improve anyone's security. Sadly, the reality is that everyone does not love each other, and we have to do our best to live with our own share of responsibility for this. Illness may bring this reality into focus.

Sometimes children of ill parents find satisfaction in caring for ill people a long way from home, where their own guilt and their ambivalence towards their parents is less aroused than it would be at home. Unless they can work to change it, for example in some form of psychotherapy, they may still have a sense of failure hanging over them which can be evoked by any client who does not get better.

BAD FEELINGS HIDING GOOD ONES...

The phantasies accompanying feelings of guilt or shame attached to illness may be so powerful and so destructive that they blot out all awareness of other feelings and other people's needs. As they are unconscious, the person may not be fully aware of them – they simply feel 'nothing', or edgy, or frustrated, or 'hot and bothered', or a desire to run away and hide. In counselling, exploration and examination of bad feelings towards the self, parents, children or partners is generally (I am tempted to say *always*) followed by a new awareness of more securely based good and loving feelings.

It is through thinking about and examining 'negative' thoughts that 'positive' ones become available – too often people think they have to block the 'negative' feelings rather than allow them to live for long enough to work them through. Positive feelings and fantasies artificially created to keep the negative ones 'down' cannot modify them; this does not offer the same sense of security as bringing the two together consciously.

Good support may be essential to allow people to feel safe enough to allow their bad feelings to be expressed and experienced sufficiently for them to be modified. Deeper phantasies need to be evoked, not just thought about, and for this a re-creation of a dependent relationship may be needed. Psychotherapy and psychoanalysis can create such relationships and evoke the relevant feelings in their current form, allowing them to be modified.

COVERING UP

Adults may say they cannot easily distinguish between a child who is covering up their anxieties, and a child who really is not anxious. The child may not know which they are. Children can be desperate to protect their parents, in particular from any knowledge which might upset them or which could bring about their collapse. The last thing they want is to expose their parents (and their internal Good Object) as weak, or no longer having everything under control. In fact, once parents begin to think at all about their children, they can often detect signs of anxiety in them.

> 'I don't think my illness affects her at all...she never talks about it. Actually, I sometimes think she's a bit, not clever, you know? She sometimes behaves in a very childish way, she's eight but she behaves and talks like a five-year-old; she also gets really wild sometimes, she'll bounce around the kitchen talking or singing loudly, not listening, it doesn't seem quite real somehow. I find it really irritating.' 'What was happening when she was five?' 'Oh, that was when I first went to hospital, when I was diagnosed. She stayed with my mother. Yes, she's the one who told me not to let it affect her. So we never talked about it. She was fine with my mother. I tried to pretend nothing had happened, really. We just carried on. It was hard at first.'
>
> 'So perhaps she is doing what you and your mother wanted her to do: pretending nothing had happened?'
>
> 'I didn't see it like that, but I suppose you are right. Now I think about it, she does sometimes show she cares. She gets really worried when my legs give way and she says, "I'll bring you a blanket, mummy." That irritates me too, a bit really. It doesn't seem right that she should be looking after me.' (This is a schematic version of developments over several counselling sessions.)

This mother was able eventually to play 'mummy goes to hospital' with her daughter and listen to her daughter telling her how frightened her doll was that her mother would die and leave her alone with a granny she didn't like all that much. They talked about the mother's sister who would actually take the daughter if anything happened to the mother, and who the daughter liked a lot, and why she had not taken her then. The mother confessed she was shamed by the way she had failed to notice her daughter's anxiety over three years. I drew her attention to my co-authored book *Helping Children with Ill or Disabled Parents* (Segal and Simkins 1996), where she could find plenty of other parents who were equally ashamed of themselves. For her child there was now a hope that her anxieties could be recognised and reduced by her mother's new ability to give her a good kind of attention. Most importantly, both she and her daughter could stop pretending and turn their considerable abilities towards living with reality as it actually was. Illness is tiring enough without the extra effort of needing to pretend.

DENIAL

In phantasy it is easy to say '*No!* It didn't happen!' and to create a fantasy world in which it did not. An unwanted idea can be 'stuffed down a well', pushed into a box and the lid shut down tightly. As long as nobody opens the box it will be all right. In phantasy an unwanted part of the self can be pushed into someone else: 'It's not *me*, it's *him*!', '*I'm* not helpless and dependent, *you* are!', '*I'm* not bad, *she* is!' A lost person can be held onto: 'My mother isn't dead, she's just gone abroad.' All of these fantasies can become unconscious and continue to govern behaviour as if they were true.

Unfortunately, of course, because they are not true they come up against reality and they may not serve well for predicting what should happen next. Very often some avoidance is needed to maintain the fiction: condolence cards would have to be hidden to maintain the fiction that a dead person is alive; and phantasies tend to draw other associations in, so after a time perhaps all condolence cards, and perhaps all cards or card shops, might be avoided in order not to have to be reminded of the death.

Denial prevents the evoked phantasies from running their natural course, which would allow them to be modified by other considerations and would bring necessary changes to ideas, assumptions and beliefs. Where people employ denial, the ideas they are keeping out of consciousness are the first panic, catch-your-breath, oh-my-god, no! reactions, which often include quite serious distortions and basic misunderstandings. They include ideas such as 'No-one can possibly love me now!' or 'This is the end of the world!' or 'This means I've lost/I'm going to lose everything!' Even where a diagnosis is not actually life-threatening, sometimes an initial panic reaction includes the idea 'I'm going to die!', where dying means something closer to being tortured in hell for ever while those you love dance on your grave, or (alternatively) fall apart and fall to pieces themselves, rather than any realistic thoughts about the ending of a life. Such instant judgements may be related to half-remembered incidents, or childhood memories or second-hand knowledge of other people of the 'so-and-so had MS and she *died*!' variety, which ignore the fact that 'she' had a long and successful life for many years before.

There are many forms of denial and it can be useful to consider exactly what is being denied in each case. It may appear to be 'I don't have an incontinence problem' or 'I don't have MS' or 'I'm *not* going to die.' However, exploration may uncover some significance to these statements which goes over and above reality, and uncovering this may enable the incontinence or MS, or even death, to be acknowledged more realistically. So 'incontinence' might be linked to ideas of being unable to keep anything inside, or of being a child with wet knickers and being totally humiliated – a fantasy derived from this is being rejected.

San said she could not pass Marks and Spencer's since her diagnosis of MS – because of the initials. Asked about what the MS meant to her she said, 'I always wanted children.' She was astonished when told that having MS did not mean she could not have children; she had assumed this was the case and had always avoided reading anything about MS because the idea of not having them upset her too much.

Mic, aged 14, similarly, refused to read the booklet about his mother's recently diagnosed MS. Offered the chance to ask questions about his mother's condition he asked many questions, but not how long she had to live; it turned out later that he did not ask because he was certain she was going to die within a year or two. Again, he was astonished when told he was wrong.

For some people what is denied is the *need for help*, rather than the condition itself. Memories of ill-treatment or humiliation by professionals or care-givers at some time in the past, whether this is an accurate memory or fabricated out of a misunderstanding, may prevent their help being accessed – the cost seems too high. Sometimes people in this situation seek their own aids, for example medication, a stick, an 'alternative' diet, a wheelchair, or glasses which they can buy over the counter without a prescription and without having to admit to anyone other than themselves that they have a problem.

Denial of a *diagnosis* is different from denial of *symptoms*. The name 'cancer' or 'motor neurone disease' or whatever may strike fear into the heart in a way that 'a small lump in my breast' or 'I've got a slight problem with my leg' does not. The diagnosis may be denied while the symptoms are dealt with perfectly sensibly. Where this is the case it may be traced back to a meaning which is given to the diagnosis, which may bear little relation to other people's understanding.

Denial of symptoms can also happen, but neurological problems confuse the picture. Someone may appear totally unaware of their incontinence to the extent of ignoring puddles or wet or smelly clothing – perhaps their sense of smell and touch has been affected, or perhaps they have just created a phantasy-world in which it is not happening.

An old lady came along the corridor in a mental hospital saying, 'There has been a flood, dear, along there [indicating back where she had come from]; I think someone should deal with it.' She had wet her knickers.

Someone who has difficulty keeping their balance but refuses a stick on the grounds that they don't want to make themselves conspicuous may really be unaware of how unsafe they are and how unbalanced they look to others. If told, they may be unable to hold the information. Is this because they *cannot* or they *do not want to*, perhaps because of an unconscious phantasy linking it with something terrible? What appears to be denial may in fact be physical damage to the capacities to see or to make connections or to feel, perhaps accompanied by damage to memory and judgement. In such situations it may be difficult but important for other people to be clear whether they think they are dealing with a *refusal* or an *inability* to see what is going on; whether the denial can be undone by thinking and talking or whether it cannot. Such issues may affect whether the person is held responsible for a refusal to accept reality, or whether they should be seen as suffering from a failure of perception or other cognitive problems. It may be harder and more distressing for a professional as well as for a family to accept that the 'denial' is neurological than to see it as something which could be got rid of if someone was prepared to try harder. (It sometimes seemed that NHS managers where I worked did not understand that decision-making and memory problems could contribute to neurological patients missing appointments and being unable to make plans for their own rehabilitation. 'Being sent back to their doctor for a new referral' as a penalty for missing appointments had severe consequences for those who struggled to remember to make one, struggled to get to their doctor and then found it hard to remember why they needed one in the first place.)

One form of denial can involve a decision to pretend that nothing is wrong. This is a strategy which some people insist on, and it may bring benefits to the pretender, if at some cost. If others can be persuaded – often non-verbally – to join in the pretence and also, crucially, to fill the gaps, such pretence can appear to work as a strategy for life. It requires that at least one person acknowledges the problems sufficiently to take action to prevent the pretender being inconvenienced or being brought up against awareness in a public way; and it requires the person who is pretending to do it convincingly. The family may not be convinced, of course, and this form of denial may simply transfer anxieties and problems to those around, including the family, along with the insistence that they do not share their concerns and do not ask for any support, advice or information about the problem from the person who is pretending. While clearly untrue, the pretence that nobody else notices or is affected may be forcefully maintained by the family, mainly out of anxiety about the effect it would have if they were forced to recognise the real situation.

My father was blind but the way he dealt with it was to pretend it didn't exist. He had my mother and he had a good memory. He could look a witness in the eye and cross-examine him just as he did before. We would go for long walks in the country and he would hold onto me tightly. I used to think sometimes of abandoning him in the middle of a forest to see what happened then. He told me never to allow anyone to feel sorry for him: 'I've enjoyed every minute of my life, and I still do.' (Sir John Mortimer on Radio 4, 'No Triumph, No Tragedy', 13 February 2007)

Mortimer's father, like many barristers, was clearly a competent actor in court. His pretence in front of his son was perhaps aimed mainly at rejecting the idea that blindness had to mean 'people feeling sorry for you'. Mortimer speaks as if, for him and his father, this was the same as blindness itself. Clearly, by holding onto his son, Mortimer's father was actually acknowledging his blindness non-verbally. He also in fact acknowledged it by travelling around Switzerland seeking cures, taking help from his wife and also obliquely when he told his son he must reject any hint of 'your poor father'. Denial is never simple, and seldom as total as it appears.

Denial may be directed at the feelings rather than at the problem. 'I'm fine like this' may be true or it may be a denial; an onlooker may have no difficulty making the distinction or they may struggle to believe the person. Heavy makeup and a bright, false smile may be a giveaway.

ASSISTED DENIAL

Denial is often helped along in one way or another. In unconscious phantasy, drugs (including alcohol) may be understood to be cutting off the voices of internal accusers – drowning, drugging, killing off, putting to sleep or punishing those internal people, 'people-in-the-head', often parents long dead, who accuse and blame and triumph over the person's suffering. They may also facilitate splitting, in which the self is separated from the internal accuser and can enjoy the accuser's torment or befuddlement.

James associated his drinking with a feeling that nobody cared for him. He was angry at the way he was neglected as a child in a children's home. His lack of care for himself in the face of a serious illness, compounded by drinking, was a complex mix of identification with an alcoholic Matron who had forced him to punish his younger brother cruelly, a punishment of himself for allowing her to do it, a desire to join his mother and father in the grave, and a way of preventing anyone currently from taking care of him. Being cared for would have reawakened memories of his life before his mother died and the enormous sense of loss he suffered when he was taken from his father. At times in his head he was also punishing his mother for leaving him and 'the Authorities' for taking him away.

Many forms of assisted denial, such as excessive alcohol consumption, can be quite destructive of the self (a 'bad' self who deserves it, as well as a 'good self' or 'guilty self' who suffers, seeing it), as well as, often, of others' comfort and pleasure, though this too may be denied. The build-up of denied guilt then contributes to the sense of despair and hopelessness. With no better means for dealing with these feelings, denial may escalate in a vicious circle.

PROJECTIVE IDENTIFICATION: *YOU CAN FEEL THIS FOR ME*

Sometimes people cannot bear to feel an emotion and they may evoke it in someone else 'instead'. This involves a set of phantasies, in particular a powerful overt denial of the emotion and also a sense that it cannot be mentioned.

A young man who looked after his mother, who was dying of cancer, told his estranged father he wanted to drive his car off the cliff.

A teenage girl whose father was ill let her parents know she was having sex in a risky way.

A young girl whose mother had cancer stopped eating.

Such behaviour creates in the parents anxieties which come close to the child's anxieties: about uncertainty, fears about the possibility of losing someone they love who is very important to them. Anxieties which will be at least tinged with guilt and a sense of responsibility for something they cannot control, involving a sense of helplessness, of being at sea – and of needing help. In each of these families, the parents sought professional help as a result of the child's behaviour and were able to regain some capacity to parent the child, whose behaviour then changed for the better.

In phantasy the feelings are forced into the other person, while the intention behind it can vary enormously. Amongst others, there may be a sense that the other person can deal with it better ('You can deal with this, I can't'); there may be revenge, or a desire to hurt the other person for some other reason; to test them and to test the feeling ('Let me see how *you* deal with it'); to just blindly get rid of the feeling, and perhaps the part of the self that feels (the specific thing, or anything at all). It can be understood as a form of communication, but for this the recipient has to be sufficiently aware.

> *'My ten-year-old shouts rude words out of the window.'*
> *'What does it make you feel?'*
> *'It makes me feel terrible…embarrassed…it makes me totally wild.'*
> *'Is it possible that he feels like this, himself, sometimes?'*
> *'I think he is embarrassed about his father, when he goes to the school. But he loves him, really loves him. He told me he wanted to buy him a racing car when he grew up, because he could drive it lying down [because his legs don't work at all].'*
> *'Does he know that his father might not live that long? Might he feel wild like that about his dad dying?'*
> *'I think he does. But he won't let me talk to him about it.'*

A teenage boy sat in my room and grunted at anything I said. I felt completely hopeless and helpless. His school nurse had brought him because he was failing to attend school and his mother had multiple sclerosis. I wanted to hand him over to someone who really knew how to work with children; I felt completely unskilled and useless. It was only the fact that I realised that the nurse had described exactly this feeling when making the appointment with me which held me back from referring him on. I took a deep breath and said, 'I wonder if you sometimes feel you need someone else to help you cope?' For the first time the boy broke out of his shell and exploded: of course he did, his grandfather had looked after his mother until he died a few months previously, now the boy was left alone to take care of a mother who was at risk of falling downstairs if he wasn't there to stop her. The nurse and I breathed a sigh of relief; now we knew what the problem was.

The feelings evoked in me felt exactly as if they were entirely mine; absolutely not his. Asking the question felt strange too, as if it was the most stupid question in the world – of course it wouldn't be true, and how could I ask such a thing of a boy who clearly wanted to keep himself to himself. The last thing he would want would be any kind of outside interference. This conveys something of the strength of such phantasies. They evoke feelings, anxieties, but at the same time forbid mention of them.

We call this process *projective identification*. When someone cannot bear to feel a feeling, they may create it in someone else and deny they have it at all. In phantasy, they put a significant part of themselves into the other person and control it there (in this case, the part that wants to reach out and cry for help).

When people cannot speak for any reason, social or physical, emotional or practical, projective identification may easily come into play. A husband, knowing he is totally dependent on his wife, may be unable to express feelings about her going out – but she may develop a serious difficulty in leaving the house while being unable to discuss it with him. Someone who is afraid of being left may evoke fears in their partner of being left without ever saying anything about it. A woman who always came off the phone feeling guilty about not loving her mother enough was hugely relieved when a counsellor wondered aloud if her mother might feel guilty for not loving *her* enough: this made immediate sense and took the anxiety out of the phone calls.

I think that in normal conversation we share, and acknowledge that we share, fleeting emotional states as they pass. I think that this process can be interrupted when someone has a very strong phantasy that says,

'I don't have this feeling: *only you do!*' This phantasy blocks the normal exchange. The recipient of the projection does feel it, and although it has been evoked by the conversation, they feel strongly that it must be their entire responsibility. Often it is only afterwards that this process can be picked up: it always makes such sense at the time that it should belong to you, not them.

Between couples there is sometimes an exchange where feeling states are divided up using this process. One gets a 'double dose' of, say, hopefulness, and the other a 'double dose' of misery. Misery and hopefulness are both recognised by each, but one is very scared of being miserable (what will happen to all the hope if any misery is acknowledged?) and the other very scared of hope (nobody will take seriously the bad things that might happen or have happened if we get hopeful). This takes place under phantasies governed by 'all or nothing' splitting. Each can become more extreme as they try to convince the other that their position is right and the other's wrong. In phantasy they try to 'push' their hopefulness or their misery into the other in order to get rid of it, to keep it safely cared for elsewhere. It may be part of a desire not to be a miserable person, but also not to be ridiculously hopeful – hope or misery may be attached to very frightening memories or fantasies: 'If I am hopeful I might be loved; if I am miserable I won't be.' But at the same time, awareness of misery cannot be forgotten, so it is important that the partner who seems less frightened of it should continue to hold it – their own and 'for' the other too. What is needed is a bit of hope and a bit of misery to be acknowledged by both, and, with the help of a counsellor who can hold both in mind at once, this can happen.

If each is happy to live with an exchange, couples can enjoy it, and it can work for many years. One can earn money and the other look after the children. One can claim to be very clever and the other to be stupid – in a way which allows each to deny that they are ever, or in any way, the other. One can take care of wider family relationships and the other deny their importance. Problems may only arise if each loses touch too much with the capacities 'handed over' and begins to feel totally deskilled, for example, or to resent the loss of an important part of the self. If the lack of support continues over time, the 'double dose' can also become overwhelming and eventually rejected. In a good relationship the fears attached to the initial division of labour may have reduced, so that either can 'take back' the aspect of themselves that they handed over, modified and changed by seeing their partner carry it for a while. It can also happen that one can become contemptuous rather than grateful for the other's contribution; and while someone may be happy to play the 'worm' for a time, they may also 'turn'.

Illness or a new disability can challenge these exchanges, as new anxieties, new roles come into play and old ones are disrupted.

CONTAINMENT OR HOLDING

In good relationships, when a baby or child cries, adults generally 'pick up' the distress and 'feed back' some understanding, such as 'you're hungry', or 'you're cross', or lonely, or some other explanation alongside other attempts at soothing, such as touch or cuddling, singing or distraction. The baby is getting rid of their feeling into the world around (by projective identification); if conditions are supportive of life, someone will be there.

Psychoanalysts such as Bion and Winnicott described the ability to take on board feeling states in this way as 'containment' or 'holding', and it is something which mothers and fathers do for their children, and partners can do for each other. Crying into a void leaves the baby feeling emptied out, with nothing inside and nothing to fill him or her up, but feelings and states of mind evoked in someone else can be understood like a good feed – the child (or partner) 'takes in' not only a new understanding, but some sense of another mind which can nurture theirs, offer them space to think and to feel, and also a sense of the importance and reality of their own existence in a social world.

Illness can disrupt this 'containment' process. The understanding may no longer be there, or the capacity to allow in another person's feelings or thoughts. Containment is important for children to grow and mature and to develop a sense of themselves as someone who matters, so losing this capacity has significant consequences.

Depression or other forms of mental illness can be more disruptive than physical illness if they take the parent's mind away from the child, leaving the child with a void where their sense of themselves in a loving world would otherwise be. Part of the distress of being a carer for someone with significant mental or cognitive problems arises from the loss of the other person's containing function.

This containing function also affects sexual development. Both fathers and mothers are important for a girl's sexual development: they can both contain some of her anxieties. Both provide role models for themselves and for partners. In addition a girl can 'try out' some of her childish sexual behaviour (just as babies 'flirt' with adults) on her father; if she is lucky, he responds in a way which makes her feel good about herself. A father's reactions to her growing up affect the way she feels about her body and her ability to attract and hold a man's attention. Boys and girls also identify with their fathers, and in their relationship with a father they may 'put' parts of themselves into their father for a while (such as their aggression, or their understanding, or whatever the father seems to represent to them). How fathers 'contain' and 'give back' whatever they represent to their children will affect the way the children grow. An aggressive father may make a child too afraid of their own aggression to use ordinary anger; a depressed father may simply not react; a firmly loving father may allow children to feel safe and therefore to be curious about the world around them. Later in life, sexual partners take over this containing function and they too can help or hinder maturation. Insecurities can be calmed in a good, containing relationship.

A father who is distressed about his own sexual problems (caused by an illness or disability) may find it hard to react to his children's developing sexuality in a way which contains their anxieties. He may not realise how important he is to his children and that his awareness of them matters. A man or woman whose sexual functioning is reduced may no longer naturally (in the course of sexual or affectionate activities) reassure their partner that the partner's body is still lovable and loving: they may need to be alerted to the need to make their partner feel loved, perhaps in a different way.

SPLITTING: *ANGELS AND DEVILS*

Doctors and nurses often find themselves viewed as 'angels' or 'devils' when patients recover or fail to recover. Family members can find themselves playing these parts too, behaving like martyrs or cruelly walking away and leaving everything to a sibling.

In phantasy it is easy to split the world into two, often to protect the 'good' from contamination by the 'bad', or to keep it safe. Sometimes we feel we are the best container for the 'good', but equally we may feel someone else is, a 'martyring' sibling, perhaps, who is so much better than we could ever be. In these circumstances it may be clear that splitting is not a neutral process; it actually involves cutting out or cutting off aspects of ourselves and the other. The reality is that we have to live with the complexities of life, of emotional states, of abilities, of hopes and failures. Under pressure from illness, and life-and-death fears, this may not for a while be possible.

Splitting is part of the 'paranoid-schizoid' mechanisms which I describe below. In this state, 'goodness' is felt to be brittle, like a beautiful crystal ball which can break if touched; it feels essential to keep any 'badness' away. When things have calmed down, 'goodness' can feel more like a sponge, able to absorb bad things without being destroyed or losing coherence or shape.

PLAYING OUT PHANTASIES

Klein learnt about children's unconscious phantasies while watching her son playing. Play can tell parents something about what their children think about an illness-related event. 'Teddy's mummy goes to hospital' is one game, but there are others.

It was when Ben made a model of a motorbike smashing into a wall, with blood dripping down everywhere and body parts scattered, that his mother decided he was being disturbed by what was going on in the family at the time. She sent him to talk to a psychotherapist and he came back obviously feeling more relaxed. He told her he had some time previously tried to talk to his best friend for support, and the friend had then told him he had tried to cut his own wrists. Ben had not told his mother about the friend.

When Klein went away for a 'cure', her small son developed fears of being poisoned by a witch. Klein realised that his 'good mother' had in phantasy become a 'bad, witch mother' because he was angry with her for being away.

74

PARANOID SCHIZOID AND DEPRESSIVE POSITION:
MOVING ON AND GETTING STUCK

It can be helpful to distinguish between two different ways of responding to anxiety based on Klein's concepts of the paranoid-schizoid (p-s) and depressive positions. I am simplifying enormously here, but we can think of it as two different sets of phantasies which can come into play.

In the paranoid-schizoid position, anxieties are about life and death. There may be underlying panic and massive fears. The life or death under consideration may be one's own or someone standing for a Good Object; martyrdom is a choice for someone in the p-s position, when their own life seems 'nothing' compared to that of a beloved person, country or belief in God.

Schematically, these are the characteristics of the paranoid-schizoid position:

- Time stands still; 'now' is 'for ever'; 'yesterday' has gone 'for ever'.
- Things are seen in terms of 'you *or* me', 'your life *or* mine'; never 'you *and* me'.
- Selfishness, which may save your own life.
- Consideration for others is cut off and out.
- 'Splitting' is common: people and things are split into simple categories, depending on whether they will keep someone alive or threaten them.
- 'Good' and 'bad' are kept separate; no 'grey' areas are permitted. Good can be felt to be at risk of breaking up if any badness comes near.
- The capacity for reasoned thought is lost; thoughts are ready-made by previous phantasies and may not be challenged.
- Apology is impossible – responsibility is so frightening it has to be disowned.
- Huge, life-threatening self-blame is covered up by blaming someone else.
- 'Sins' are felt to be so bad they should be paid for with a life – so in order to save their own life, someone may deny their sins (or try to kill someone else).
- Forgiveness is not an option.

- Other people may be felt as dangerous, threatening, intrusive.
- Other people may be used or manipulated or threatened, as a way of getting rid of terrible anxieties into them and out of the self.
- Other people may be seen as cartoon characters: Perfect Angels or Monsters, Saviours or the Devil himself.
- Pleasure is experienced in a manic way, covering up or displacing fears, and can 'crash' into despair.

People aren't always aware that this is how they feel, but it may be possible to deduce it from their behaviour and what they say.

In the paranoid-schizoid position, guilt and blame can become persecutory:

- Too much guilt cannot be felt; it can only be pushed into or onto someone else.
- Blame (originally and secretly) directed at the self is redirected at other people.
- Other people are then felt to be blaming and accusing.
- Guilt increases, and is increasingly denied, pushed onto someone else.

When someone is ill, their partner, their child or their parent may be terrified about what will happen to their own lives. Paranoid-schizoid mechanisms can mean that the ill person is blamed for their own illness, and for ruining other people's lives.

When things get better and anxieties reduce, people can revert to 'depressive position' mechanisms. In the depressive position:

- There is a sense of time; of present, past and future being distinct.
- A sense of concern for others returns.
- Other people are experienced as more real, more whole, more human-sized and less cartoon-like.
- Sorrow and apology become possible as guilt becomes more realistic and less frightening.
- People can reach out in a caring way.
- There can be hope for a more realistic outcome.

- Other people do not seem so ideal, either in a bad way or a good way.
- There is less idealisation of the self.
- Fear is less powerful and more realistic.
- The experience of pleasure is less manic, more secure.
- It becomes possible to think, and to hold in mind more than one idea or feeling at a time.

People can move from one position to the other, as their anxiety levels are raised or lowered. Depressive position functioning also involves feeling sad and sorry about the attacks made on people, thoughts and ideas in the paranoid-schizoid position; but it brings the possibility of either working through these, or of manically denying them and reverting to a modified version of the p-s position. Panicking is exhausting and frightening. Although the depressive position involves feeling 'sadder but wiser', it also feels safer and ultimately allows a more secure relationship with reality.

WHY DO CHILDREN BEHAVE BADLY WHEN THEIR PARENTS ARE ILL?

One would think that children would behave particularly well when a parent is ill, especially if they have frightening phantasies of losing or injuring them by their own aggressive feelings. Sometimes they do: they can try to be 'extra good'. Unfortunately, their anxieties and their stage of development can make it hard for them to react with anything other than paranoid-schizoid mechanisms. It is not possible to be 'extra good' all the time: this requires that a child reject all their normal, not-perfect, reactions to daily life; it requires that they make no demands, that they truly 'give up' themselves for others. So they deny – they blot out thoughts and feelings, either 'bad' ones, for fear of them being (not just 'becoming') true, or 'good' ones, because it is impossible to hold both good and bad at once. They despair at their 'failures', and moments later idealise their own capacities, feeling enormously powerful and good.

They also project their badness into others: brothers and sisters may be treated as 'baddies' when they quarrel and disturb the mother, seen as ill and too weak to cope; so the 'extra-good' older sister shouts at them with all the viciousness at her command – and realises that she has gone over the top and maybe her little brother and sister will never forgive her.

Unable to tolerate and hold onto bad thoughts for long enough, children find grieving very difficult. It is not clear if this is *because*, or only *if*, they are not helped by adult understanding, or if it is just a characteristic of children. (Erna Furman's book *A Child's Parent Dies* (Furman 1974) shows that, with the help of adult understanding, many children can grieve successfully for the loss of a parent, and that the outcome of the grieving process depends on the pre-existing relationship with the child's 'Good Object'.) Adults in my experience can find it very hard to help their children to think about losses and to work through their meaning, particularly if the children are very small. They may try to ignore changes or assume their children will 'forget', which leaves the children prey to very frightening and unrealistic fantasies of their own. At the same time, children's view of adults is clearly not the same as an adult's, and they attribute both much more and much less power to them. This colours their phantasies, particularly when they try to deal with anxieties about a parent's survival by in phantasy becoming the parent or taking over their characteristics or capacities; the parent a parentified child is trying to be bears little resemblance to a real one.

In my experience, children can be terrified that one parent has 'made' the other one ill; or they can be angry with an ill father who seems not to be supporting their mother, more anxious about her (phantasied) weakness than his (real) illness. The illness of one parent can threaten the child with loss of both; and the child may protest and punish a parent felt to be guilty. Because the child is driven by often quite unrealistic phantasies, it may be hard for an adult to understand what is going on in their minds.

Roald Dahl had an amazing capacity to understand particularly the unpleasant sides of children's minds, and *Danny the Champion of the World* (1975) illustrates an omnipotent fantasy of a parentified child. Danny takes over when his father breaks his leg. In the story the father is not even provided with a stick to walk with and becomes almost totally useless, while Danny becomes enormously resourceful. This is a good example of splitting: Danny's capacities are enhanced and his father's diminished, exaggerating the contrast between them. And it is clear that this is not a lasting solution: a small boy can look after his rather impotent father for a while, but his father's potency is actually needed in the long run. Danny succeeds in poaching hundreds of pheasants, but he cannot live alone with his father on poached pheasants for ever; he needs to have friends and go to school too.

Sometimes it is clear that a child's bad behaviour is a case of projective identification, that the child is ensuring that the adults around feel something of their own despair, horror or terror that the world is coming to an end. Sometimes it seems the child is expressing their guilt, and wants to be punished; or is blaming someone they feel has caused the problem. More than one phantasy can be involved at once, so all of these may be expressed in one action, such as running away or threatening to kill themselves.

Daily refusal to help, too, can be a way of expressing the sense that the child needs someone else to help who is bigger than they are. 'Why can't Dad help? If he doesn't, why should I?' implies a desire for a 'proper' dad, not one who mysteriously 'does nothing' around the house while not going to work either. The illness is discounted and the boy simply has a 'useless dad', an object of contempt, not even pity. But since the boy identifies with his father, it makes him 'useless' too, and where does that lead?

A sense of 'badness', drawn from anxiety, seems to exert a pressure to be expressed in one way or another; and illness makes children as well as adults feel anxious and bad.

SUMMARY

In this chapter I have explained what I mean by phantasies and tried to describe some of the phantasies involved when people have to cope with (their own or another's) illnesses and disabilities.

CHAPTER 3

Understanding

'I don't understand him. I wouldn't behave like that. If I were ill, I'd want to tell all my friends. He won't let me tell anyone. He thinks they'll be sorry for him. But when he doesn't even lift the shopping, because they don't know, they just think he's being a bad dad.'

'I wouldn't mind if she made an effort but she just sits there doing nothing. She won't even do her exercises that the physio gave her. I think you should try to help yourself, not just wait for someone else to do it for you. It really irritates me when people expect others to do things for them, when they could do them themselves. It would be different if you couldn't do something, but...'

'How can I make her more positive? When I ring her up she's always so negative. I tell her there must be something she can do, but she won't do anything. She's still working, but she complains all the time. I'm a positive person, she's always been a bit negative...yes, I am afraid it will make her worse.'

'I don't understand why his brothers don't do anything to help. They just leave it all to me. None of his family cares.'

'Why don't I do something in the afternoon? Because I'm exhausted by then. It takes me two hours to get up in the morning, and then I have to go back

to bed to recover, and by the afternoon I've had it. People think I'm just sitting around, well I am, but it's because I haven't got the energy to do anything else. And then people complain I don't ring them. They say they get tired too, as if they know, but they haven't any idea what fatigue is.'

'Childbirth is the worst pain you've ever had? That's nothing! When I went into labour I thought I was just starting a mild sickle cell crisis; I didn't take much notice until it was a bit late. Most of the nurses think we exaggerate the pain because after you've taken pethidine you relax immediately and can start chatting. They say pain doesn't go like that, but when you've taken it [pethidine, only available in hospital], you know it's going to go. And chatting helps distract you.'

INTRODUCTION

Mutual understanding can be put under threat from the moment an illness or new disability emerges. Partners, friends, professionals and colleagues, even the local newsagent, may have their own 'cure' or recipe for salvation, and may find it hard to grasp the fact that the ill person has their own ideas about what will make them better, or their own feelings about being left to themselves or needing company. Differences of opinion about how one should behave, either as someone who has a health problem or as their carer or family member, are felt not as neutral, interesting differences of opinion, but passionately, as reasons to take up cudgels, if only in the mind – to accuse, to complain, perhaps even to fight or to cut off relationships entirely.

Some professionals and some partners may feel an obligation to at least try to understand; others pride themselves on an 'understanding' which makes no concessions to misfortune or to any form of grieving process. Having little patience with their own illnesses or their own pain, they neither expect it from nor offer it to others. Equally, some people who have to cope with severe changes in their health status want to be understood, while others would much prefer it if they could hide the changes and prevent anyone ever knowing. Some want others to know all the details; others want to gloss over any difficulties and continue to occupy the same place in social life and in the minds of others that they have occupied previously. These positions can change, sometimes from moment to moment, but certainly over weeks or years.

Illness and disability can arouse very strong desires to control: to control the environment which has suddenly slipped out of normal control; to control unruly emotions which threaten to destabilise relationships; to control the person you love who is threatening their own and your lives (because of the illness); to control the self, who has to deal with unwanted changes. A need to control or subdue the world often lies behind abuse of one kind or another. Understanding can sometimes help to defuse the risk in such situations – although in the heat of the moment, understanding may not be accessible.

In this chapter I look at some of the factors which can make it hard both to understand and to be understood by others where an illness or disability is concerned.

DIFFERENT EXPERIENCES

Unfortunately, understanding other people is notoriously difficult. Normal processes of understanding include 'putting oneself in the other's shoes', but illness and disability create differences between people which make it hard to know what their shoes really feel like.

First, outside and inside may not tally. A person who looks ungainly to others may feel they are effectively covering up a balance problem and, by not using a stick, are ensuring they remain 'normal'. However, to the onlooker, the sense of imbalance, of insecurity and anxiety provoked by watching them lurching from side to side, may be terrifying and far from 'normal'. Equally, a scar on the face may distort appearances from the outside while the owner sees only the reflection in others' faces.

Hidden disabilities can cause the opposite problem. It may be easy to forget that someone cannot see or hear properly if their face looks normal. Cognitive confusions, loss of insight or loss of memory may not be immediately obvious: it may be difficult to be certain they are real in the first place; it may be almost impossible at times to determine whether they are a characteristic of the person or of their illness; and it may be difficult to remember they exist. Neurological problems are particularly tricky. Legs may feel strange, sexual function be disrupted or mood affected with nothing being evident to anyone else. It can be very hard to understand how peculiar a person can feel when their limbs show no signs of a problem. Diagnosis can be a problem in this case too, with people suspecting that 'it's all in the mind' and some finding it difficult to believe that reported symptoms are real, or, if real, caused by a physical illness rather than a psychological one. Someone suffering from certain kinds of damage to the brain may appear or sound normal, and may be able to carry on a normal conversation so long as it goes no further than 'Hello, how are you?', while serious losses of function are hidden. So a message may be left or an appointment made with someone who appears and sounds perfectly competent – but who is incapable of writing it down or passing on the information.

'I spoke to your husband, didn't he tell you?'

'The doctor told my husband he should write to the DVLA to tell them he has frontotemporal dementia. He said he would but he hasn't of course.' (This is an illness characterised by loss of insight – as the doctor must have known.)

'I always feel guilty because I think the other mothers think I should be able to make cakes for all the school events. They don't realise I'm not working because I've got MS [which meant that at the time she had to sleep much of the day in order to be able to function when her children came home from school]. I can't go round telling them all. I'm not sure I want to, either. People think if you're not in a wheelchair there's nothing wrong with you.'

Time

Time also creates different experiences. An illness or disability can become familiar over time, while creating shock in those who see it for the first time. Those who have become used to it may become impatient with those whose responses have not had time to blunt or be modified by experience. They may also dislike the reminder of their own initial distress, or of the gulf between 'then' and 'now' evident in another's facial expression.

Even a partner or family member can forget a new or erratic hidden disability: any time within a year of onset, or even longer, if the disability is not thrust into their view on a regular basis, their internal image of the person can easily revert to a previous 'normal'.

Identification and separation

One of the fundamental differences which can get in the way of understanding for a couple is the fact that being the person with the illness or disability is not the same as being the partner or family member, yet both are affected. This may seem obvious, but couples can find it hard to separate and distinguish their own situation from their partner's. Discomfort with their own situation can make it hard to listen or to think about the situation of their partner; equally, preoccupation with the other's problems can distract from one's own.

The ongoing illness of a previously healthy, active person can hit their partner in two distinct ways: first, in identification, the ill person's losses are deeply felt and understood; second, and no less painfully, the partner may feel their own loss (and may be either less or more understanding about this). In my experience, neither sex is more or less likely to be self-preoccupied than the other in such circumstances.

Very often partners feel guilty for caring about their own loss: 'It's so much worse for them, how can I be so selfish?' Losses unacknowledged by either can cause anger and frustration to emerge indirectly, where the connection is less evident. On the other hand: 'I hate it when they remember it's hard for me too: they have got enough to cope with as it is.'

Quite often, couples find it hard to fully acknowledge that both have lost something by the illness and settle on the idea that one is justified in complaining and the other much less so. One may 'martyr' themselves for a while, successfully hiding their distress or other feelings. As a short-term solution, this can work for short-term illnesses, but has serious flaws in the long term. Not only can resentment build up, but so too can other serious consequences of self-neglect.

Some couples do manage to continue to care for each other in spite of their own pain. However, for others, the illness exposes cracks in their relationship which were always there.

It can be objectively hard to decide when someone's illness should take priority and when the life of those who care for them should come first. For some there are rules: Jewish law says that, at a crossroads, a wedding should always take precedence over a funeral; and for some it is clear that young children should take precedence over old people. But an elderly mother-in-law may not agree. Should a carer's or a child's visit to the dentist or to a friend or the gym take precedence over a visit to the hospital? Guilt and resentment can build up over many such decisions – or alternatively a shared awareness of the difficulty.

The differences between being the person who is ill and the person who loves them are brought into sharp focus if one person has been unconscious or at the edge of dying, and the other has been waiting, not knowing what the outcome would be. After recovery, life does not go back exactly as it did. The partner may have disengaged from the relationship in response to the expectation of being left, but there may also be a reluctance to discuss what it felt like, and a complete failure to understand the other's position. Lying in intensive care, on the verge of death, some people feel nothing, or a pleasant dream, while their partner is going through terrors, worrying about how they will now live. It can take a huge effort of will to bring this up in conversation later and to put oneself in the other's shoes: imagining nearly dying is not the same as doing it.

A friend woke up from seven days in a coma. Her husband told her he had been terrified she would die, whereupon she said, cheerfully, 'You'd have found someone else!' At this point she did not realise she could not move, nor understand the seriousness of her condition.

I discuss this in my paper 'Flirting with death' (Segal 2009).

Influence of internal world

Mutual understanding is threatened by the sense of having to fight one's own corner. If one is unable to express sympathy for the other's situation and behaves as if they are the only person to suffer, the other may feel a need to shout all the louder about their own losses. Neither can listen to the other – they are in a situation of 'either/or' rather than 'both/and', where competition leaves each feeling more and more desperately alone. Ill-health can turn people against each other. In addition, the loss to any children in the family may increase their distress – or may be ignored by one or the other.

If either or both suffer from a chronic tendency to always see other people as better off than themselves, they may find it very hard to understand certain aspects of the other's point of view. They may see only those aspects which make the other seem better off, and only those aspects of their own lives which make themselves seem worse off. Where both partners do this, it may be a recipe for a vicious circle of mutual attack.

On the other hand, where each feels there is some hope of being understood by the other, there may be less need to draw attention to their own loss and more trust that the other will continue to care for them and to hold in mind their losses. The sense of being under attack by the illness is in this case mitigated by the other's concern, and a benevolent cycle of mutual support is encouraged. Neurological illnesses can threaten this belief if they cause character changes such as loss of concern or loss of empathy.

What may make the difference is the strength of a 'mother-in-the-head' or Good Object figure (see Chapter 2) which underpins belief in love and support. Maintaining a memory of a loving partner as their mind deteriorates may be much easier for someone who had a loving relationship before, based on a good relationship with loving parents (or substitute). A real partner may only be able to function supportively as far as these internal parent-figures allow. It can be very hard to support someone who has no belief in such a figure. Even really helpful and supportive actions may be misinterpreted as attacks; as undermining or taking away potency, for example.

> '[My mother's] only offering to help because it makes her feel good. She just wants people to think she's helpful. She likes to feel important. She tells everyone how she helps her disabled daughter, but she's never there when I want her. She doesn't do anything for me really.'

Interpreting motives is notoriously subjective. Clearly, the most obvious assumption is that others are behaving in a certain way for the same reasons we would be ourselves. Sometimes mothers become the symbol of everything unpleasant or disliked in the self, so there may be little insight into the fact that a scathing description comes quite close to a version of the self. Some mothers clearly do behave badly, and their daughters may work hard to distance themselves from their behaviour, with varying degrees of success.

In such descriptions it can be hard at first to tell if the mother really does do 'nothing', or if the shopping, cleaning, supporting or cooking which she does is simply being dismissed as 'nothing' by an irate daughter who, like an awkward teenager, is so angry at being unable to do it herself that she cannot bear to admit that her mother really does do 'something'.

> *'She's trying to stop me driving because she's nervous; she was in an accident once.'*

The man who said this was actually suffering from loss of insight and loss of judgement as a result of his neurological disease. Both he and his wife found it very hard to admit that his mind was affected as well as his body. He attributed all his problems to her difficulties and denied he had any. Accusations like this are one of the more distressing aspects of any form of dementia. One of the most common accusations is: 'Somebody stole my keys!' This may represent a sense that some aspect of life and responsibility, and the 'key' to understanding, to functioning, has been lost. Unfortunately, it seems that the 'natural', most primitive form of understanding involves attributing agency to someone else rather than recognising either fault with the self or 'not knowing'. Being the person who is accused is most uncomfortable. It seems so normal and so real that the influence of the illness may be completely overlooked. The partner may find themselves shouting back, defending themselves or making a counter-accusation, before they remember that communication is now taking place on a different level, and that a more appropriate response might be some version of a more empathic 'You hate the feeling of losing your mind...'

'Your mother says I can't drive any more because the doctor won't let her drive.' (Because she had had a stroke. What this sly father omitted to mention was that for years he had been falling asleep at traffic lights and his wife had woken him up when they went green.)

In Chapter 7 I discuss the importance of grieving processes in helping to restore belief in loving internal parent-figures after some significant loss. An early loss which has not been adequately grieved may mean that this loving internal parent-figure is not available for use, which may contribute to later relationships breaking up if a loving belief and trust cannot be sustained. Mutual understanding is affected by past experiences, which leave traces both in direct memories and in expectations of others.

'Her dad was ill when she was a teenager. When I got ill she said she wasn't going to go through that again. She wouldn't let them make any changes to the house. I can't go upstairs now; she won't let them put a handrail in.'

'My dad died when I was two. I only connected it after I'd been in therapy, but all my relationships until my mid-thirties lasted about two years, then we'd break up for some reason or other. I thought my therapist was going to die or throw me out or something then, but he didn't. I've stayed with my husband for ten years now.'

Therapy can allow important grieving processes to take place and modify the internal world which we use to understand the external one.

PEOPLE USE THEIR OWN EXPERIENCE TO UNDERSTAND OTHERS

Clearly people use their own experience to understand others; this functions in many different ways.

'I know what it's like not to be able to walk, I broke my leg once.'

Past experiences which seem superficially similar may in fact be very different. A broken leg heals; it carries no implications for long-term disability; it is unlikely to affect long-term employment prospects. How one deals with a broken leg may be quite different from the experience of dealing with a neurological disease which shows itself in a difficulty walking. Thinking about the similarities and differences makes it clear that there are differences, but normally people make assumptions without thought. Under many circumstances thought would take too long or would be unnecessary – our minds work in such a way as to allow us to make associations on the basis of superficial similarities, and these associations are often close enough for us to 'get by'. However, in order truly to understand, thought may be required, and such thought may have to challenge the original assumption. Some people can do this and others cannot.

'A colleague of mine had MS. He really hated having to give up work. That is one of the worst things for anyone with MS, it threatens their job, it would make them feel useless, impotent...'

Not only one's own experience but also other people's may have a lasting impact, creating a powerful image of the consequences of an illness which are then generalised. The person who said this was totally convinced that this was the most important issue for *anyone* with MS. He found it very hard to imagine that some people with MS might actually want to give up work, or might find that the least problematical aspect of the illness. It is also possible that he was himself concerned with his own impotence or with a threat to his own job. Sometimes people use their own experience in a way such that they (and others) do not always recognise it as theirs.

'I don't think it's fair, my dad doesn't have to lay the table. He's just lazy. I don't see why I should do it when he doesn't.'

This was said by an 11-year-old boy. He was judging his father's behaviour by his own; if *he* did not lay the table it could have been attributed to something like 'laziness'; he found it very hard to imagine that his father's reasons (a neurological disease) could have been quite different.

'I wouldn't mind being at home like you. I have to go out to work. I'd love to be able to play tennis in the afternoon.'

This was said to Alice, who had given up her job to look after her very disabled husband whose health was gradually deteriorating. One book about the experience of caring, *The 36 Hour Day* (McEwen 1985), conveys something of the relentless effort required from waking early in the morning to dropping into bed worn out late at night. Alice had been persuaded by her social worker to take up tennis because she was spending all day every day lifting and moving her husband, washing, cleaning, cooking, dealing with his faeces and urine, with mechanical equipment which needed servicing, with social services, with paid carers and with helpers who frequently failed to turn up or to do their jobs properly. It was wearing her down to the extent that she became suicidal and afraid she would intentionally damage her husband in fury and frustration. She did not tell her friends about her experiences because when she saw them she wanted a break from thinking about it, and she did not want to burden them. Her friend could see no further than the tennis; the rest was beyond her experience.

UNDERSTANDING AS HEALING

People often talk of their need to be understood, in particular by their partners. They may also assume that one or both of their parents would or should or could understand them. Some are angry when this understanding does not happen; others have grown up with the knowledge that their parents do not and will not understand. Sometimes there is an idealisation of non-verbal understanding, with a sense of grievance if understanding has to be helped along with words.

Understanding the effects of an illness can help to locate a loss, to place it where it belongs rather than somewhere else. Counselling can provide a space to allow understanding to emerge over time.

'When I came to you I was angry and upset about my daughter moving out and leaving home, but I think really what I was upset about was my health. I didn't realise how frightened I was. I'm not upset about my daughter at all now: I'm glad she's got her own home. I am afraid I might have a stroke if they operate. I just didn't let myself think about it then.'

'I was afraid my husband was going to leave me, and I was being horrible to him. I now think it was because I hadn't really got over my father's death. I could have made him leave, I was being so awful. I think I was afraid he was going to die like my father did.'

Understanding can also throw new light on an illness and its effects, which changes the way it is perceived.

Alice said she got very angry with her husband and wanted to hit him when he began shaking, which was a symptom of his condition. Careful thinking with a counsellor about when this happened allowed her to notice that it was when she was about to go out: he would shake himself out of the wheelchair just as she was about to rush out, late for her game of tennis. Once she had recognised this, she was able to talk to him about her going out without him and ask if he was jealous. He denied being jealous, but his shaking lessened.

Understanding can also assist the development of a new relationship with parents, which can lead to a greater capacity for accepting help and for feeling supported.

Juliet had a deteriorating neurological condition which took her to a counsellor. She complained at great length about her mother, saying how much nicer her father was and how she would have rather gone with him and his new partner when she was small, rather than stayed with her mother. She had made no secret of her resentment at not being allowed to go; she looked like her father and was very attached to him. She attributed his numerous lovers to her mother being 'boring' and him being 'a man'.

After some work in counselling the counsellor wondered aloud if her mother had in fact disliked Juliet. Juliet was horrified, saying it was not acceptable for a mother to dislike her child. The counsellor agreed, and suggested it might have been hard for her mother to admit too. After some thinking about her relationship with her own daughter, Juliet realised that her mother could well have disliked her, with good reason. Her relationship with her mother changed dramatically, and for the first time she was able to ask for and take help from her.

Juliet's new understanding of her mother's situation – although it was most uncomfortable at first – enabled her to change her own expectations of herself and her relationship with her daughter. It changed her picture of her mother in her mind, and this changed her picture of herself too, as well as of her daughter.

Ibrahim, a highly intelligent young man, 'knew' he had caused his brother to be born with a club foot because he used to use the word 'spastic' as an insult while his mother was pregnant. It was not until he was an adult that he recognised this and understood that it was not true. He felt as if a huge burden had been lifted from his shoulders.

The sense that a significant or disturbing or anxiety-provoking idea or thought is held and understood by someone else seems to be important. It is as if certain ideas require something to be done with or to them, and until some change has taken place they irritate, annoy, demand attention. 'Witnessing' seems to be an aspect of understanding which somehow involves sharing responsibility for knowledge. People speak of the burden they feel lifted when they have managed to put into words some distressing event or thought or feeling which they have kept within themselves for many years. Simply having an idea held up for inspection by another mind can mean that it is looked at from a different point of view and may be instantly seen in a very different light. In this way, understanding can allow new ideas to grow and develop.

Understanding facilitates grieving processes, in which an outdated view of reality is given up and a new one embraced, without doing violence to the self and without losing vital aspects of insight or life or the self which otherwise might be forgotten. Just as a gardener giving a cutting to a friend can provide reassurance that a loved plant can be replaced if it dies for any reason, so knowing that someone else understands seems to take away a burden of responsibility for the well-being of an important aspect of the self and all that goes with it. Somehow people have a sense that understanding allows some part of themselves to be lodged or deposited with the other person, where it can be allowed to live, needing less attention from themselves. Other ideas, other aspects of the self, then have more space to develop and to live.

A sense that someone else understands also seems to support and strengthen the feeling that there is a friendly, understanding parent-in-the-head who is there to be called on when needed. This understanding parent-figure can create something which feels like 'space-in-the-head' in which thinking can take place. It facilitates not only understanding of the self, but also, perhaps, understanding of others too.

'Since you made me think how it was for my mother [when I was a baby and she gave me away] I feel quite differently about her. I told my sister she needs to grow up and stop calling my mother a witch.'

'You made me think about how other people see me. I never did that before. I see things from other people's point of view now; I never used to do that.'

PROBLEMS WITH UNDERSTANDING

Unfortunately, understanding can be problematical, and either party may resist understanding for good reason.

Illness and disability can create many misunderstandings which can be extremely aggravating. People may lack the patience or the knowledge or the openness of mind to explore and really try to understand someone else, without jumping to unjustified conclusions, putting themselves into the picture too quickly or taking over a conversation. Particularly if the illness interferes with thinking or speaking, understanding may be forced to rely on non-verbal communication, which I discuss below. Illness can slow speech down, making it hard for a stressed partner to take the time to listen. It can also raise levels of distress, making it emotionally painful, disturbing or frightening for the listener.

'He won't sit and listen to me.' 'Because she always says she wants to be dead.' 'Yes, I know he hates it when I say that, but it's how I feel sometimes.'

It can take some courage for a couple to go further with such a conversation, in an attempt to understand exactly what is being said: this conversation took place with a counsellor in the room. It can be impossible for someone who is deeply involved as a member of the family, or who feels personally accused or blamed. It may be a lot easier for a professional than for a partner; easier for an older adult child listening to a very elderly parent than for a young child listening to a young adult parent. There may also be a sense that telling a professional or an outsider makes distressing thoughts slightly less risky; the professional goes away after a while and the thought may go with them. Once a partner really understands, however, what was said can never be taken back. Many thoughts and ideas are true only at certain times, under certain circumstances, and a few moments later, after they have been taken in by the listener, they in fact change – sometimes to the opposite. Unfortunately, a partner who has been told they are useless or they should leave may be too distressed to wait for their loved one to say that this isn't what they feel all the time, or even most of the time. They may just avoid all conversation as far as possible, for fear of what they might have to witness.

> 'My mum keeps telling me God will heal me. I don't think she wants to understand that it's not curable.'

In this case there were obvious reasons why the mother might not want to understand her daughter's point of view; equally the daughter did not want to understand anything from her mother's religious point of view. Such mutual refusals (or inabilities) to accept the other's point of view can create a sense of isolation, frustration and, at times, fury and despair.

Such misunderstandings can also be a way of expressing conflicting beliefs: both daughter and mother may understand each other only too well, but both be terrified of admitting that this is the case. The mother would not want to admit any part of her, any moment's thought which did not insist on her belief in God – for fear He might not cure her daughter, and if not, it would be her lack of faith which caused it. The daughter might be equally afraid of being caught up in her mother's form of religion which she saw (when she was feeling at her best) as superstitious, punitive and primitive – but which she felt herself slipping into when she was feeling unwell, weak and vulnerable. Other examples of this arise when one person has a powerful belief in 'positive thinking' and the other in 'expressing the negative'; or when one insists they *can* do something and the other is afraid they cannot. In each case, avoiding understanding the other enables an idea to be held more tenaciously, with contradictory ideas rejected repeatedly and loudly.

Some ideas are just too painful to be understood.

'He said he wanted to buy a racing motorbike as soon as he got out of hospital, and drive it as fast as he could. I was really cross with him: he knows how dangerous motorbikes are!'

This teenage boy was in hospital with terminal cancer; his mother did not want to understand his implied suicidal wish, though her angry response allowed her to express some of the distress she felt, hearing it.

Being told that a person you love wants to die hurts. People who are ill or struggling with a new diagnosis or a new impairment often feel they don't want to wake up, though they may hide this out of consideration for those they love. Sometimes it turns out that the partner has 'picked it up', feeling guiltily that the person would be better off dead, or that they even wish they would 'get on with it' and die, and bring to an end the terrible waiting, or the cycle of hoping and having hopes dashed again and again. Such a feeling may not be easily shared in a tactful, loving way with a partner. Mutual concern may prevent sharing of some of the struggles accompanying illness. Each may tacitly understand this, or they may not – it may be impossible to find out without breaking the silence.

Understanding can also bring new responsibilities. In the days when nobody realised that children could be badly affected by separation from their parents, parents could send even small children to boarding school in the belief that it would be better for them. Now we know more about the effects of such separation, we have an obligation to take notice of children in a new way.

Similarly, parents who used to hit their children when they were small may be forced to understand this in a new way as their children become old enough to tell them. Confrontations with irate children can be distressing for parents, who may feel they must either admit their sorrow and their guilt or reject the child and risk being abandoned in their own old age. An illness may provide a trigger which brings old resentments and ill-treatment into focus: an angry child may feel they must justify their refusal to visit a parent in hospital, for example, or decide how much they are prepared to become involved in an ill parent's care. The parent who once was all-powerful is transformed by illness (or by old age) into a potential victim of a child they once made to suffer. As the child grows into an adult this cannot feel very safe.

APOLOGISING FOR MISUNDERSTANDINGS

Apology may help. If someone felt aggrieved at being misunderstood, but that their grievance has been sincerely 'taken in' and accepted by the guilty party, a true apology can function like a kind of new understanding. Although in a sense little may have changed in the outside world (for example, if no compensation can be offered), in the inner world a lot may be changed by an apology. A grievance seems to cause irritation: it niggles or hurts or annoys; it brings regrets and a sense of loss and sadness as well as injustice; it may not be allowed to 'rest' until there has been some kind of closure. An apology means knowing that the guilty party feels their guilt, and perhaps also the annoyance, the irritation, even the hurt (to their self-esteem, perhaps), as well as the regret and sorrow. The burden has been in some important way shared, the misunderstanding corrected.

An apology somehow seems to mean in phantasy that justice has been done. Misunderstandings often feel unjust: the daughter who accuses her exhausted and ill mother of 'doing nothing'; the childless friend who says 'You didn't ring when you said you would', without knowing what it means to have an ill husband and children clamouring for attention. Anger with injustice means, perhaps, anger with a primitive phantasy of a father-in-the-head, the powerful controller of justice in the world, who (in this context) may represent an internal judge and jury. This 'judge' is vindicated: once again in agreement with the external world. Until there has been an apology, there may also be secret anxieties that the internal judge is actually not on your side at all – worse, that you might actually be wrong. Ill mothers are very vulnerable to believing they 'do nothing'; and, perhaps, trying to be a good friend as well as a good carer-wife and mother might have to be given up for a while. Clearly, belief in the self as well as trust in others and in the world in general can all be to some extent restored by an apology which establishes agreement about what happened and why, preferably without excuses, though perhaps with clarification and reasons.

HUMOUR: SHARING OTHERWISE UNACCEPTABLE THOUGHTS

Joking can play an important part in mutual understanding by allowing the most distressing or otherwise unacceptable ideas to be expressed in a way which makes them tolerable – perhaps.

> *'She told me to push her under the nearest bus, so I said I couldn't because I'd got my best suit on and I didn't want it splattered... We had a good laugh and I think we both felt better.'*

Within a friendly relationship it can bring into the open unbidden thoughts which need to be discredited. Sharing them as a joke implies that 'of course' they are not being kept secret in preparation for action. A more serious conversation would imply that there was a chance that such ideas should be taken seriously. In Chapter 6, under the heading 'Physical pain standing for emotional pain', I give an example of a joke which allowed a husband's unconscious insight about his wife's pain to be brought into consciousness and shared very helpfully.

> *'Because I'm not working any more either we can go out a lot. There are plenty of places you can take a big wheelchair. He fell in the canal once, when he was still driving himself. I was walking ahead, with some friends. He didn't shout or anything. He was just lying there... A man on a narrowboat pulled him out. It was scary at the time, but we all laughed about it afterwards. We teased him: "Were you looking for the fishes, Pete? Wanted a swim, did you?"'*

The balance between risk and pleasure has to be negotiated; humour can help people to cope in a way which enables pleasure to be retained.

Joking can also backfire. If the 'bad' thoughts seem too real, not held in check by other, more powerful, friendly ones, they cannot be laughed at: they become too serious. Joking can be used to express barbed, accusatory thoughts and wishes; to attack in a way which is not friendly at all. Part of the difficulty with joking may be that both speaker and listener need a 'friendly super-ego' – a benevolent mother- or father-in-the-head, who permits and encourages play, does not come down like a ton of bricks on any fault or sense of guilt, and knows that these unbidden, aggressive or 'bad' thoughts are not the only, nor the most important, ones in the mind of the speaker. Not only illness but also loss of any kind may threaten this friendly figure and replace it, if only for a while, with a less friendly one – even with a bullying or attacking parent-in-the-head. At a time when joking may be most needed, it may be unavailable for use.

Joking can also be used to sidestep or avoid the emotional impact of understanding; or to 'put a foot in the water' in such a way that it can be removed rapidly if the response is bad: 'Only joking!'

> 'He won't be serious. I tell him I'm feeling ill and he makes a joke of it. It makes me really angry sometimes.'

> 'He said he wanted to get out, to leave me, and I was really upset. I asked him later if he meant it and he said he was only joking, but he wasn't. I can't forget it. I couldn't manage without him.'

Where some groups of women friends may be more likely to have serious discussions about illnesses of their members, joking is an important part of the social 'glue' which holds other groups together, for example in a pub or a warehouse or a factory. 'Ribbing', or joking about the illness or disability of someone in the group, can be a reassuring statement about them being a full member of the group, allowing closeness while retaining distance. Such joking can depend on mutual understanding of a high order which at the same time respects and maintains privacy, but it can also slip into baiting, scapegoating and cruelty – it has a powerful capacity to either include or exclude people from the group.

Illness, death and family relationships can be subjects for humour, which in some settings may allow open communication about serious matters in a relatively light way.

NON-VERBAL UNDERSTANDING

Non-verbal understanding can be a powerful means by which people communicate. Babies and children who cannot put their thoughts and feelings into words depend on those around to interpret their feelings or other things they want to say. At its best, this process can work very well, with parents and children in harmony, with the child feeling they are understood and the words they are given the right ones. However, the potential for mismatching, for misunderstanding, for manipulation and confusion, is enormous. So it is for adults who lose their power of speech.

Non-verbal communication can work by the appropriate feelings being evoked in others. Mothers may feed their children when the *mothers* feel hungry, and send them to bed when the *parents* are tired or begin to be irritated by the children becoming hyper. Parents can often be very accurate when they identify with their (small) children and instantly recognise their feelings or their needs in this way. Carer partners can make decisions about when to eat on this basis too. If their needs match reasonably, this can work – couples who have been together for a long time know how often their partners need food and know whether they need to watch a clock or their own appetite.

What people do with their understanding of someone else's needs depends on their beliefs and culture, and the way they respond to their own. So parents may feed their children when the children (and their parents) feel *sad*, rather than hungry, for example (perhaps interpreting the feelings as 'It's the monsters in your tummy coming to get you...'). When a child behaves badly while their new brother or sister is being fed, a parent might try to ignore it, get angry or respond with comfort: 'You're jealous' or 'You're feeling left out, come here!' or 'You're cross with me, I know.' Adults too, feeling left out or jealous (of the baby, of their children), or just angrily envious of the care which someone else is getting, can communicate feelings they do not want to recognise by evoking them in others, as I described in Chapter 2, under 'Projective identification'. And carers can understand, or can be completely confused: 'Why does he always call me just when I'm about to feed the children?' or 'He knows I'm about to feed the children: he's just like a child himself, he wants all the attention.' People do sometimes revert to childish feelings and behaviour when they are ill, and those around them can understand in these terms, particularly when using non-verbal cues. A dependent adult may for a time lose touch with their more adult self: both they and those around sometimes need to be reminded that they are *not* children, and that their *understanding* (and, perhaps, their capacity to wait for attention without feeling they are being abandoned for ever;

as well as their capacity to show concern for their carer) is still that of an adult. However, attempts to convey this message non-verbally may be misunderstood as neglect, for example, and lead to an increase in childish behaviour. Some messages need words.

Feelings of loss (past, present or future), of fear, of anger, of hunger, of desire, of loneliness, can all be communicated by expressions, by slight movements of the head, the eyes, the hands. It may be such uncomfortable communications, perhaps only fleeting, or only conveyed to some visitors, not others, that make it hard to visit some people in hospital or when they are ill. Counsellors have the task to put such feelings into words; family members may feel a greater need or pressure to ignore or to misunderstand or to avoid very distressing feelings which are aroused in them by a non-speaking ill person. In particular, fears awakened in childhood may be evoked, in the patient and/or those around, and these have a particularly terrifying aspect to them which makes them very hard for an adult either to bear or to challenge.

David Rieff, in Swimming in a Sea of Death *(2008), describes how impossible it was for him to talk with his mother (Susan Sontag) about her imminent death, although both believed they had a commitment to truth and the value of words. He felt forced to maintain a fiction that she would recover. He was also unable to write at the time, perhaps because writing would have confronted him with the real truth about her illness and his feelings which neither he nor she could bear to admit.*

(Sontag's father died of TB when she was a small child, and she was preoccupied with ideas of dying herself. Death seems to have represented something totally monstrous to her; perhaps, I suggest, coloured by unexamined 'frozen-in-time' ideas and fantasies of a three-year-old who had lost her father and could not get on with her mother. She could take no comfort in thinking about 'those left behind', and she was unable to comfort her son, who was left agonising over his helplessness. Poignantly he shows, without quite admitting it, that, once they had been shorn of their connection with truth, words could not help his mother. I wrote about this in 'Lies about death' (Segal 2013).)

Sontag's life, as described by her son, also perhaps shows how children can learn ways of dealing with loss from adults in childhood.

In her personal life she seems to have tried constantly to 'move on' and leave the past behind her, which seems to have been the way her mother and step-father handled her father's death. She could not bear to think of leaving her own life.

There are plenty of other ways of communicating which can be used if the problem is only loss of the physical capacity to speak, though these may depend on the willingness of others to take the time and make the effort to find means of communication which do work. They also depend on some kind of shared universe.

Physical touch, for example, can convey meaning in a powerful way, but this meaning may not be shared. For one it may be a comfort and fulfil a need for friendly closeness: for the other it might be the same – or it might threaten a disturbing invasion of their bodily boundaries and space. Attempts to touch may produce a very different reaction from that expected. The 'toucher' may feel rejected and hurt and not know why their attempts to 'reach out' produced such a powerful reaction. Long-term partners usually know enough to be able to understand each other's reactions, and they may be able to act as a translator or boundary-holder for each other.

Conversations through a computer can enable understanding, though the person-to-person links will be different. Using primitive devices in the 1980s and 1990s, I found that, in counselling sessions, people tended to go straight for important issues, mainly, I think, because 'chatting' through a Lightwriter screen did not seem worth the effort. People who spoke very slowly, too, tended to make each word count – sometimes, if I had counselled them before they lost their speech, they could convey significant feelings or memories to me by evoking past conversations with one or more words, or simply a gesture.

Understanding becomes compromised if someone is so ill that they cannot convey their feelings except through minimal movements, or none at all.

Towards the end of his life, Alison sometimes could not tell if her husband was ok or bored or depressed as he lay in bed for hours, unmoving. A friend said he would be depressed if he did nothing all day, but she felt her husband wasn't depressed, except perhaps occasionally when she thought he was sad. Mostly she thought he was ok, though saying she thought him 'content' would have been going a bit far. She remembered his previous self too well to believe that he could be content with his lot, but there was no sign of agitation or irritation.

Powerful non-verbal communication can take place at the same time as conversation and loud talking. Even very ill patients can be aware of the manner in which a nurse handles them, while changing the bed at the same time as talking to her colleague. Behaviour is often interpreted as non-verbal communication. A lot of meaning is attached to whether or not a partner visits in hospital.

Stan did not visit his wife in hospital. She was philosophical about it and said he couldn't manage it. He had a bad time when he was a child, she said; his mother left his father while he was in hospital and nobody told him. He did not want to talk about it.

Michael's (much younger) wife did not visit him while he was recovering from a stroke; he said she was just too busy. The nurses thought she had a new partner and did not want him back.

Clearly, there is a level of uncertainty which must accompany reliance on non-verbal communication where there is a minimal level of feedback.

While Darren lay in a coma his parents and his wife fought a battle through the courts about whether he should be allowed to live or die, with his wife saying he would not have wanted to live and his mother equally insistent that he would never have wanted to die if there was the slightest hope of his recovery – or even if there was none.

In such a battle, families can feel that violence is being done to the person they love, with their passion fuelled by the sense that violence is being done, not only to a part of *themselves* that they cherish, but also to their internal Good Object, their whole world, too.

A sense of peace or acceptance can also be communicated non-verbally. Sitting quietly with a relative who is accepting of their lot, whatever it is, can bring both comfort and forgiveness.

LEARNING TO UNDERSTAND

It is possible to enhance understanding of others who have certain illnesses or disabling conditions. Books, films, plays and songs which describe others' experience can all contribute, as well as talking with people affected themselves. The main risk is that the experience of one or a few may be generalised and assumed to stand for all, when in fact everyone comes to their own illness or disabilities in their own way, with their own background, their own anxieties, experience, hopes and fears. I sometimes say to people that being told someone has multiple sclerosis is like being told they are French: it means that they are not English, but that is virtually *all* it means. Within that, the variation is extreme.

I offer a course for those working with people who are ill or disabled, in which I invite participants to think, first, how they would feel if they had an illness or disability themselves. Second, we move on to how they would feel if they were a partner or family member; and finally we look at their role as a professional in this situation. In this way they listen to colleagues' experiences and expectations and so widen their knowledge of the different ways in which people react; they are often astonished at how different these ways can be. They also improve their ability to distinguish their own reactions from those of their clients or patients.

SUMMARY

Illness can bring many misunderstandings in both the external world and the internal world: it is so easy to 'get it wrong'. Against this, good understanding may be one means of offering real help or support to someone who has to live with ill-health in themselves or another. It can make or break a relationship. It may be resisted with all the power at the person's disposal; or it may be welcomed with open arms. Understanding someone else is not easy and requires, probably, both some understanding of the self as well as a real awareness that others can be very different. When it works, it can be very satisfying.

CHAPTER 4

Will We Survive?

INTRODUCTION

An illness or increasing disability may be absorbed into a current relationship, albeit with changes; or it may, through subtle or less subtle means, bring the relationship to an end. Understanding some of the processes involved may bring them more under conscious control and reduce the chance of ending a relationship prematurely, as a result of temporary difficulties which actually could be overcome.

IMPORTANCE OF PARTNERSHIPS

It is interesting how much difficulty people can have in verbalising their role in a partnership. Asked what they do for their partner, men in particular may stumble after they have listed – proudly, indignantly, angrily or sadly (because it is no longer true) – 'earn money' and, perhaps, 'sex' (by which they mean penile penetration and orgasm). Particularly when their earning capacity is under threat, they may not recognise the many other things that they do for their lovers, their wives and their children. Women too may have difficulty recognising the multitude of parts they play in their partners' lives.

When pushed, it becomes clear that partners can do many things for each other. They provide comfort, attention, concern, pleasure (not only through wider sexual activities but also humour, solid reliability or interesting unpredictability, for example). They help each other to think, to make decisions; they share responsibility for painful or difficult tasks such as handling children or their own parents or siblings; they challenge and support, take over certain tasks and hand over others; they encourage growth and development of new capacities. They support life in ways that are both practical and symbolic, whether these are given high status by society (such as earning a large salary) or lower status (such as cleaning toilets or washing up or keeping track of clean clothes). The fact that somebody is happy to see you when you open the front door can be a source of enormous comfort and reassurance in a hostile world, although people may only recognise it when they can no longer rely upon it.

Some of these elements of a relationship depend on physical capacities, others on emotional ones. Some are threatened by illness. Some can be taken over by the other, but at the price of considerable changes in the relationship. Some can be retained, others will be lost, owing either to the illness or to reactions to it. New talents can be discovered, but people may also be surprised to find things they or their partners cannot or will not do. Aspects of the self previously 'seen in' or 'projected into' each other may have to be 'taken back'.

Partners also, of course, may attack or undermine each other, make each other uncomfortable, make demands or control, manipulate and exploit, in ways that are not life-enhancing and are not to mutual benefit. Even in this situation there may be some comfort in the relationship. Such partnerships sometimes survive because they are familiar, they mirror childhood upbringing and fit into a sense that this is how things should be, or have to be – that ill-treatment is deserved or is a sign of superior standards which are to be admired, for example.

Partnerships also restrict choices and limit behaviour, either of which may be felt as an advantage or a disadvantage – or both at once. There is a relief in not having to make decisions and being able to hand responsibility to someone else; but this depends on the capacity to trust that the person who takes responsibility truly has the best interests of those who matter at heart. Whether the self is included as 'someone who matters' depends on the individuals concerned.

People come together in partnerships for many reasons and in many ways. In my first book, *Phantasy in Everyday Life* (Segal 1985), I discussed some of the phantasies involved in relationships. Very often there seems to be some set of anxieties which partners share, but which each has solved in a different way. (For example, one partner may deal with anxieties about money by spending, the other by saving; together they may reassure each other that the money will not run out, and can be enjoyed.) There can be huge reassurance in finding someone else who will facilitate the creation and maintenance of a shared view of the world. People tend to choose someone who 'fits' in some way with pre-existing views (or unconscious phantasies) of the way people are, and of the way the self should be treated. They take the place forged by relationships with parents, other close adults and siblings, who helped to create phantasies of the 'mother-in-the-head' (or 'father' or 'sibling'). These phantasy people also include parts of the self, often disowned; they are not faithful matches to the real people but are truly 'unconscious fantasies', sometimes nicer, sometimes more cruel than the real people ever were. These links can create a deep attachment and underpin a relationship which on the surface may seem to offer little in the way of pleasure or support. They can also explain why it is that sometimes a small, seemingly insignificant disability can disrupt a relationship while a much larger one does not.

FITTING DISABILITIES INTO RELATIONSHIPS

As described in Chapter 1, when any change happens in a relationship it may be followed by a period in which the change is resisted, a period when one sees the need to change and the other resists, a period when change and experimentation takes place, and, eventually, a new phase in which the changes have been made and have settled in so that they no longer need discussing and each person is sufficiently reconciled to the new status quo. These phases overlap as one change after another is absorbed into the relationship. One of the threats to relationships is that people are often unaware that their feelings about their current situation will change over time. They talk and think as if 'now' is 'for ever'. In fact, these changes may happen over years rather than months.

Initial attempts to keep things as they were, with the minimum of changes, are perfectly normal. Problems can arise when one person is doing this and ignoring the pressures they are putting on others.

'I don't want to use a stick, I can lean on my son. He likes it.'

For about a year after he could no longer drive it, Chris could not bear to part with a car which needed both hands and working feet. He said it represented the ability to get out, to be free from dependency on others; although in fact it required someone else to drive it, and taxis actually meant more freedom. His wife was prepared to be his driver for a while but she had very mixed feelings about his hanging onto the car. They could have used the money, but she understood what a car could mean for a man and did not want to see her husband 'reduced' in any way.

A few, with a different agenda, seem to leap at the chance to make massive changes, some well before they are actually necessary.

'My mum gave up work the minute she was diagnosed. I don't see why she did that, it put pressure on Dad, he hated his job. She could easily have gone on working.'

One family member often sees the need to change before the other. They may have to struggle not only against their partner's resistance, but also against their own. They may find themselves overstating the case for change, while the other overstates the possibility of keeping things as they are. Until the changes have been discussed or have actually happened, they may feel so big that any thought of change becomes impossible.

For Mina, the idea that she had MS was unthinkable. Her grandmother had MS; she was now unable to talk or walk or look after herself. Mina was so frightened of being like this that she was unable to take any steps which involved admitting she had anything wrong with her at all. This meant she was unable to go out since her walking was no longer stable but she was unable to ask for a stick or crutches. For Mina, making any change meant becoming exactly like her grandmother. This kept her more affected by her disability than she needed to be. Once she was able to separate herself in her mind from her grandmother and admit her difficulty walking, she could use a stick and she no longer felt unsafe. She was able to go out again.

Mina's husband had been unable to talk to her about her walking because he could feel her resistance. He was worried about her but did not dare to challenge her. He felt quite hopeless and almost paralysed himself. He too saw her as about to become like her grandmother, although there were 45 years between them.

Virginie's father bought her mother a new buggy to replace one which had been damaged in an accident. Virginie saw her mother crossing the road in it, nearly knocking a cyclist under a lorry. She asked her mother if she had seen the cyclist and her mother clearly had not. There had been several other accidents. Virginie later said it was one of the worst moments of her life, when she told her mother she was taking the keys away and returning the buggy to the manufacturers. Her mother looked as if she felt her life was ending. She told friends, 'My sons think I shouldn't drive because I'll kill myself; my daughters say I can't because I'll kill someone else.' This was because her daughters knew that, since her stroke, she had felt ready to die, in spite of not being ready to give up driving.

Sometimes the ill person can feel forced into exaggerating their health difficulties in order to obtain some kind of acknowledgement from a family in denial.

'When I'm dead you can do what you like...'

'The family forget I'm ill, so sometimes I make a point of limping even when I don't have to, just to remind them. But then they say I'm not really ill at all, just pretending, so it doesn't help.'

Since the exaggeration is easy to challenge, this kind of fight can also be a way of maintaining the status quo while beginning the process of bringing to the surface the need for change. Over a period of time new solutions to old problems may arise, some by default, some as a matter of thought or discussion.

GRADUALLY, OLD DEFENCES MAY NOT
ONLY FAIL, BUT BE SEEN TO FAIL

After a time, the pressures arising from trying to pretend nothing has changed may become too much. Equally, people can get tired of always putting their own needs on hold if an ill family member is exaggerating their disabilities or using them to exploit others. Somebody may react in a way which brings change. A partner who has 'gone along with' a fiction for a long time may eventually realise that this is not in the best interests of the family, and may seek some way of making changes. Depending on their own circumstances, they may be able to do this *with* their partner, or they may be forced to separate themselves and change their own role within the family, perhaps admitting that they have to take on new responsibilities, regardless of whether their partner agrees or not. Being in this position can be very challenging and painful and may require support from outside.

Sometimes a child provokes change by (mis)behaving in a way which brings in outside attention, and the possibility of support.

Anger arises when someone thinks a change *could* be made, or perhaps that a change *does not have to happen*, when it is already happening. Bitterness and despair are more hopeless, and imply that a terrible change has happened, and nothing can make it any better, often that someone is to blame for it and could take it away if they didn't deliberately refuse. Bickering and nagging tend to arise when there is no hope for improving the situation, and may be aimed at hurting or irritating others rather than bringing about a lasting change. Any of these emotions may precipitate change.

Change can also happen more quietly in some families. If one parent has been 'martyring' themselves, adult children may notice and take action – though interfering in parents' relationships is notoriously difficult. Part of the difficulty is that people seldom do things entirely for themselves: their reactions nearly always involve fantasies about the people who are important for them. They may fight hard for the right to 'save' someone who stands for their 'good object', even if it means they themselves must suffer. Children do not always want to see how much parents care for each other.

Arguing, fighting or serious discussions may take place as each member of the family is gradually forced to become aware of their own discomfort, to name and locate its causes and to seek necessary changes from others as well as themselves. Power relations matter here: what happens may depend on who is given power and respect in the family, rather than on what would be best for everyone. Illness changes power relations, though exactly *how* depends on the individual family.

When people are too afraid of their own anger or bitterness and they despair of changing anything, they may simply withdraw. They may seek outside sources of comfort, though they may feel too guilty, bad and miserable about themselves to do this. A serious withdrawal may be the catalyst which makes a couple talk to each other and find new solutions, but if each is too afraid of what they or their partner will say, they may need help from outside first.

Susie had always been the kind of person who liked company. She liked having friends, she adored her partner and he was totally committed to her. When she became increasingly disabled with multiple sclerosis she found herself having to rely on her partner more and more. He reacted badly at times. A more solitary person, he was working from home and felt his life was in danger of being taken over by the MS and by Susie's demands. In a counselling session, Susie agreed to take over responsibility for organising her own carers. She also agreed to an arrangement whereby Richard would not be disturbed by her for any reason during the hours of 10.00 and 12.30, and 2.00 and 4.30. Richard felt this arrangement might work. Susie seemed fine. Some days she felt quite competent and other days she did not, but this day it seemed she was reasonably optimistic about finding other people to help her if Richard could not.

Suddenly she burst out in distress, accusing Richard of bullying her and being horrible to her. What emerged was that she was terrified that if she allowed Richard not to help her, he would shut his door and never emerge again; that she would be cut out of his life entirely and he would become deeply withdrawn and depressed. Building in arrangements which ensured that they would have time together helped her to feel safer. Anxieties about too much closeness and anxieties about too much distance both needed to be addressed, as did the depression which threatened both of them. These came to light only when Susie was unable to keep her distress hidden (from herself as much as anyone else) any longer.

Siobhan's husband constantly nagged her to do physiotherapy exercises to improve her walking. He was overweight himself and he also needed to exercise. Siobhan hated going to the hospital to see the physiotherapist because it reminded her that she was ill. Hospitals also made her think of people dying. She worried about her husband's weight too. When they argued, both felt more alive and less depressed – as if they were actually doing something about their situation.

Pavel had been struggling to keep his job and his family life, but was finding it hard as his fatigue got worse as well as his walking and his coordination. His wife was trying hard to be positive about things but was finding this, too, increasingly hard. When he was asked what he had lost, Pavel burst out 'Everything!' and held his head in his hands. At this point it became possible to look at what he had actually lost, and at what he still had. 'Everything' was an exaggeration, but it was a correct description of what he felt at that moment. His wife's attempts to keep positive seemed to him to be a denial of his feelings of despair. She was terrified that if she acknowledged his despair she would be put in touch with her own, which was being just kept at bay in her struggles to remain positive.

The sense that the world has fallen apart, that the boundaries are no longer there, that a way of life has gone for ever and nothing will ever be safe again, can be felt by both, in which case it can be frightening and almost paralysing. J.R.R. Tolkien, in *The Lord of the Rings* trilogy (Tolkien 1954, 1955), evokes this feeling when he describes how the hobbits return to their homeland after their adventures and find it changed beyond recognition; the hobbits set about restoring something good of the past. The feeling of despair and loss of a whole world must have been familiar to the child Tolkien, who lost his homeland and his father at the age of three, and his mother when he was 12, but he was able to make something creative of it.

Either the ill person or their partner may be more robust psychologically, and more ready to face living with disability. One partner

111

often takes the lead in finding ways to live with a loss, and may find it hard if the other fails to respond.

> 'I could cope with his difficulty walking, but what I can't stand is his refusal to try anything that might help.'

Understanding this position can be difficult, but there may be an explanation if they have the patience to find it.

> 'I know I've lost my erection: I'm being the best partner I can, but Harriet isn't interested in any other form of relationship, sexual or otherwise; she says she can't bear to touch me any more and she just wants to leave.'

Again, finding out why she feels like this may help to change it; but Harriet would have to be prepared to join the exploration, and in this case she refused. Struggling to adjust to a new reality, there are times when people want to run away, physically or psychologically.

Guilt, frustration, resentment and other reactions to loss have to be handled in one way or another. For a time, both the ill person and their partner may find themselves actually hurting each other (or themselves); having thoughts of ending it all; hitting or mocking or attacking each other or themselves in their mind, or in reality, in more or less dangerous ways. Although unusual, even attempts at murder and suicide can take place when people feel pushed beyond their limit by an illness or increasing disability and insufficiently supported by those who they feel could or should care.

As long as the desire for life is strong and they have a sense of being supported by internal parents (probably with some representation in the external world), people can find ways of managing even powerful feelings of loss. They develop interpretations of whatever has happened which enables them to go on living in hope. For some, religious ideas help; for others simply a powerful sense of life being worth living; or a commitment to a partner which is strong enough to outlast deterioration; or a recognition of their role in their children's or friends' lives. Past history plays a huge part here, in enabling people to feel loved and loving: though for some, their own history makes this impossible. Working through past losses and the residues of past bad experiences may or may not be possible.

As old ways are given up and new ones replace them, many people feel their losses more as sadness than as anger or resentment or bitterness. The feeling that everything has not just gone but been *taken away*, that all is *lost because somebody is at fault*, can gradually shift. New accommodations are made, new skills learnt, and a relationship moves to a new phase. Pleasure is no longer rejected because it would 'mean' that 'everything is ok', when it isn't, but is allowed to emerge alongside the sadness.

The sense of 'badness' may still arise in various connections, but differently, and with more awareness of the fact that 'goodness' or pleasure can exist alongside it.

As awareness of the loss grows, questions are raised about the survival of the relationship. If the old world has gone, how can a relationship survive? Will the partner want or be able to love a new, less attractive self? How could anyone else want a body or mind which is a burden to its owner? The interesting (and sometimes astonishing) thing is that people surprisingly often do. Even though a body is now falling apart and a mind wavering, the person is so firmly rooted in the body and soul of their partner that the relationship does hold. The phantasy 'husband-in-the-head' or 'partner-in-the-head' may survive illness and deterioration for many years. Although there may be a gradual or stepwise metamorphosis into a different relationship, the old links with childhood and young adult phantasies remain and continue to provide a source of nourishment which can maintain a sense that the relationship is worth something.

WANTING AN APOLOGY

People often come for counselling seeking an apology from someone. They have done their best to make the other person see how guilty and wrong they are, and are at their wits' end because it seems to make no difference. I find myself explaining the difference between *persecutory guilt* and *apologetic guilt*. If guilt is too strong it can feel like a requirement to grovel, perhaps to kill oneself, to utterly abase oneself to a point of no return; more realistically, perhaps, to admit that the accuser is right, always was right and always will be right for evermore. The response clearly has to be 'Not me!', 'I didn't do it!' or perhaps 'You did it!' or 'They did it!' The person may truly not feel the guilt, only fear or paralysis or a desire to run away.

It is only if the guilt is *less* strong that it can be felt and an apology given. So reducing the guilt may help.

Sometimes all that is required is to say in some way, 'I understand, we are both at fault; it's not the end of the world, I only want you to admit to a little bit of responsibility, feel *a bit* guilty.' Often this works.

Unfortunately, in some relationships it would backfire because the level of underlying guilt is so great that it cannot ever be accepted. The guilty party cannot bear to admit to any guilt at all. The reaction to any admission of guilt by the accuser will be to load *all* guilt onto them. If this is the case, it tells something about the relationship, which may have survived for many years with one openly always 'in the wrong' and the other 'in the right' at least overtly. The desire for an apology has to be given up; it will never happen. It may be dealt with by humour: 'The position of a husband/mother/wife is in the wrong...'

EMOTIONAL BLACKMAIL

> *'How can you go out and play football and leave me here on my own? You know I'm not well.'*

> *'When I came in I found her on the floor. She's not supposed to try to get out of her wheelchair on her own, but she sometimes does it when she knows I'm out enjoying myself. I feel awful when I see her like that.'*

Emotional blackmail happens, it seems, when someone feels powerless, their complaints repeatedly dismissed or never put forward in such a way as to produce a long-term solution. The intention seems to be to make the other person suffer, to maintain a situation of misery, perhaps even to demonstrate that there is no alternative (even when there is) rather than to bring about change. Some families live like this, not knowing any other way to be. It can be hard to change these situations if there is no real interest in reducing suffering. However, if complaints can be taken seriously and addressed seriously (rather than avoided and dismissed), sometimes a better accommodation to circumstances can be found.

The possibility of actually separating may be more real than either partner realises in these circumstances; the difficulty may be in confronting this when one person is seriously disabled and deteriorating.

Hana's husband constantly complained about everything he had to do for her; he particularly seemed to hate it when she took herself out on her wheelchair and got involved in local issues. He just wanted to sit at home with his books. Hana knew she did not have long to live; she wanted to arrange to 'take herself to Switzerland' (i.e. end her life) in order not to put him under more pressure. In counselling she realised she did not actually have to stay with him for the last months of her life; her brother and his wife had offered her a home. She became excited at the thought of leaving and living with her brother. Suggesting this to her husband, she was astonished when he resisted strongly. She was able to tell him how distressing it was when he constantly complained. He stopped complaining. The counsellor noted that his income actually depended on Hana's personal pension, which he would have lost if she left, though Hana herself completely discounted this as a motivation.

ANXIETIES ABOUT THE RELATIONSHIP

This could be the last straw

Relationships which are already rocky may be pushed to the edge by a diagnosis of a serious illness, or by some unbearable symptom.

Sanjit often behaved badly towards Vena, but she tolerated it while he was out at work all day. When he became ill he was home all day and his behaviour did not improve. Vena seriously considered leaving.

Juanita married Darby because he offered a home for her and her small son, and a passport out of her own economically struggling country. Darby saw her as a carer for his declining years. When his illness threatened Darby's earning capacity, Juanita seemed to have no sympathy for him but ignored his difficulties and berated him for failing to provide her with the money she needed. He equally had no sympathy for her in her distress at leaving her family, and was angry that she wanted him to help around the house. He felt he had done enough by providing the house they lived in and a future in a rich country for her and their son.

Both Mark and Alicia had had affairs in the past. Each had tolerated the other's infidelities. When Alicia started to behave unpredictably, at times aggressively, her mind wandering, Mark became very angry with her and sought comfort with his secretary. He became afraid of his own aggression towards Alicia, arranged for her to move to a nursing home and visited her there. He did not stay with his secretary and, in spite of some effort on his part, did not find a new partner for a long time.

Even where either has reason to complain about the relationship, and where the illness makes it worse, a partner may find they cannot leave. Many factors keep couples together in these situations: guilt at leaving a partner when they are helpless; lack of anywhere to go or anyone to go with; financial considerations; unrecognised emotional dependence; the hope of improvement; a sense that the end cannot be too far off – any of these may hold people in the same house, caring with more or less good grace.

Jahan, who was a doctor, said she would have left her husband several years earlier if he had not been ill. Their children were fond of their father and she could not face their reactions and their blame. She did not have anyone else and felt she could (just) put up with his behaviour for a while longer. She hated the feeling that she was waiting for him to die, and was grieving for the good relationship they had lost many years before.

Zak had left his wife but came back when she was diagnosed with a terminal condition. His wife's son was sure he had only returned in order to inherit the house and prevent her children getting it, which he succeeded in doing.

Some couples give the impression that they stay together in order to enjoy punishing and taking revenge on each other. Roald Dahl describes a man who does this to his wife in a short story entitled *The Way Up to Heaven* (Dahl 1960).

116

Can he/she cope?

One of the biggest anxieties can be that a carer will no longer be able to cope. The idea of professional carers or a nursing home of some kind is reassuring to some but frightening to others.

Sandy had been looked after in children's homes as a child. He hated the idea of having to move into a nursing home.

Maureen told her family she would 'come back and haunt them' if she was put into a nursing home. She also told her daughters they were never to feel they should look after her. She died when her husband was beginning to feel he could no longer cope. The family wondered if the doctor had helped her to die: they suspected she might have asked him to.

Rose moved into a nursing home after years of complaining about being uncared for, in spite of devoted care by her children. She found herself surrounded by people she liked and got on well with, and told her children they should have sent her there a long time ago.

Being a carer can be exhausting and dispiriting, particularly if the person being cared for is not getting better. The physical effort involved is often underestimated. Moving someone's legs or feet, fetching drinks and food several times a day, or just tidying up after them may not seem much but in fact add up to a huge physical effort. Even living with someone who is ill can be stressful. Watching someone you love who is ill, particularly if they are deteriorating visibly and perhaps reacting badly to the changes in their own bodies, can be depressing. Identification processes mean that the healthy partner may feel that, 'inside', at least half of themselves is ill, collapsing or perhaps dying too. Anxieties about whether a partner can cope may include not only worries about the practicalities but also about psychological or emotional resilience, and about whether the love or other bonds between the two are sufficiently strong – or, perhaps, too strong – to allow a much-needed separation.

In spite of all the difficulties, it can be very hard for a family carer to recognise that they cannot cope – so someone else may have to tell them. People put up not only with high levels of irritation and frustration – living with someone who has memory problems or is deaf or very controlling can be very irritating indeed – but often with actual abuse too, which they allow 'because s/he is ill'. Back pain (which might be not only physical but also symbolic of an inadmissible burden) or other kinds of physical pain may force some kinds of caring to come to an end and help to be brought in. Some eventually recognise they have to leave out of fear of their turbulent emotions: afraid of what they are doing or might do in the future, either to the other or to themselves. A sudden fantasy of committing murder or suicide, for example, or an overwhelming reluctance to go home, may trigger a realisation that the situation has to change. Some leave at this point; some seek help. Some feel they cannot leave because the guilt will remain with them for the rest of their lives. Others stay on, but plan an exit strategy.

A young man said he had left the girl he loved best because he had just been diagnosed with MS and thought he would be a burden on her. He hadn't told her why. Later, he recovered more than he had expected. He married someone else and had mixed feelings about leaving his first love.

Particularly where one person saw the other as weaker or more vulnerable in the past, there may be anxieties about whether they can cope.

Mabel was a lot younger than Fred, who had always looked after her in a fatherly manner. She had actually had a responsible position before her marriage, but enjoyed playing up to her role as 'the weaker vessel' in the marriage. When Fred's illness meant he became unable to continue taking care of the house as he had before, she did not want to take over. She liked being looked after. She was very angry with him for becoming ill. She was also afraid that if she showed she was capable, Fred would take advantage and hand over everything to her, whether he could do it or not, just as she had handed everything over to him, including things she could have done herself, when they married. Unable to discuss this reasonably, they got into fights in which she shouted at him that he was useless. She found it very hard to distinguish what he could and could not do in reality.

The fear that a loved person will not be able to cope can be a very powerful motivation for staying alive – or for a suicide pact of some kind. People are not always clear who is more able to cope and who is less.

Frank, a very disabled man who had always taken responsibility for himself, was sure that his wife would not be able to cope if anything happened to him. To an outsider it looked as if this was a fantasy; that it was he who would not be able to cope if she left or if anything happened to her. It also looked as if this fantasy contributed to him feeling his life was of value.

If the relationship breaks down, who will care for me/them?

People often worry about who will care for them or their partner if their current relationship, however unsatisfactory, breaks down. Since people generally judge others by themselves, this can be a particular anxiety for those who suspect that, when they were healthy, they would have run a mile if someone with health problems approached them. In fact, of course, not everyone does 'run a mile' in such circumstances. Severely ill and disabled people do start new relationships. Family members who assume all is well, or that they should not interfere while someone is married, sometimes offer more support if there is no partner around. Living in residential care may be dreaded, but it may not be as bad as expected and can also lead to unexpected friendships and pleasures. However, breakdown of any relationship generally leads to at least one person feeling worse off, certainly for a time.

Clearly if there is a breakdown in the relationship, an ill person will have to be cared for in another way. People worry that their children will be put in a position where the bulk of the burden falls on them, whether they like it or not. On the other hand, partners who move out often continue to care and to take responsibility for the welfare of their ex-partner, even though they feel they cannot any longer live with them.

Power relations and physical violence

The balance of power in a relationship is often in fact unconsciously underpinned by physical strength as well as emotional capacities and finance. Illness may change this.

'I must see a counsellor. My husband fell over in the toilet and I left him there, I didn't try to pick him up. I feel terrible. I was so angry with him. Well, actually, I pushed him, to make him fall over; he always asks me to help him with his trousers when he doesn't really need me, he just wants me to be there, he can't bear me to have any time to myself.'

'I hit him yesterday.' 'Was he hurt?' 'I don't know. I couldn't look. I don't think so, but I hit him really hard.' 'Can you tell me what happened?' 'He sits there in his wheelchair, looking at me, he said I didn't care about him. I spend all my life doing nothing but looking after him, and he says I don't care!' 'And after you hit him?' 'He just laughed at me. I think he wanted me to hit him.'

Women discovering a capacity for physical violence in themselves can be very distressed and frightened. They may not dare look to see what damage they have actually done, nor tell the doctor, so they do not know if it is serious or not.

One of these husbands did seem to provoke violence. He had always liked to test his own strength: as a young man he was diagnosed with diabetes and was determined not to let it get in his way. In counselling, his wife was eventually able to overcome her own appalling guilt to think about what was happening. It seemed as if he was testing his strength against his wife's; when he provoked her to hit him, pummelling his chest or his upper arm, he always laughed and, she eventually realised, he seemed somehow satisfied. We wondered if it was a way he could express his own anger and frustration now so many other outlets were closed to him. He seldom complained directly and always expressed a strong desire for his wife to be happy.

Counselling enabled his wife to make a more realistic assessment of her own physical attacks on him. When she was fully supported by her own GP, a social worker and her counsellor, she did not hit him. Over a period of a few years, when one of these was absent, she sometimes did. In spite of this they were able to have a good life together for many years. We discussed whether he should be moved to protect him from her attacks, but thought he might continue to provoke attacks and be at more risk if at the mercy of people who did not love him as she did. Eventually he lost the capacity to provoke in the same way and the hitting stopped. When his wife finally had to admit she could no longer care for him and moved him to a nursing home, he died.

It is perhaps controversial to maintain that physical violence can take place in the context of a good relationship. But physical and cognitive disabilities can mean that what previously would have been expressed verbally now can only be demonstrated through action. And projective identification, whereby another person is 'made' to feel emotions one cannot bear to feel oneself, can be used as an outlet. In this case, the husband never admitted how angry and frustrated he was; he considered it a matter of pride to be able to bear 'anything'. He also knew he was totally dependent upon his wife. It made sense that he might need her to express his fury, and that he might feel better after she had 'cracked' and after he had shown, yet again, that he 'was man enough to take it'.

Women hitting men is different from men hitting women. Normally women do not cause as much damage because they are not as strong. Even when hitting as hard as they can with their fists on his chest or upper arm, they are unlikely to damage a man as much as would happen when a man hits a woman. Exactly where and how the hitting or other attack takes place is significant: punching a shoulder is different from punching the face or head, for example, and the distinction is important. The involvement of weapons is much more dangerous.

The situation is very different if a partner knows they no longer *want* to stay. An incident of violence which is confessed to a doctor might be a means of calling outsiders to help bring the relationship to an end. Even here there may be ambivalence, and social services may decide initially to offer more support to the attacking spouse. A 'victim' may not report such an incident for fear of having to leave home or lose their partner, and neither might a carer for the same reason.

A wife withheld medication from her husband, who could not reach it himself. He was ambivalent about reporting this because he depended on her totally; if she left she would take their son. To his surprise, social services offered her support, and for a while this allowed the relationship to continue.

It was not until Rohan threw a hammer at his small son that his wife finally recognised that she had to move him into a nursing home. She had been able to live with an escalation of verbal attacks over a period of several years, mainly by ignoring or discounting the emotional meaning of them. She did not at first recognise the seriousness of the hammer-throwing, and it took a neighbour to point out that she needed to take action. She was very distressed at the quality of the nursing care available, and took considerable trouble to visit her husband regularly in spite of his continued abuse. She remembered how much he had loved her before his illness began, and felt she owed him a debt of gratitude for his support in the early years of their marriage, when he encouraged her to start her own, very successful, business. She found it very difficult to tell family members why she had had to stop caring for her husband at home, because she did not want to diminish him in their eyes, and wanted to hide the extent of his deterioration. This increased her feeling that they blamed her, as she blamed herself, for being unable to care for him until the end.

In a sense, the relationship between Rohan and his wife never really broke down; she continued to care for him although she had to move him out of the family home. From Rohan's point of view, however, she was cruel and unfeeling and he was furious that she would not let him come home.

Nick, increasingly, though slowly, disabled by multiple sclerosis, said he was going to murder his wife 'because then he would be free'. She represented all the restrictions which his illness imposed on him – he thought that without her complaints and carping his confidence would return; without her, he would not be disabled. In prison, he thought, the food would be better than at home and he would get the right medication which was denied to him outside. Discussing this with his counsellor, Nick said he did not really mean to do it; however, both agreed that he could wake up in the night and 'forget' that he did not mean to do it. He agreed that his wife should be told, in the hope that she would then help him to move out into his own accommodation.

His wife refused to believe that the relationship was so bad, and took no action. Some time later she woke up to find him standing over her with an axe in his hand. She had to make all the arrangements for Nick to move to sheltered accommodation because he was not capable of organising it himself. It seemed to the counsellor that without such concrete, drastic action Nick had been unable to 'get through' to his wife how serious his distress was.

In both of these cases it was extremely difficult for the partner to make a distinction between behaviour which had to be tolerated 'because they are ill' and behaviour which had to be taken as a serious and real threat. Illness confuses people: interpretations of behaviour are changed. Normally hammer-throwing might be recognised as a sign that action needs to be taken; however, once an illness is involved, judgements are affected and the significance of behaviour (or other forms of communication) somehow more easily discounted.

Partners' judgements can also be affected by, for example, shortage of sleep, or their own health conditions or medication. Where someone believes they are the only acceptable carer for their partner, feeling they cannot cope any longer can trigger thoughts of killing: the self or the ill partner or both.

Ill-health can truly threaten lives. As mentioned in the introduction, there is evidence that people who are in ill-health are more likely to suffer physical abuse from their partners. Illness can make it hard for a partner to fulfil their partnership obligations: it can interfere with sexual relations or other ways of 'making up' after a quarrel; it can shorten tempers, make someone appear 'lazy' or uncaring or selfish; or damage their ability to argue coherently or to remember a significant piece of information. Being unable to make a decision can be extremely irritating for all concerned. No longer representing a 'good mother' or 'good object', illness can switch someone into representing a 'bad' one, evoking, perhaps, memories of 'bad', uncaring behaviour by parents or other carers in the past. Illness may cause people to provoke attack for all kinds of reasons: perhaps challenging a partner or adult child to let the world know how badly they have behaved towards someone who was ill (and *therefore*, in their eyes, 'deserved better'); perhaps to show 'I can take it'; perhaps to revenge themselves on a (in phantasy) neglectful partner (perhaps confused with a parent) in the most painful way they can, through his/her own conscience. Illness can make people more at risk from attacks which normally would not have harmed them. Seeing someone damaged by a previous attack can enrage the assailant and increase their desire to attack again, on some level to punish the injured party for making them feel bad, or to get rid of the evidence of their own shocking guilt.

Illness itself feels like something bad, both inside and outside. It often makes people feel they are bad; distressingly, it can make them behave badly too. It also takes on moral connotations, changing the way behaviour is judged. A carer judging the behaviour may have difficulty allowing themselves to see truly dangerous or bad behaviour correctly, out of a belief that an ill person cannot be held responsible for their actions, and that to do so would make *the person judging them* a 'bad' or 'intolerant' person.

INSECURITY

Some relationships seem to be threatened more by anxieties than by reality. Insecurity can make people behave badly in one way or another, and a husband or wife who is expecting their partner to move out at any minute may behave very badly indeed.

Ally and Chris had different deteriorating health conditions. They had lived together for many years, increasingly acrimoniously after the loss of a child. Ally often threatened to leave, and had done so once several years ago. After discussion with a counsellor, Ally finally decided to stay with Chris. Once Ally had made this decision, Chris stopped behaving so badly.

It might seem that a partner who was afraid of being left might improve their behaviour in order to keep the relationship, but this is not always what happens. Anxiety about being left can increase anger, accusations and shouting, for example. There are many reasons why this should be so. The waiting may feel unbearable; living in constant fear of being left at an unspecified time may feel worse than 'getting it over with'. A sense of hopelessness, or a desire not to keep someone who does not want to stay, may play a part. There may also be a desire to protect a loved one from a burdensome illness. A desire to protect the 'healthy' partner may be mixed with anger and resentment that they could leave the illness behind, that they have a choice, when the ill person may feel that he/she has none. Previous experiences of being left, perhaps as a child, may also play a part, creating an underlying sense of hopelessness and putting the current abandoning person into the same category as a parent who abandoned their child.

In particular, anxieties about being left may provoke attempts to increase control over the other person, even though excessive attempts at control may cause more problems. Sometimes the belief that the other person is about to leave arises more from the fantasy of the ill person; sometimes it is a thought which often passes through the mind of the partner, and which may be expressed in a way which allows it not to be taken quite seriously. In this situation, relations can improve enormously if the partner makes a final decision to stay – or to go – and makes it clear that this is not going to change.

A quarrel may break down the inhibitions which prevent the naming of a 'worst fear'. The naming of the problem, whatever the outcome, can somehow be felt to 'lance the boil' – to bring to the surface something frightening which is festering beneath the surface. It can also enable new solutions to be discovered. Unfortunately, while supposedly expressing 'how I/you *really* feel', more ambivalent or nuanced feelings, or those buried underneath angry ones, may be forgotten. The person *saying* it might feel relief and a new awareness of different feelings, but the person *hearing* it is in a different situation. Splitting allows good and bad to be separated and is useful at times of danger; however, it is not a recipe for good long-term social relationships. Like clever propaganda and fake news, quarrels distort perception, simplifying and exaggerating elements of truth into massive untruths. The relief of a quarrel which 'clears the air' may be short-term, as the effect of cruel or harsh words spoken (from the paranoid-schizoid position) becomes a new source of resentment (when perceived and understood as having the force of reality).

SEEKING HELP OUTSIDE THE RELATIONSHIP: JEALOUSY

Some people who know they can no longer provide everything their partner needs encourage their partners to seek solace elsewhere. There may be some comfort in retaining the sense of control given by planning; there may be a realistic awareness of the partner's current or future needs and a real desire to continue to take care of them, if only by proxy. The encouragement may extend to planning for their sex life. I take up issues around sexual relations in the next chapter.

The cost of such encouragement may be high. Feelings of jealousy may be hidden rather than acknowledged for fear of stopping the partner seeking essential support. If hidden, they can be expressed in less obvious ways, like the husband who always developed a serious tremor just when his wife was about to go out. Jealousy in particular is often denied to the self as well as others, although it may be obvious to an observer. People often feel that jealousy is as bad as envy: that it must imply an unreasonable desire to control the other; that it makes bad feelings where there should only be good, loving ones.

Jealousy is a reaction to someone you love loving another person, and is one of the most basic, natural feelings. It is painful for the sufferer, and causes problems when a jealous child wants to interfere with a baby sibling's comfort, or tries to stop one parent cuddling the other, so it is not surprising that children learn that jealousy is 'bad' or shameful and want to hide it rather than acknowledge and tolerate it. However, it does arise from love, and as a child grows jealousy can be mitigated by a growing love for the sibling as well as by accepting that parents can love more than one child. In the case of adults being jealous of (for example) the physiotherapist helping their partner, or a carer partner going out dancing, jealousy can be mitigated by knowing that the partner still loves them, and that (probably) they have no real intention of eloping with the physiotherapist or dancing partner.

It can be hard for some (and impossible for others) to accept that they are not the only person in their partner's emotional life. The line between normal and excessive jealousy may be hard to negotiate. Illness, perhaps bringing nights apart and intimate physical or emotional contact with attractive therapists, can bring to the surface issues of trust and control; it is natural that jealousy, overt or covert, should arise. Often couples can laugh about it, but it can be painful, particularly if someone actually falls in love with their nurse or doctor to the extent that they neglect their partner. Sexual attractiveness can be exploited by unscrupulous or naive care-givers (who can also fall in love with those they care for); and older people can fall for younger ones, in the (unconscious) hope that this will keep them young (or alive). The neglected partner may be torn by the desire to say 'You take them!' and the fear that the relationship is not reality-based, and that someone they loved is about to get seriously hurt.

Jealousy can also be used in the service of emotional blackmail, keeping a partner from contact with friends and family while they collude partly out of fear, partly out of awareness of the desperation and vulnerability of the controlling husband or wife. There may be cruelty involved, which may or may not be recognised.

People do not always distinguish jealousy from envy, but it is helpful to recognise that the desire to spoil someone else's pleasure because you do not have it is envy, and is not necessarily involved in jealousy. The capacity to bear some jealousy (and perhaps also some feelings of envy towards others) is essential if we are to allow people we love to enjoy life in the company of others – or allow them to visit the osteopath or the doctor or the therapist or friend who might offer them some relief which we, sadly, cannot provide. As such, it is something adults have to learn. In good relationships the pleasures or relief obtained in this way can counteract the pain of not being the person who provided it.

WANTING TO DIE

Knowing that someone who is about to die is ready for it, prepared and no longer fighting it, can be a relief for everyone who cares for them. Being able to talk about it can help people do their best to bring their life together to a good end. Relationships go on after one person has died, and a good ending helps the relationship to develop in a loving, sustaining way, after the death. People go on 'talking' to someone they love for a long time after they have gone, and knowing how the other felt about dying – in particular, knowing they cared for those left behind – can affect the rest of the survivor's life.

However, if death is not imminent, relationships can be threatened in a particular way by one or both partners feeling they want to die. Although rationality might suggest that we should end our lives sensibly, at some unspecified but obvious point, relationships are not governed purely by 'rational' thoughts. Hearing someone we love or care about saying they have no desire to live any longer can be shocking and distressing, even if they are disabled or in pain. This is one of the situations where the interests of one person may be different from the interests of those who love them. It is complicated by the fact that everyone involved may in fact have contradictory wishes and desires, and that they can (confusingly) attribute their own wishes or desires to other people.

Many people express a wish to bring their own lives to an end rather than allow their illness (or their life) to run its course. There are conditions which end most unpleasantly, and it makes sense that nobody wants to suffer in that particular way. Children might well not want this for their parents, and adults hate to see those they love suffering. However, seeing the suffering is one aspect of illness which helps mourners to accept the fact of life coming to an end – without this, it can be harder. The problem is that people have feelings about the life and death of others, even if they are not actually in close contact, but particularly if the person in any way represents a Good Object in their life.

It is very hard to be told that someone who has been your 'rock', your lifetime support, someone you have had complex feelings about, including love, no longer cares for you – and this is how a desire to die is often interpreted. This situation touches so many of our anxieties: are we good enough, loving enough? Are we a bad person? Did they ever care for us or love us? Does anyone love us? Are we worth anything in the world? At the same time there can be worries: I didn't realise it was that bad; is it selfish of me to want them to live? If I love them, I should let them go. But am I letting them go too easily? Is this a test to see how much I want them to live?

When someone we love wants to die – particularly when we cannot see why this should be the case – the relationship can be threatened at a very deep level. Death can easily feel like an abandonment; a death which is chosen can feel like a *deliberate* abandonment.

There are people who have been independent or in control all their adult lives, who find it difficult to understand that anyone might care if they took leave sooner than they had to. I have the impression that thinking loses some of its clarity in these situations, and people have little real idea of how important they are to others.

In counselling, people speak about not wanting to be a burden or depend on others for care beyond a certain point. When I ask who would miss them, the response has often suggested a feeling that *someone* is not caring for them as they should. A family member hearing this would perhaps be justified in feeling that this is an implicit attack on the 'someone' and their capacity to care, whether or not it is intended in this way. This conversation often ends in a realisation that killing oneself would in fact be terrible for someone: 'I have to wait until my mother has gone', '*Someone* would have to find my body', 'I do know someone whose mother killed herself; she has never got over it – I couldn't do it to my children, however bad it was, at least not until they are much older.' Such thoughts suggest that the capacity to think about and care for other people is alive and well, and relationships still matter.

How someone dies affects those left behind. Dying brings to an end any hope for future development of a relationship with a living person; bad relations cannot be made better. In addition, it carries the threat, at least for a while, that a good and loving person may become in the mind an accusing, bad one. Angry and hurt feelings of being abandoned and deserted, which are normal when anyone dies, may be harder to deal with if someone truly had a choice about when and how they went and chose their own (dis)comfort over that of their children or partner or parents. Close friends too are faced with distressing feelings if they missed the signals or somehow feel they failed as a friend, or were simply discounted, when they thought the relationship meant more. Judging the relative importance of one's own and the other's feelings can be difficult at the best of times; under the influence of illness and medication, and in the absence of anyone else's opinion, other people's interests may be forgotten or misperceived.

Feelings of wanting to die may in fact pre-date the health condition and may reflect much earlier problems.

Although people can benefit in many ways by a death happening sooner rather than later (for example, financially, in time spent caring for a sick person, and in the possibility of beginning a new life with a new partner), a parent choosing a premature death over one which is forced upon them leaves their children with complex feelings. Partners 'left behind' also have to deal with the meaning and significance of such a choice. Gratitude may be involved as well as distress arising from many different sources.

LIVING WITH SOMEONE WHO IS DYING

Living with someone who is dying slowly can be incredibly stressful, particularly if they survive repeated close brushes with death. Sometimes dying can take years as a robust body is kept alive by tube feeding and intermittent antibiotics, while the mind and the soul gradually fade away. This can be hard to live with.

Carers must watch ebbing away not only the life of someone they love, but also their own secret hopes for a replacement lover or marriage, for a chance to pick up the pieces of their own lives before they are too old, perhaps to have more children or to start again. To openly grieve for this loss may feel unfair, and it may be impossible to share it with the partner whose illness, not him- or herself, is the cause of the problem. They may at times envy the ill person who has no decisions to make, no choice in the matter, who is not torn by the same ethical and practical dilemmas. Anxieties about their own health, suffering under the strain, may increase their difficulties.

Where the person exists in a state of half-life, perhaps in a coma, perhaps seriously paralysed and cognitively deteriorating, kept alive by medical science rather than their own natural resources, grieving may take place in a piecemeal fashion, as different aspects of the person are lost over a long period of time. Sleeping with the person in the same bed may remain a source of comfort; however, this may become impossible, for reasons to do with the body, with feelings about the person, with incontinence or spasms or with the need for a specialist bed, for example.

The relation with the dying person may remain strong but more and more based on the healthy partner's phantasies and less on actual input from the dying partner. Attempts to understand the partner's state of mind may require careful thought and observation, rather than the normal assumptions of a long-term relationship.

It may be possible to recognise certain symptoms, such as agitation or a spasm requiring some immediate remedial action always arising when the telephone rings, as reflecting a conflict over jealousy or anxiety or anger, for example; but this recognition may have to struggle with a natural inclination to interpret it angrily as an unreasonable punishment for the partner, or simply 'bloody-mindedness'. For some couples, a fiercely loving relationship can be maintained over many years in these circumstances, while life revolves around the ill partner. Others find themselves withdrawing and disentangling themselves sooner, making more use of assistance and building up alternative sources of support and life outside the relationship. Others, again, simply exist in a half-life of hopeless despair verging on self-neglect.

People often blame themselves when they are in a bad situation. A strong sense of badness, of 'this is not right!' which actually belongs to the fact of the illness, may be attributed to the self ('I must have done something wrong') or to the ill person ('They brought this on themselves'), or to professional carers who can easily be seen to fail in some way. Just as ill people often feel ashamed of their illnesses, carers, with equal lack of justification, often feel worthless, even when they are caring very well for an ill partner – it is as if they feel that the illness itself is a sign that they are not good enough. Some find support and reassurance from the ill person themselves or from their own good sense. Others deflect their own unrecognised guilt and self-blame onto others.

Sometimes partners feel they are so bad that they are convinced the patient would be better off without them. In their head there may exist an ideal carer, who would not mind hospital visiting, remembering to bring things, making endless phone calls to doctors who do not reply, and would be able to make the right decisions easily. Such feelings of worthlessness can contribute to their decision to leave, or even to a carer partner's own suicidal thoughts.

Living with someone who is or may be dying can also bring with it a strong desire to bring the situation to an end. Wanting the person dead is one aspect of this, which may be accompanied by terrible guilt and sense of unworthiness. It may also be accompanied by anger with those who could help to bring it to an end: to hospital staff who refuse to give more morphine; to those who insist on inserting a feeding tube which cannot be removed. There can also be a fear of being pushed to the limit and doing something lethal 'accidentally' or on purpose. Carers' groups can help with such feelings if they can bring them into the open, allowing members to share both the experience and the guilt. Sometimes carers take matters into their own hands, with or without the open encouragement of the dying person and the connivance of the medical profession. Living with the knowledge of such an action may not be easy, however justified it seemed at the time.

SEPARATING

Whether or not an illness is terminal, the stress of staying with an ill partner can be too much for some to bear. Anxieties about their own life and health may increase with awareness of growing resentment. The losses sustained by the partner can resonate too powerfully with losses in their early life, bringing fears of loss of self, of existence, of security, of everything, which wipe out all other feelings and mean that the person effectively runs away.

Often, however, separating involves long, hard and careful thought as well as open grief. Concern for the person who is left has to be dealt with in some way. It may become buried by guilt, anger or fear, but it may have to be openly acknowledged and accepted. Staying may mean sacrificing the self, and separation may truly be seen as life-saving. Other people may be considered: how would a mother feel if her only child gave up his life to becoming the carer for someone he was never seriously attached to? What about hopes for having children or grandchildren? Is one permitted to 'fall out of love' with someone? Would they actually be better off with someone who did not resent being with them? If small children are involved, a departing parent has to consider the effect on the children: are they in fact at risk? Is it better for the children to stay or to separate? Or is there only a 'least worst' option? Conscience, the desire to be a good person and the realities of what that might entail will all play a part. Leaving may be very hard; but staying would be, too.

In my experience people who leave generally try to ensure that the person they have left will be taken care of, particularly if they are still ill. They may wait to go until the person is sufficiently recovered to look after themselves. If the person has a recurring illness, the partner may try to leave during a quiescent time, when they have recovered from one attack but have not begun the next. They may also continue to care from a distance. The problem may be living with the illness and its effects, rather than a loss of all affection or concern for the person.

For the ill person, such concern may not at first seem like concern at all, but a form of cruelty. To the normal feelings of being left may be added anxieties about how to cope with their own illness and with their new status as a person who is or has been seriously ill. They may be terrified of being alone for the rest of their lives, convinced that no-one can possibly want to make a new relationship with an invalid or even an ex-invalid who may be ill again, or who is 'damaged goods'. There may also be sheer indignation: 'How can they leave me when I am in such a state of need? What kind of a person does that?' Friends and relatives may find it easier to understand and forgive a man leaving than a woman; a female nurse or doctor may feel she can never leave, however much her invalid husband provokes her. How could she hold her head up in society ever again? However much he ill-treated her, she would be expected to excuse it as part of his illness – which she is supposed to tolerate. In fact, many people do not leave but become excellent carers. And some who stay either physically or emotionally abuse or neglect their invalid partners when leaving might be better for all concerned.

However, I have also known ill women who leave their husbands on the grounds that, if they are going to be ill, they would rather only have to worry about themselves, not about their husband. Some accept separation philosophically and with understanding of the conflicts suffered by the healthy partner. An illness may be taken as a 'sign' that a change is overdue, and living arrangements reorganised amicably. Separations are not always as they seem to an outsider.

Indignation at being left can affect attempts at rehabilitation. Sometimes people want their ex-partners to see what they have done by the act of leaving. In despair, and more interested in punishing the partner (in real life or in their minds) than in regaining a life of their own, they may make little or no effort to pick up the pieces of their own lives, though they make some effort to ensure that the partner hears how much suffering they have caused. The ex-partner here may also stand for a cruel parent-figure who has never been forgiven.

Separation can in fact lead to new relationships, though of course it can be hard for anyone to start again. A new relationship may be able to incorporate the health history better than the old one did. Even without an illness it can take two years before someone is ready to look for a new partner. People also sometimes decide to live alone and learn to enjoy its benefits and tolerate its difficulties. Living 'alone' may not be an option: carers may always be present, requiring relations with them to be managed, but sometimes this feels preferable to managing other kinds of relationships.

'FLIRTING WITH DEATH'

I discuss a particular kind of separation in my paper 'Flirting with death' (Segal 2009), which I have mentioned before. I came across several relationships where people left or had affairs unexpectedly after being faced with the real possibility of losing their partners through death.

The partners were all intelligent, well-educated people who could not understand what had happened. While they had been ill, on the verge of death, their partners had been 'wonderful'. They had visited, taken care of life outside hospital; and they had obviously been very upset. What was astonishing was that when the crisis was over and the threat of death lifted, with the ill partner home and able to take care of themselves again, the relationships suddenly foundered. One partner left very suddenly, taking out of the house all of his furniture, which left the house almost bare. Another began an affair for the first time (after many years of marriage) six months after his partner came home from hospital. Another became cold and distant, withdrawing to his own room and leaving his partner alone in the evenings, when previously they had always spent the evening together.

When they thought their partners were about to abandon them by dying, I think that these people had suddenly had the rug pulled from under them. They were faced with an end to a relationship they had expected to last until the end of their lives. The feeling of shock, disbelief and horror which they created in their partners was, we suspected, just what they had felt, watching their partner 'flirting with death'.

Understanding the abandonment as a form of communication made sense, and some of the no-longer-ill partners were able to use the insights to recover the relationship.

SUMMARY

Illness can bring many threats to a relationship, at any stage of life. It may mean a complete transformation of practical living conditions; it may mean a significant change in emotional and psychological transactions, a need to develop new defences, new phantasies, new assumptions about the way life is to be lived. Many relationships survive this, perhaps with a struggle; others founder in one way or another.

CHAPTER 5

Illness, Disability and Sexuality

INTRODUCTION

Sexual relations have both physical and emotional effects. 'Making love' is one of the clearest ways that couples demonstrate that they love each other. Within a good relationship sexual activities can be enormously comforting and affirming, implying that the body as well as the mind, the inner self as well as the outer shell, is wanted, loved, cared for and functioning in a good way. Touch is often felt to be healing as well as pain-relieving, and there is some science (Krahé *et al.* 2016) to back this up. Sleeping together can feel safer than sleeping apart: in the context of many illnesses such as epilepsy, this is real and serious. A good sexual relationship tends to imply a sense of value and worth in other areas too; it can be a source of pride and self-respect. In the early days of a new relationship, it can make the skin, the largest organ of the immune system, glow with health. In order to achieve any kind of sexual activity, ordinary worries have to be put on one side for long enough to begin – though at some point the sexual urge itself may take over and all else be forgotten. Not only orgasm itself, but also non-orgasmic sex can be followed by physical relaxation, sleep and relief, if only temporary, from daily worries.

All of this remains true in the face of a physical illness. However, illness and disability can complicate matters enormously. Representing life and creativity, when illness can seem to foreshadow death and loss, sexual relations can become hugely important for both partners when one is ill, asserting the reality that life goes on, and that neither is alone, at a time when both reality and the partnership are being called into question. For someone of any age with health problems, sexuality as a sign of love may be a source of pleasure which remains after others have been lost. It can also be 'put on hold' during a crisis, at a time when nobody feels like it.

Sexuality pulls people together and keeps them together long enough to form an attachment which will lead to them caring for each other, 'in sickness or in health, till death us do part' in old age. Even though they know that this frequently fails, people continue to live in hope. But if the attractiveness of youth is squandered on someone who leaves, what else will bring in a new partner? There are actually many reasons why people choose to live together or become friends, but people often fear that sex is the only or the main one. Sexual attractiveness is an expression of a willingness to engage with the give-and-take of relating to someone else intimately, and as such it signifies something important about how much closeness is tolerable. It is something which is felt to keep a partner from straying; it is seen as a wifely duty, a husband's right – and vice versa. Often seen erroneously as belonging only to youth and beauty, sexuality can in fact play a huge part in the lives of people of all ages and all health conditions. And people can be very afraid of the implications of losing it.

Although everyone knows that sexual relationships are not governed by entirely rational feelings, people can be surprised by the unexpected impact on themselves and on partners of changes in sexual behaviour and sexual feelings. Men who lose their erections often feel they have lost power and potency in other ways, and may behave in such a way as to demonstrate or 'prove' this. Women who thought they were not bothered about sex may realise that their attractiveness to their partner does matter to them, particularly after they have begun to show signs of no longer being fertile, when they may be newly suffering from the 'social invisibility' common to post-menopausal women. Both can find themselves caught out by their (or the other's) reactions to infidelity.

Loss of sexual responsiveness is often covered up, partly in the hope that it will go away, partly in the fear of what it might mean. It is also often (mis)interpreted as loss of affection. Men who judge their feelings by the behaviour of their penis (as if it had a life of its own) may interpret loss of erection as meaning they must no longer love their partner. A new or changed reluctance on the part of either to engage in sexual activities can be 'read' as a rejection rather than a response to a changing body. A fight may be provoked at bed-time in order to avoid awareness.

Sexuality is not always a casualty of illness or disability – powerful sexual thoughts or behaviour may also become part of the defences against the anxieties created by physical changes. Mid-life crises could be seen as attempts to fend off anxieties about growing physically (and mentally) older: they often involve falling in love with a younger person. 'Wild' sexual behaviour may be an attempt to 'prove' someone is still alive and potent – and that a neglected partner is the one who is growing older and at risk of being alone and unloved.

Under the stresses of living with illness or a new disability, sexual relations can be threatened, and with them, the whole relationship.

SEXUAL RESPONSES CAN BE AFFECTED BY GRIEVING

Grief and loss in general affect the body as well as the mind. Not only are people more vulnerable to coughs and colds after a bereavement, but they may also 'go off sex' for a while. Avoiding all feelings in order to deny the importance of a diagnosis or symptom will in particular interfere instantly with sexual responses; turning in on oneself in response to grief means turning away from everyone else. Anger and resentment, both common reactions to loss, and both of which can be hidden, get in the way of sexual activities. On the other hand, sadness may allow comforting behaviour which can lead to sexual activities.

(During an adjustment period, even small attempts to reduce the load carried by a carer partner can reduce anger and resentment. 'Isn't it time you got yourself a cup of tea and sat down' at least implies a certain level of interest, concern and care which can later be rewarded by warm feelings and desire for closeness rather than irritated rejection. Unfortunately, attempts to minimise feelings about the high level of debt owed to the partner for all the work they have to do, by claiming that what the partner is doing is 'nothing' or 'not a lot, really', may have the opposite effect.)

Feeling dead inside kills off any desire for sex, which might threaten to awaken more alive and painful feelings. At a time when they feel uncomfortable, anxious, rejected or 'in the wrong' with internal parents or with their own bodies, people may find it hard to make a sexual partner feel anything but uncomfortable, anxious, 'in the wrong' or rejected. These feelings are by their nature difficult to discuss, and they may contribute to an increasing distance between partners, particularly if one tries to deny the feelings and the other is left with a sense of being entirely responsible for them. Acknowledging shared distress is not easy when it involves feelings which are very threatening to a relationship.

An affair may suddenly seem attractive to someone who feels they have to 'protect' their ill partner from their own sexual or emotional demands. They may be afraid it was these which caused the illness; they may believe, rightly or wrongly, that the ill person cannot or should not be 'subjected to' sexual demands, felt to be dangerous, and which cannot at the time be reciprocated. Such an affair, of course, would also provide an opportunity to punish a partner who is secretly blamed for being ill. Simply banishing the suffering partner from the mind for a while can be a relief, but the guilt and sense of betrayal that returns later may seriously compromise the relationship with the self as well as with the other. An excess of guilt can lead to attempts to drown it out, sometimes by repeating the original offence.

SEXUAL RESPONSES CAN BE AFFECTED DIRECTLY BY CHANGES TO THE BODY

Sexual responses can also be affected directly by changes to the body. Stroke can destroy sexual responses temporarily, though previous levels of functioning usually return. Alcohol, diabetes and prostate operations are well known to cause loss of erection. Paralysis or spasm in the limbs, tremor or pressure sores can mean that a body has to be carefully manoeuvred or anti-spasmodic medication taken in advance. Hormonal changes affect mood, with testosterone in particular affecting both aggressiveness and enthusiasm for life in both men and women. Loss of testicles and ovaries causes a change in hormones which affect lubrication as well as having significant symbolic meaning which has to be worked through. Physical responses to sexual thoughts and activities can change as a result of hormonal or other chemical changes to the body. Desire for sex may be affected, or the capacity to achieve or enjoy penetration, ejaculation or orgasm. Spinal injury can change the erotic responses of the body, with pleasure points sometimes relocated. Many neurological conditions can cause massive fatigue, and, confusingly, may have varied and changing effects on sexual responses. Pre-existing sexual behaviour may be exaggerated (people can become 'more like themselves') after the onset of a neurological condition, making the role of the illness itself unclear.

Medication (such as Viagra) which allows men to regain or maintain a lost erection may or may not help either them or their partner to enjoy sex. Some say it is as good as the real thing; others say it is not. It cannot bring back lost sensitivity. Equally, there are many forms of lubrication on the market for women, though it may take considerable experimentation before one is found which works well enough. A vagina normally moves into a different position during foreplay, ready to take a penis; if this does not happen for any reason, penetration may be uncomfortable.

Women who have neurological damage to their genital region sometimes complain that nobody considers that their sexual pleasure might be important to them. To their unavoidable loss can be added a more avoidable feeling of outrage or distress or unfairness at the lack of acknowledgement or understanding.

> 'I told my doctor I wasn't getting the same sexual responses I used to and he just shrugged his shoulders and said it was the MS. He didn't seem to think it mattered. He would have been different with a man!'

Sexual responsiveness can be significantly affected by the hormonal and other changes of the menopause, but this does not mean that older women have lost all desire for a sexual relationship. Over several years they may have worked through their feelings about their loss of youth and all that goes with it, and have found ways of managing their new physical body without losing all the benefits of a good sexual relationship, now, perhaps, freed from anxieties about pregnancy.

Sexual desire can also be increased by illness, through various mechanisms. Damage to certain parts of the brain can reduce or remove inhibitions, so that a man or a woman may demand sex in socially unacceptable ways.

A teenage girl was horrified to hear her mother inviting the taxi driver in for sex.

A young physiotherapist was busying herself in the office when a patient was waiting for her in the gym. The team counsellor asked her if there was a problem, and she confessed that the patient had previously made lewd suggestions to her when they were alone and she had not been quick enough to handle them well.

SEXUAL RESPONSES CAN BE AFFECTED INDIRECTLY BY DAMAGE TO THE BODY

People can react in many ways to the physical changes in their partner's body. For some, there can be a pleasure, if guilty, in relating to a newly helpless body or personality.

A husband confessed that he found his wife more desirable when she was unable to move herself. He was not sure if this was a good thing or a bad thing.

For others, sadly, physical changes can be too disturbing; though in my experience this is less often the case than people fear. It seems that the unchanged image held in the partner's mind is often more powerful than the reality of bodily changes, and this may carry the sexual relationship.

More commonly, people fear that the opposite sex will no longer be attracted to them sexually if their bodies are damaged in some way.

Sofia refused to have a catheter put in because she thought it would stop her having sex. The specialist discussed it with her and her husband, and eventually she was reassured that it would be no problem. She was hugely relieved when this turned out to be true.

Amina did not want a colostomy bag although toileting was a real problem. Her concern was that she would be losing her sexual attractiveness.

Men often seem to believe that the only form of sexual behaviour which interests women is penile penetration and orgasm. There is plenty of evidence to suggest that, although this may be true for some, for many women it is not true.

Lack of sexual responsiveness may not actually take away the desire for some kind of sexual relationship with a loving partner. Some people are able to enjoy their partner's pleasure even when they physically feel little themselves; others are more irritated or annoyed by it, or feel that it simply heightens their own sense of their own loss. Some women want to continue having 'normal' sex with their partner even though they no longer respond, out of a desire to please and satisfy someone they love. Others do not want their partner to have pleasure they cannot have themselves and may even go out of their way to spoil a partner's pleasure out of resentment or envy or despair.

Medication, particularly anti-depressants, can often take away sexual desire and responsiveness. This is particularly unfortunate since sexual activity is an excellent anti-depressant, and these medications are sometimes prescribed for conditions which do not themselves damage sexual function.

LOSS OF SEXUAL RESPONSES CAN AFFECT LIFE IN OTHER WAYS

Loss of erection can make some men feel there is 'no point' in living. (Whenever a male client has told me they see 'no point' in going on, I have found that they are actually not having erections. People can use symbolic language without realising it.) Women too can feel like this when they first lose their sexual responses. People are at times quite basic creatures. Having good sex can mean life is worth living; without it, the very meaning of life comes into question. For others, sexuality has a different value.

Ralf (55) would not go to the pub after he lost his erection. He felt he was no good to anyone and that he couldn't talk to women any more. Exploring this in counselling enabled him to return to his previous sociability.

Sue (53) was quite pleased to give up 'all that' and was glad when her husband 'stopped bothering her'. They lived together quite amicably.

141

Stan (45) was certain that loss of erection meant he would never find another partner.

Maureen (35) was devastated at the loss of her sexual responses. She had never been married and had never had children, and felt that this loss meant she would never be a wife or a mother.

BELIEFS ABOUT SEXUALITY AND ILLNESS

There are many beliefs about sexuality and illness which affect behaviour. Depending on the state of the 'person-in-their-head' as well as the body of the ill person 'out there', a partner may feel they have to give up sex prematurely, or feel that they have permission and encouragement to continue the relationship, perhaps under different conditions.

'Ill people can't have sex' – maybe they can

Sexual relations can also be affected by the belief that ill people aren't supposed to have or want sex. This may be true if the illness is flu, but many people with neurological diseases do want it in whatever form they can enjoy. The more basic forms of hugging or holding may be highly significant symbols of affection and love, and when the illness or some side-effect takes this away they can feel a serious loss.

A severely disabled young man who liked dressing in ladies' tights was unable to buy them for himself. He struggled to work up the courage to ask a carer to buy them for him and put them on him.

Hospital beds, unfortunately, while preventing back problems for carers, may remove one of the few remaining pleasures for someone who is seriously paralysed, that of sharing a bed. Professionals may not even think of this, particularly if they are young and a patient is old and, perhaps, no longer beautiful. With the single bed and professional carers, the last opportunities for skin-to-skin touch, or for bodily affection from a partner, may be taken away without the professionals even noticing. Both partners may be too embarrassed to mention it, or simply think they have to put up with it, that they have no right to make a fuss, or that the professionals (or their adult children) would think there was something odd about them wanting to share a bed.

> *'I refused a hoist and I could still carry her up to bed. By the end it was the only form of physical contact we had, and I know she enjoyed it as much as I did.'*

A woman in her eighties confessed that she was pleased her husband, suffering from Parkinson's disease, 'wanted' her even at the end of his life. She found being a carer a great strain, 'not being one of nature's nurses', and her husband could be difficult, but this was a source of pleasure.

'Sex might hurt/damage her/him' – are you sure?

Sexual arousal or sexual activity can be felt to be dangerous – liable to cause a heart attack or a urinary infection in a vulnerable person, for example. A responsible carer or the ill person themselves may repress their sexual urges in this situation. These fears may be realistic or they may be based on misinformation, or on an assumption that sexuality is only for the young and healthy. On the other hand, sexual activities can also be known to be healing, facilitating physical relaxation and sleep for both the ill person and their carer – if either have the energy. An exhausted carer may understand that their partner would like some sexual play, and that it would be good for them, but be too tired, with too much to do, too anxious or too angry or too pressured to initiate anything. The ill person may also be exhausted and afraid of what their sexual demands might do to the already-overburdened carer. Where one partner normally initiates but can no longer, or is too tired to do so, it may take some time for the other to take over. Initiating sexual relations means taking responsibility for sexual desires, and this may not come easily. Sexual feelings can be fraught with unrealistic implications (such as 'naughtiness', or 'dirtyness', or even a frisson of wickedness). Becoming the person who admits to *wanting* sex may be a huge step for someone who always saw themselves as *submitting* to it.

Tiredness can sometimes be overcome by an erotic response, but a too-frightened or too-concerned carer may not find this out.

'You can't be a carer and a lover' – yes you can

People sometimes say that they cannot combine the role of carer and lover; that looking after a partner's intimate care needs, or exposure to their bodies and their 'bits' on a daily basis, takes away all the mystery and prevents them looking at the partner in a sexual way. However, my experience suggests that, while this may be true for some, it is certainly not true for everyone. Many people combine both.

There may be many reasons why a carer may not want sex. Caring is exhausting if it becomes a 24-hour, seven-day-a-week responsibility for another person's life. Sexual relations need to be given a priority if time is to be allowed for them, particularly if the complications of paralysis or loss of muscle power have to be taken into account.

> *'I gave up making the effort: it was me that had to do everything, and though I know he liked it, I lost the will. I was always tired.'*

Sexual relations require a certain amount of peace of mind and ability to focus, if only for a brief time. For a carer, time off may be difficult to arrange, for both practical and emotional reasons. There may be resentment, anger, shame or even contempt for the ill person, or a desire to keep a distance between the two bodies when one is felt to be 'polluted' or 'dangerous' or 'deformed' in some way. Anxieties about 'passing on' the illness may or may not be realistic. Resistance to physical closeness may arise from idiosyncratic implications of changes to the mind or body in the carer's fantasy. However, inhibiting feelings or phantasies may sometimes be uncovered and changed by counselling.

'We two have become one'

There is a kind of emotional closeness which can be created by illness and caring, for example where the carer has in their head a fantasy, conscious or unconscious, of their partner as someone who is at risk of dying or being very angry indeed *if the carer is not with them*. (The nature of this fantasy suggests that it arises from separations at an early age which have left their mark on the carer or their ill partner.) This can make it impossible for the carer to 'switch off' their responsibility or take time out and leads to a feeling of being totally taken over and unable to free themselves. Work on separation 'in the head' may be needed before the carer can allow themselves to relax at all. Even where there is no illness, people can feel totally bound up in each other, taken over, and suffocated by the other person to the extent that they feel they 'have to' get out of the marriage. In relationship counselling these people may be helped to separate 'in their heads', to distinguish their partner from aspects of themselves or other people in their inner world which had been projected into the partner. They no longer, then, need to separate physically.

My experience with clients who had to cope with illness or disability suggested that the same process occurred for them too. The 'suffocation' experienced by some carers could be relieved by distinguishing more clearly between the ill partner 'out there' and the one in the carer's mind, as well as by examining thoughts about 'keeping them alive' by 'being there', and about how angry the partner would actually be, openly or secretly, if they went out for a while.

Sexual relations can be affected by such feelings of suffocation. Anxieties (or resentment or anger) about being taken over altogether can interfere with the desire for the physical and emotional closeness of sexual activities.

'We were one; now we are two (or three?)'

The stresses of caring are real, but their effect on sexual desire may be exaggerated by a partner who is disengaging themselves and has replaced the ill person with a new sexual partner but does not want to admit it. Worse, the partner can believe this is the case when there is some other problem. A male carer who is drinking too much or is developing diabetes may have problems holding an erection but not want to admit it to himself or his partner: this is a different kind of disengagement, in that it involves hiding an aspect of the self from the ill partner. 'I didn't want to worry her/him' is a common reason people give for beginning to separate their own lives from that of an ill partner.

Worrying about each other appropriately is part of many good relationships, and feeling that one has lost both the right and the duty to worry or be worried about can be linked with feelings about being bound together or loosening the bonds. Worrying alone distracts from sexual activity; sharing worries can be a prelude to it.

'You just have to be more careful'

Patros (a large man) was afraid his (small) wife was totally at his mercy; he found this arousing but was afraid to have sex with her because he could not always tell whether she liked it or not. He was frightened of his own power over her, of being carried away and hurting her, while she would be unable to stop him.

Janice continued to give her husband Viagra and to have sex with him for some time after he lost the ability to talk or move himself or to show much in the way of pleasure. He had often expressed the wish earlier in their relationship that she would continue to love him, which he equated with her desiring him and wanting him sexually. At that time, anger had often prevented her from wanting sex; now he no longer made her angry she was glad, though sometimes a little guilty, that he could still give her sexual pleasure when so much else had been taken from him. Discussing this example, some (young) medical students considered the wife was not justified in doing this since her husband could not give permission. (I hoped that they would have learnt better by the time they qualified.)

FERTILITY

Sexual difficulties can also be caused by feelings about having children or getting pregnant. Illness or disability can affect people's desire to have children. Not only may they fear that the child will get the parent's condition, but they may also be afraid that a baby will compete for attention or add to the difficulties of coping with the condition. The question of whether or how they would be able to look after a baby worries some very much; others less so. Some blame pregnancy for the start of their own or their partner's health problems and fear, correctly or not, that another pregnancy will exacerbate it. In any of these circumstances, particularly if fears cannot be discussed openly, difficulties may arise with sexual relations as a way of avoiding pregnancy while simultaneously avoiding discussion.

For others, having a baby is something which is still possible and a potential source of joy, particularly if other sources of creativity, hope or pleasure have been taken away. Questions of care for the baby may be addressed realistically and sources of available support and help arranged in advance.

For some people, however, particularly if their thinking has been affected by their condition, having a baby seems to take on a more fantastical aspect, where the baby somehow represents their own salvation – a new chance for their own life, rather than a potential person in their own right. (This can also happen for people who are not ill or disabled. It does not augur well for the child.)

LOSS OF FERTILITY

Loss of fertility as a result of an illness or other physical problem may be a huge source of sorrow and grief and require considerable reworking of beliefs about the self, about life and about the world. Sexual activities may be affected: rejected perhaps for a while because they simply remind the couple or the individual of the babies or children they will now never have; or manically desired in a 'last-ditch' attempt to prove the doctors wrong.

Being unable to have a baby has a different significance for those who feel they have enough children or grandchildren and those who do not. Loss of the possibility of a future choice can anger or upset even those who have decided not to have children. Distressing feelings about losing one or more babies in the past, evoked by a new loss, can take people by surprise; grief which was avoided earlier, perhaps by the thought that 'I can have other babies', may now have to be faced. A miscarriage in her twenties takes on a new meaning for a woman of 36 losing her fertility without having had the children she wanted. Distressing feelings about loss of fertility may have to be worked through before sexual relations can be enjoyed.

Talking about the effects of her illness on her life, Marcia mentioned in passing that she had had an abortion at an early age. She suddenly found herself weeping for the baby she had never had. She realised that throughout her life she had carried many hidden feelings about it which made sense at the time, but now, 40 years later, could be reassessed. She reported a huge change in her feelings about herself and about her life, including her illness, after this session.

Working through the feelings and memories in counselling can bring a new look at the events surrounding the loss, and can change many of the associated thoughts and feelings. A secret which once felt very guilty may feel less so when it has been shared in later life. An older self may be better able to understand and forgive a younger self – and in some circumstances may also be able to understand and forgive adults who did bad things to a younger self.

After all such associations and feelings have been worked through, more ordinary sexual desires may return, perhaps in a different form.

Partners who themselves do not feel so distressed about not having a child in the future may require considerable patience while they wait for the grieving process to run its course. It can help if they realise this is what is happening and that it will take many months, possibly years, as the pain gradually moves aside to make room for other interests. The presence or absence of existing children belonging to one partner and not the other will have an effect: perhaps permitting parental feelings to be expressed as a step- or adoptive parent; perhaps for a while increasing the sense of being in 'different places' as far as the loss of fertility is concerned. As with any such grief, neither partner may fully recognise the other's feelings, particularly if it becomes a forbidden topic, and pleasure in closeness of a physical kind may be affected. Where thoughts cannot be spoken, physical sex (or its refusal) may express them. The hope is that the couple understand each other sufficiently that the message is understood, and correctly, in a loving way; the risk is that it is misunderstood. Is it a sign that 's/he doesn't really care', or that 's/he loves me even so'? And is it the case that 'if you have to ask, you can't really love me/know me'?

'BAD SEX'

Having sex does not always mean making love. It can mean 'fucking' or more aggressive forms of activity, with or without the permission of the other. Sexuality can be used as a means of domination and control; to get rid of aggressive and damaging feelings into somebody else. For someone who associates sexuality with punishment, dirt, threat or abuse and indulges this with (male or female) prostitutes or a partner, for example, it may be an important means of maintaining a fragile hold on self-worth at the expense of others. There may be fears of retaliation from people who were actual victims or from others who represent them in some way. Where people have been abused or have used sexuality in aggressive or attacking ways themselves, loss of sexual desires or responsiveness may have very mixed meanings.

Where couples have played with more aggressive forms of sexual activity, anxieties that the 'play' has caused damage can interfere. Domination and control as part of sexual fun takes on a different connotation if one partner becomes very dependent and really unable to control their body or events. Dangerous, degrading or humiliating forms of sex may be idealised (and 'vanilla' sex derided) by couples who rely on each other's support to maintain what both feel is a fiction, that it is 'the best'. Loss of this support may threaten to face them with very frightening unconscious fantasies indeed and may impel them to find alternative partners. If such activities have been hidden from a partner, illness may threaten to expose them, with unpredictable consequences.

When a child becomes ill or is born 'with something wrong', in unconscious phantasy the parents can be convinced this is to do with 'something wrong' with their sexuality or their sexual activities – with 'bad sex' or sex which has damaged their insides or their sexual apparatus and which may have taken place entirely within their conscious or unconscious fantasy. The difficulties involved in uncovering, acknowledging and sharing such anxieties with a partner add to their distress.

LOSS OF SEXUAL INHIBITION

Where an illness causes loss of inhibition there are problems for those around as well as for the person themselves, though they may seem unaware of them. Other adults may be unable to control wild sexual behaviour of a family member, the consequences of which can be serious. The first difficulty may be in recognising that it is happening; while once this is recognised it may not be at all clear what to do about it, and who, if anyone, has any responsibility or capability of taking action. Mostly, in my experience, people behave and speak as if the person is 'making their own choices' and as if they had no right to interfere unless young children are clearly at risk. The days of confining to a madhouse women who proposition every man they meet are over. There are other interpretations ready for a man who behaves in a similar way.

Loss of inhibition and loss of insight are two areas where our attitudes to illness and disability become morally awkward. The line between maintaining liberty and protecting the vulnerable changes with generations and raises difficult questions which have to be considered on a case-by-case basis. The question of whether to take away a driving licence from someone who seems to have lost all concern for others and all insight into their own behaviour is an example where the wider society leaves the family on their own. In general, doctors will not take a wife's word for it that her husband is no longer safe on the road; she has to manage the situation without professional help. The same applies to sexual disinhibition. The person concerned may not be 'safe', but the family may simply have to live with this. Determining whether a teenage boy living alone with such a mother is 'at risk', or what action can or should be taken to support him, is a morally and socially challenging question.

FEAR OF AGEING

Ageing does not mean loss of sexual responsiveness, but loss of sexual response may be taken to mean that ageing has begun. 'Getting old' can be associated with being 'on the scrap heap', unwanted, unlovable, out of the loop, irrelevant. The associated unconscious phantasies (and conscious fantasies too) can be cruel. These anxieties lie behind many break-ups of long-term relationships. A new, younger partner can assist in the denial of an ageing process, 'proving' that 'I'm still young and vigorous!' The abandoned partner is left to carry all the fears about a lonely, rejected old age on their own – although the break may not be complete. Such separating couples may stay more connected than they realise if each feels they have left part of themselves in some sense 'in' the other. Affection may live on, or a desire to know what is going on with the other, or some desire to retain control, based on a sense that bodies which once entwined sexually retain elements of each other when apart.

> *'I can't expect her to stay with me, she's always liked sex and I can't do it like I used to.'*

More lucky couples are able to share their anxieties about growing old together, or are less concerned about sexual activities.

> *'I asked him if he wanted to leave me for someone who was still ok, but he said he didn't. He said there's more than one way to skin a cat...'*

FINDING SOMEONE ELSE...

> *'I'm not sure if I should tell him to find someone else to have sex with, now I can't. I wouldn't mind if I was sure he wouldn't leave me. I feel I'm being selfish, but I couldn't bear it.'*

> *'If I couldn't have sex I wouldn't mind if my husband found someone else to have sex with. It's just an itch he'd have to scratch. He wouldn't leave me.'*

> *'When I'm gone, you must ask Sandy to marry you. You couldn't live on your own and I know you've always fancied her.'*

> *'When he's been with someone else he always comes back and is really nice to me. I don't know how long it will go on though, he might find someone he prefers to me. He says he won't, but I'm not sure.'*

Ideas about 'finding someone else' while remaining with their partner pass through the minds of many people. Thoughts of infidelity are normal, and an illness or disability which affects sexual relations for any reason plays into fantasies about sex with other people. Talking about this, the intention is nearly always for the partner to keep on looking after and caring for the ill person. People often believe that one can have sex which involves the body only and not emotions or the mind.

Having observed these relations over years, I am sceptical. There may be people who can manage these relations, but my feeling is that they are much harder than people expect and have consequences they claim not to want. Attachments are forged in bed. Sexual partners are not discarded without trace. The partner who is no longer being touched or held physically in the same way may be very well aware of missing out. However, all of this may have to be accepted as a 'least worst' solution to the situation. There may be a trade-off in which some non-sexual care continues in exchange for sexual freedom. It may be better if the ill partner could be more free themselves to find someone else (a solution desired by many unfaithful partners) but this may be an unrealistic hope, or the continuing attachment may prevent it happening.

Carers often feel the need for help and comfort for themselves which may or may not be available from their ill partner. They may not want to ask for support for fear of putting a strain on the partner, or a previous level of support or help or comfort may no longer be available because of physical or cognitive damage or other constraints. If they feel that their main problem is the partner and their behaviour, the partner may not be the person who can provide a shoulder to cry on while they make their complaint. They may not wish to upset them, or they may have no hope of being understood.

The risk of a comforting relationship becoming a sexual one is obvious. Carers need support and help in their daily tasks; they also need to get away, and they may turn to others to confide in if the partner is no longer able to perform this function. Such a relationship may become sexual almost by accident: unsatisfied sexual desires plus the opportunity becoming available plus a desire for a moment to forget the miseries of the ill partner's condition and to forget the situation of the carer – together these may prove too much to resist, particularly if either has been unfaithful in the past.

Whether such an event destabilises the relationship may depend on how the relationship develops. Sometimes people do manage to maintain threesomes, in which the ill person is looked after by both their partner and a lover. Where I have come across this (more than once), the lover came on the scene initially as a close friend of the ill partner and had a pre-existing commitment to them which survived.

Where this is not the case, for a carer to maintain a commitment to the ill person and at the same time to another relationship can be very difficult, though some people manage it. If the situation continues over a long period of time, one or other may eventually break: the lover may eventually tire of always coming second; the carer may find their conscience does not allow them to walk away from their ill partner and may abandon the affair. Others do leave an ill partner, either justifying themselves by continuing care for the ill person from a distance, or (also perhaps justifiably) blaming the ill person for bad behaviour or for causing the abandonment in some other way. In some cases the bad behaviour could be linked to the illness or diagnosis; sometimes it seemed independent of it. The opprobrium attached to leaving an ill partner (by family, friends and the self) may be harder to bear than in a normal divorce. Several women have told me they had initiated divorce proceedings but felt they had to put them on hold when their husbands became ill.

What I have noted through 35 years of counselling is how often (though not always) people follow one of their parents. Someone who had a parent who had an affair or left when they were small is more likely to have an affair themselves or to expect (or even provoke) their partner to have one; those whose parents stayed together seem to be more likely to stay together. Illness and disability in my experience play less of a part in deciding whether a couple will stay together than parental behaviour.

An ongoing illness itself, particularly if it threatens an imminent death, may be felt as a kind of betrayal although neither partner may have been at fault. It can take away in particular the certainties of the future, however illusory, as well as important pleasures and benefits of the relationship, leaving the struggles and the conflicts. The presence or absence of sexual activities may play a part in affecting this balance, or may become symbolic of attachment or detachment. The illness itself may be like a third party in the relationship; it may also bring in numerous professional health workers or carers of one kind or another who complicate matters. In this context, talking to someone else about difficulties in the relationship, or seeking the kind of help which the partner used to provide, may be felt as a betrayal – but one which is essential in order to cope with the original betrayal.

THE VIEWS OF THE WORLD...

Where there is a legitimate partner, sexual relations with someone else are likely to be understood as a betrayal, whatever arguments are used in justification. Other people can be very harsh. Some have been tempted themselves and felt they needed the support of social condemnation in order to remain faithful; others fell from their own high standards and want to punish others who do the same. Some people think that an ill person should have whatever they want, that their desires should take precedence over the life of a young and vigorous partner, whatever the cost. They cannot forgive those who take new partners while their current one is ill, or those who leave an ill partner.

However, others are less harsh. They will not 'throw the first stone', not being without guilt themselves. They may recognise the stress under which partnerships are placed by illness, particularly if cognitive problems are involved, and they know that some people cannot survive alone. They sympathise with the struggles of conscience of the defecting partner and do not condemn those who choose to make a new life before illness swallows up their old one. They recognise that nobody can have everything they want, whether they are ill or healthy; that relationships are complex and can never be fully understood by an outsider; and that people have to make very difficult decisions in appalling circumstances, in which there is no wholly good outcome, just some that are less bad than others.

Children may be torn between indignation at the abandonment and anxieties for the health and the life of the 'carer' partner. Some older children may encourage a more healthy parent to move on, others may accuse them of not caring. Children will ask themselves what they would do, and can be very judgemental towards themselves as well as towards their parents. If they can talk about the situation their views will change as they grow up; otherwise their beliefs and ideas and the unconscious phantasies derived from it may remain at the level of the age they were when events happened.

SUMMARY

Previous sexual activities and sexual feelings can be a casualty of illness or new disability which may have to be lost and mourned before (or while) a different relationship can be developed. Salvaging some aspect of sexual relations, perhaps in a modified form, can be of huge significance to individuals and couples: without this they need to find other ways of demonstrating on a daily basis that they still love each other. There may be considerable practical and emotional difficulties which get in the way. Sometimes, all that is needed is determination; sometimes, this is not enough.

CHAPTER 6

Pain

INTRODUCTION

Living with pain or living with someone who is constantly in pain brings with it a particular set of difficulties. Pain affects people: it affects their capacity to think, in particular to think about others; and it affects their judgement – their sense of time, justice and sometimes even rationality. Watching someone else suffer physical pain hurts, but how we understand and perceive this hurt depends on the complex phantasies involved.

Pain is one aspect of illness and disability which can make people feel particularly bad, physically, emotionally and morally, whether they have it themselves or are close to someone who has it.

Pain can seem so demanding and so urgent, requiring attention at the expense of almost everything else, that it often creates conflicts around priority. Can another member of the family legitimately ask for any attention for themselves if one person is in pain? Would they be heard anyway? Should an ongoing, chronic illness count for more than, say, another family member's toothache? Or is it the other way round? What does it depend on? Many pains, both physical and emotional, can be neglected as a result of one pain being allowed to override all others, perhaps unintentionally. These minor forms of neglect may have a long-term cost, but even the emotional struggle to find and insist on the rightful place for a lesser or different pain itself takes energy and thought which may not easily be available. This is one of those situations where there may not be a right or wrong, only several unsatisfying and uncomfortable partial solutions.

'I'm never sure whether his pain is so bad that it destroys all consideration for others, or whether he just uses it as an excuse to allow himself to ignore all consideration for others. I don't know how much control he has over his behaviour when he's in pain. I don't like not knowing. That makes me feel guilty and angry and confused too.'

In this chapter I look first at pain from the point of view of the person who has it, then at the point of view of someone who cares for them, before picking up some shared concerns.

IT'S MY PAIN...

Loss of capacity to think straight

'It does my head in; I can't do anything, I just want to curl up and lie here and hide from everyone. I know I get really ratty so I warn my family to keep out of my way – at least that is an improvement, I never used to, I just used to shout at them before. My daughter never knew if it was her fault or my pain then.'

Although certain kinds of pain can focus all of thought on itself, we are also capable of overriding pain. For example, a bone only starts to hurt some time after it has broken, which gives time to get to safety or to seek help. And pain can also be forgotten, sometimes quite quickly after it has passed – and the need to go to the doctor may also be forgotten if a pain comes and goes.

'I always think it's gone when it isn't there. Then it comes back again and I realise it hasn't.'

Ongoing pain may be ignored for a long time, half-forgotten but ready to reawaken attention if it changes. People often carry their bodies in a certain way in order to prevent a well-known pain recurring; sometimes the way they do this gives rise to skeletal problems which cause different pains in another part of the body. Sometimes people know that a certain movement, or sleeping or sitting in a particular way, will bring on a pain, such as back pain; they may find themselves 'forgetting' and bringing on the pain. There may have been a good, though unconscious, reason for doing this at this particular time; usually people deny this at least until they have reflected for a while. They may be right to deny any intention, or they may be completely unaware of their own unconscious motivations.

All of this can be confusing. Can I or should I override or ignore my pain? How urgent is my need? Am I being selfish, or can I really not think? Have I brought it on myself? A sense of morality and of rights, duties and obligations all play a part in reactions to pain and affect the way it impacts relationships. It is not surprising that people can become very edgy and angry when they are in pain.

Interpretations

Pain is something which always holds significance; physical pain may be understood to represent an emotional pain, and vice versa. Emotional pain can trigger physical pain.

> Counsellor to Selma: 'I can't take your pain away, but sometimes other aspects of people's lives make them "wind" the pain up or down. For example, if you are angry, your body might tense up and it can make the pain worse, the anger stops you relaxing and letting go of the pain. My hope would be that, by talking about the things that make you angry, we may be able to help you feel better about them, and that might make the pain more bearable at least. At the moment the pain makes you angry and then you are reminded of all the other things that make you angry and that makes it worse.'
>
> Selma, one year later: 'I'm much calmer now. I'm not angry with my mother or my step-father any more; I've really forgiven them for what they did to me. When I saw you [for counselling] first, my pain was about 11 on a scale of 1–10. Now it's about 4. And I'm getting on much better with my mother and my daughter. And I've gone back to the doctor to ask if he can refer me to the pain clinic. I couldn't do that before.'

Counsellor to Dave: 'I've noticed that whenever we talk about your father you reach for a joint.' (The joint was cannabis, to relax his muscles. I was seeing him in his own home: he kept forgetting he was not supposed to be smoking at all while I was there.)

'No, it's just my legs hurting.'

'You tell me you aren't angry with him, but your wife is, and when you talk about him it seems to me that you could be very angry with him if you let yourself admit it. I think you don't want to be angry with him, and you tense up to stop the anger and that makes your spasms start up and they hurt and then you want a joint to relax again as well as to help you forget how you feel.'

'I went to an osteopath and he touched something in my back and it made me cry, and I was crying about my mother; she always had back pain. I hadn't realised how it had got inside me... I couldn't bear it, there was nothing I could do for her, I was a child. I left home as soon as I could, I think it just made me feel so guilty.'

'Whenever I rang my sister – which wasn't very often, I didn't like ringing her – I got cystitis. After I realised this, it stopped happening. I haven't had it since. She did irritate me dreadfully. We get on better now.'

Physical pain standing for emotional pain

Sometimes physical pain can draw attention to emotional pains. I have found that back pains are often linked with mothers, and thinking about this link can modify the pain for some people. A 'pain in the backside', or a 'pain in the neck', may be a response to someone *being* such a 'pain', for example. Many other pains also have symbolic meanings which might be 'read' and understood, perhaps by someone else.

Ann hurt her foot badly on the way to bury her father's ashes. The pain increased over the next few days. Her husband heard what had happened and said, 'Oh, you wanted to give him a last kicking!' The pain began to subside straight away as Ann laughed and realised she had indeed been very angry with her father without realising it. (This is an example of humour allowing unconscious insights into consciousness: her husband had intended it as a joke.)

Some months earlier she had been afraid she was getting arthritis; all over her body joints were hurting. She went to see a psychotherapist to talk through some important issues around her father's death. During the session she realised she was tense with unadmitted feelings towards him: on coming out of the first session she realised her physical pains had all disappeared.

Pain can reinforce an identification with a parent who had a similar pain or can represent some aspect of feelings towards them. By holding onto or constantly re-creating the pain, the adult may be keeping alive something of the relationship which still needs working through. A doctor or partner or other family member who just wants them to 'be all right' may be frustrated at the apparent lack of response to their treatment. The problem is that significant emotional pain has to be dealt with differently if it is not to be expressed physically. An understanding person who is willing and able not only to share and 'contain' the pain, but also to allow it to emerge in the first place, may be essential; this may have to be a therapist of some kind. Close relationships may allow expression of painful truths, and may offer both understanding and containment, but the fear of damaging a good relationship can make people hold back their worst anxieties.

Pain can be experienced as a deserved punishment.

Selma had been sexually abused when she was a child and was angry with herself for many reasons, including feeling she had revenged herself on her cruel mother by seducing her mother's boyfriend. She found it hard to seek help for her arthritic pain and tended to discard painkillers after taking them once or twice.

There are other situations in which painful memories or experiences are 'kept alive' in a physical pain: such pains may move about the body and be difficult to describe precisely. Sometimes people feel they are not being taken seriously and become angry when they are told a particular pain has no physical cause: others are relieved to be given the opportunity to uncover and talk about a loss or an abuse which has left emotional scars in the form of physical pain.

Masochism: attack on internal object

There are people for whom pain inflicted on the self can be felt to be 'really' inflicted on someone else who is located in the person's own body. A punch on the head may be experienced as punching the cruel person who is constantly telling them off and whispering rude things about them. To an onlooker, this process can seem mad and incomprehensible. It is of course more complex than this suggests. It may involve not only the pleasure of making the other person suffer (in conscious or unconscious fantasy), but also a pleasure in being able to survive punishment, which can seem to turn the tables on the punisher: 'I'll show you who's in charge around here!' Control has moved from the attacker to the victim. People can feel as if by withstanding the pain of an illness they are somehow standing up to a fantasy person or deity who made them ill. They may be less interested in getting rid of the pain than in surviving the worst that can be thrown at them.

Selma sometimes felt she was carrying her mother inside her body, that it was her mother twisting her up; at times she felt the pain was attacking her mother inside her, not herself. This way of dealing with it gave her a kind of triumphant satisfaction and momentary relief. During counselling she began to see her mother as a young abused woman herself, in a very difficult situation when Selma was a young child. For the first time she felt empathy and sympathy for her, and her desire for revenge on her mother disappeared.

If your right hand offends you, cut it off (Matthew 5, 30).

SOMEONE ELSE'S PAIN...

Watching someone in pain can be agonising, particularly if there is a loving relationship involved. We really do not want those we love to be in pain. Some mothers wish they could 'take the pain themselves' and spare their child. Others do not. Partners too may desperately want to take the pain away, or may feel guilty and despairing because they cannot – or because they know they are, perhaps secretly, hugely glad that it is not them who is suffering. We understand pain through our own phantasies, and this applies to others' pain too. In phantasy we can for a while obliterate the pain, or the knowledge that it hurts, or the knowledge that it is *someone we love* who is hurt – the possibilities are endless. Many of these possibilities create phantasies which leave us feeling worse afterwards.

One of the ways of getting rid of awareness is by responding with some kind of denial, helped along by a distracting emotion or phantasy. Real concern and care can be pushed under by more aggressive feelings such as irritation and annoyance: 'Get over it!', 'You're not the only person suffering around here!' Another person's pain can also satisfy envious feelings: 'Ha! You thought your God would save you!', 'You thought you were better than me, and now look at you!'; or jealous ones: 'Now Mum will love me more than you!'

Awareness of less acceptable feelings can make people feel guilty: either *so guilty* that they compensate by denial, or *just guilty enough* so they can confess and apologise or laugh at themselves. Knowing that the 'bad' feelings are never the whole truth can help, although *at the moment* it can feel as if they are.

Over time, responses can change. People may get used to knowing that the other person is in pain and no longer feel it themselves in the same way. Sometimes they forget. Other people's pain is much less present than one's own, and someone else's may be more easily forgotten. Having to remember without the physical cues is hard, but carers or other family members may feel they *shouldn't* forget.

A six-year-old felt terribly guilty because she caught herself forgetting that her mother was in pain all the time. She thought this meant she was very selfish and tried never to forget again.

Sometimes a partner can be tiptoeing around, thinking anxiously that the pain is still there when it has in fact gone, but the person forgot to say. It can sometimes take a considerable effort of conscious thought to notice both when a pain begins and when it has gone; telling someone else means admitting it is there and is serious and that it is taking up time and brain power which everyone would really rather use for something else. Asking may not help: people can be irritated if they are constantly asked whether they are in pain or not, as well as irritated if simply spoken to when they are in pain.

Allowing moments of enjoyment while knowing a partner is in pain can cause pangs of conscience: if they can be confessed, the partner's reaction can be a surprise. People have different attitudes towards whether they want someone else to remember their pain *all the time* or not: the partner or 'parent-in-the-mind' may differ in this way from the one 'out there'. People can also give mixed messages about it, depending on whether they are in pain or have forgotten it for a while, or on whether they are feeling loved and loving or irritated and irritating, perhaps.

Some people *do* want their partners to experience the pain too; others very much *do not*. Some fluctuate between wanting (and even trying) to inflict it on the other and wanting and trying to spare the other person.

'I'll hit you with my stick and then you'll know what it's like!'

This may be experienced as a reason for divorce or as an understandable temporary blind fury caused by the frustrations of physical and emotional pain. The tolerance of the partner themselves towards emotional pain and aggression, and their experience both of current and of past relationships, may all affect which interpretation takes precedence.

Clearly, many people can get pleasure at times from knowing someone else is suffering; and not only small siblings, or soldiers waging a 'just' war. The 'Tom and Jerry' type of cartoon, in which creatures chase and escape and watch improbable damage being inflicted on their torturer, probably taps a relatively 'normal' version of this enjoyment.

'I hate seeing him in pain. He tries to keep quiet when the children are home but he can't help crying out at night, and it tears me to pieces. He's such a loving father and husband, I know he doesn't want to upset us.'

'When he's in pain I just wish he would go away and keep in his room. He always wants to be with me, but I hate it. I know I shouldn't, but I do.'

163

'I stay in my room upstairs as much as I can and I leave him in bed downstairs. He makes things as difficult as possible for me. He calls me all the time, especially if he hears me talking to someone. He says he's in pain, but I don't know. I don't always go. He left me when the children were small, for another woman, then he came crawling back. I don't know what he thinks I'm supposed to do. He still wants me, but I don't want anything like that. I think it's disgusting at his age.'

'When she cries it makes me think of my mother; she was ill all the time and I used to sit outside her door listening. Now I just want to leave.'

Doctors and allied professionals can get inured to watching other people's pain. This can lead to dismissing pain. A cancer nurse spoke of her feeling that her own children's pain was 'nothing' compared to the pain her child patients felt, and I worried for her children. A general practitioner said he couldn't do his job if he thought even for a moment what kind of emotional pain his patients were going through.

SHARED CONCERNS

Who caused it?

The idea that pain is caused by someone or some thing is very powerful. If this were so, all that would be needed would be for them to stop doing it. Perhaps if they were propitiated in some way, asked nicely? Or shouted at, threatened with revenge? Blown up? Anger evoked by this mythical pain-creator can be redirected at a more human target. A Hindu man told me his illness had been caused by a Muslim neighbour – 'foreigners' are an easy target. So too are mothers (perhaps in the guise of witches or mothers-in-law) or 'chemicals' or genetically modified crops. New guilty parties are found on the internet every day.

To show it or to hide it?

When someone is in severe pain they can lash out at other people, regardless of whether this is a wise or kind or sensible thing to do. Some believe they have a right to lash out, that it is somehow better to express it than to hide it; others prefer to keep their pain hidden. Some succeed in keeping their pain secret; others feel they are being stoical but let out hints and are angry or upset when those hints are not recognised.

Martina said she wished her husband would admit it when he was in pain; she often knew he was and felt cut out and rejected when he pretended he wasn't, though she thought he was doing it to protect the family.

Clearly the capacity to bear others in mind is affected by the level of pain involved as well as by personality factors and beliefs and phantasies about the best way to behave. In some relationships and some subcultures, lashing out is expected and tolerated or even approved; in others it is not. Predicting how people will behave may not be easy.

Claire was astonished when her Afro-Caribbean midwife told her firmly to stop making such a noise during labour. A German midwife, several years earlier, had encouraged her to vocalise her pain. In both cases Claire's beliefs about the midwives' cultures were challenged. She did as she was told. It hurt either way, but what she remembered most was being disbelieved by one midwife and being treated kindly and with respect – and effective local pain relief – by the other.

Relationships may be affected badly if people have very different views of the ways they should bear pain.

'He thinks it's all right to shout at me when he's in pain; he says it's not meant personally; I should know he's just shouting because he's hurting, but he says such awful things and they do hurt. He says he can't help it, but I don't think it's true, I think he just thinks it's his right. I don't know if I can take it much more.'

In this case, the husband was eventually persuaded that he *could* control his reaction by pointing out that he did not shout out if he was in church when his pain hit. Eventually too, his wife threatened to leave him if he did not tone down his attacks on her, and he began to take seriously her insistence that she could not bear it. Just as he expected her to discount the meaning in his expressions of pain, so he was initially discounting hers. He did in fact still care for her and, having finally recognised that she was truly hurt by him, he was able to find less aggressive ways to react to his pain.

People can be quite contemptuous of others' reactions. One who has been brought up to be quiet when in pain may attach a moral meaning to their silence; equally, the more dramatic and flamboyant methods of expression of pain may be accompanied by secretly despising the stiff upper lip.

Jane felt one should keep quiet when in pain; and that this was better because it caused less trouble for others. Her husband complained that it meant that he never knew if she was or was not in pain, and it actually meant he felt guilty all the time not knowing. He felt she wanted him to know without being told. If she let him know, he said, he would feel less obliged to guess and hold her in his mind all the time. This discussion helped Jane realise that her mother had behaved like this: she was suddenly hugely relieved to understand she no longer had to feel constantly on edge in case her mother needed her to notice something 'without being told'.

Juan did not think his wife was really in pain because she did not make enough fuss.

Sara thought her husband pressured the children too much with his loud expressions of pain. He was surprised that she thought they cared.

Interpreting other people's pain

> *Speak roughly to your little boy,*
> *And beat him when he sneezes:*
> *He only does it to annoy,*
> *Because he knows it teases.*
>
> (Alice's Adventures in Wonderland, 1865)

Lewis Carroll was writing a satire when he described the Duchess ignoring her baby's howling, but in real life signs of pain in children are often interpreted as 'behaving badly'. Clearly any adult can give the impression that it is bad to complain or express any emotion distressing to the adults around, but 'needing attention' may be defined as bad for reasons arising from a child's own judgement as well as (or in spite of) the way adults responded. In the nursery, older children as well as adults may greet signs of pain or even empathic responses with scorn, as if they belonged only to 'babies' or 'girls' or some other socially despised category. Sadly, such responses may last into adulthood, with nobody ever pointing out the *mistakes* (as distinct from the cruelty) in taunting others in this way.

Social status, including relative ages, as above, may play a part in deciding whether pain is to be derided or treated with respect. A nurse may respond quite differently to the pain of a helpless woman in a hospital bed and to the pain of a doctor colleague, but pain itself can also transform people, lowering their relative social status. Many people want to distance themselves socially as well as emotionally from anyone who is in pain; caring responses seem to be more difficult and are often seen as having to overcome a 'natural' revulsion. The image of birds mobbing and killing an injured member of their own species may remind us that humans too can behave like this; however, we also know that dogs and elephants can care for injured members of their tribe, and we have heroic stories of people devoting themselves to others, even at great risk to themselves. These stories testify to the enormous range of responses which people can have to the pain of others and they can influence how people expect themselves to behave both in times of crisis and in ongoing chronic situations. The reality may or may not match up to their ideals.

'My husband was very even-tempered and never got angry, so I was shocked when he reacted to my illness by shouting at the boys. I thought I depended on him for sanity; I hadn't realised how much he depended on me.'

People who have been badly treated themselves as children, perhaps as orphans, can become professional carers with the laudable conscious intention of giving care to other orphans in a way they were not cared for themselves. Unfortunately, lack of care and attention as a child can leave people with a low capacity to give others real care and attention –

to see others as separate real people, with their own feelings and desires. They may see their charges only as split-off parts of themselves and be unable to take seriously aspects of them which are different. Worse, when their charges behave 'badly', perhaps by showing signs of discomfort or pain, or any associated feelings such as anger, this behaviour may take them out of the category of 'goodie' – they can be re-classified as a 'baddie' and treated as the enemy.

A nurse in a mental hospital told a nursing assistant not to give more porridge to a woman who was dying of cancer and calling out for more to eat, because 'it only feeds the cancer'. She listened, apparently unmoved, to the woman's moans and cries of obvious pain, saying that 'she always does that when anyone changes the bed' as if this was just the woman being difficult. When the assistant remonstrated at the way the nurses spoke about the patient over her bed, she was told that 'the doctors do it'.

On the other hand, pain can be interpreted in other ways.

> *'I can't bear it when she's in pain. I get a terrible stomach ache. I think it upsets me more than her. It comes in waves, and she's ok when it's over, all perky, but I'm feeling shaky for hours afterwards. I think it's because it reminds me of my mother at the end of her life; I'm afraid she's going to die.'*

> *'We're used to it now. She likes me to hold her hand when it's bad, and I sit there with her if I can. It's ok if I'm not doing anything else. It makes her feel better. We just get on with it, don't we?'*

Whose pain is it?

Carers truly suffer in identification with those they care for. At times they may not be clear whose pain it is, particularly if they are caring for someone they have known for many years and with whom they are identified. Loss of speech forces people to understand each other non-verbally, and this kind of communication is vulnerable to misinterpretation. Particularly if there is a strong relationship between them, there is the potential for near-perfect understanding – and also the potential for confusion between self and other, so that the carer's feelings, thoughts and responses are attributed to the partner who cannot speak.

Carers can worry very much whether they are understanding correctly; for example, whether they are giving the right level of analgesic at the right time. Some do not worry. Where two different members of the family are both trying to understand another who has lost the power of speech, each may be certain that their own view of the person is the right one.

Siobhan was certain that her father wanted morphine after a serious stroke which took away his power of speech; her mother was equally certain that he did not. They found it almost impossible to talk to each other about it. Her mother would hide the morphine which Siobhan left for her father.

STRUGGLING WITH PAINKILLERS

It'll cause trouble in the long term

To many people it is obvious that painkillers should be used when pain is present. However, for others this is not the case. The hospice movement had a real struggle at the beginning to allow patients to use morphine-based painkillers even at the end of their lives, while the idea that they should be allowed to regulate their own medication levels was a further battle which had to be fought. The anxiety seemed to be that anyone allowed to control their own medication would use more than they really needed and become addicted. In fact, studies quite quickly showed that they felt more in control and needed less. Knowing that help was at hand if and when required relieved the anxiety for patients of having to predict how long it would take a nurse to respond, how much argument would be needed for which nurse before sufficient medication was given, and whether the analgesic effect of the current dose would have worn off before the new dose took effect. When controlling their own dose, they only had to predict when and how much their body would respond.

When a long-term condition is involved, people sometimes express anxieties that the body will become habituated to the extent that a medicine will no longer have the same effect. Just as many people fear spending any money in case their savings run out before they die, so they can fear 'using up' their allowance of painkillers on a lesser pain (which perhaps could be borne) and being faced with a more serious pain later in life which then has no remedy. This can lead to conflicts within the family, with different family members feeling different anxieties, often unable to verbalise the precise anxiety, but aware of a great fear or anger. When the person controlling the medication is not the person suffering the physical pain, there may be an issue of the patient feeling on the one hand deprived and made to suffer needlessly, or on the other, bullied, controlled or forced to take a pill they do not want, as the carer tries to take into account, perhaps, 'what the doctor said', or remembers (while the patient forgets) what happens when the pain recurs.

People sometimes prefer to suffer their own pain rather than get rid of it, and they may not recognise the effects the pain has on them (which irritate or distress others); or they may even 'forget' that they can take a painkiller.

Stanley believed his father had suffered pain stoically for many years before he died. He had always wanted his own father's respect and he resisted taking even aspirin for his arthritis, feeling it made him less manly and lesser than his father if he had to take even one.

Chris resisted taking aspirin when she had a headache on the grounds that she 'wanted to know when the pain had gone'; she told the doctor she did not want to cover up a pain which could be, she believed, a sign of a 'real' illness such as a cancer. She was able to take aspirin more easily after he laughed and told her that it would not touch such a pain: she would certainly know if she had anything serious, however many aspirins she took.

Frank often did not give his wife aspirin for her arthritis. Both had memory problems and forgot she needed to take it regularly. Frank believed she would become habituated to it; his mother had relied on homeopathic medication and he had inherited a general distrust of pharmacology which his own experiences had increased rather than decreased. He remembered more often when he was told that aspirin reduced inflammation and prevented more damage to the joints, as well as relieving pain.

Choosing constipation or pain

Many analgesics unfortunately have side-effects including, in particular, constipation. Embarrassment may in this case prevent family members being told the real reason why painkillers are not being used.

Frank's daughters were exasperated with him for not giving their mother sufficient analgesics, so that she cried out with pain whenever she moved. Eventually he was forced to tell them that the stronger one they wanted her to take gave her severe constipation which hurt her and was difficult for both of them to deal with because her hands were very arthritic. A very private man, he found it embarrassing even to say the word.

Fear of pain

Misunderstandings can arise between people, whether in the family or in a professional relationship, from different attitudes towards pain. Some fear pain above all else; others fear loss of awareness or loss of consciousness more.

'I loved pethidine: it didn't take the pain away but it meant I didn't care any more.'

'I hated pethidine. It made me feel sick and helpless. I'd rather have the pain any day.'

'If I'm in pain, give me morphine. I don't want to know what's going on. You can look after yourselves. Don't come and see me either; I don't want people to see me like that.'

'I want to be conscious, I don't want to feel fuzzy and confused. Even if I'm in pain I still want to know what is going on. I want to know who's there.'

'When I had a fever as a child I had hallucinations; I don't want anything that might give me hallucinations again. I don't care about anything else, that's the worst thing for me.'

Worse, people can feel differently at different times. Before the pain starts they may say 'don't give me painkillers'; once it has started they may cry out for them. When it is over they may be angry that their request (not to be given them) was ignored. Even when they have the best of intentions, pain and illness can still put people in the wrong.

Such differences matter more in situations where people assume that others are like them and where they are unable to hear each other's differences. Both family and professionals can find it hard to really register that this particular patient may have feelings about pain which are different from theirs, or from another patient or person they knew. It may not be possible to find out how someone is 'really' feeling, particularly because this changes; if it is possible, it can still require knowledge, tolerance, time and patience to find out. These may all be in short supply when someone is ill.

It may or may not be acceptable to give someone a painkiller because a carer is distressed by seeing them in pain; this can happen without being noticed.

Medical professionals as a source of painkillers

Relations with medical professionals can be powerfully affected by their role as a provider of medication. Painkillers can be just what a patient wants from the doctor, and there may be pressure on the doctor to offer them without examining too closely what has caused the pain. However, this is not what the doctor is supposed to do, and a struggle may follow – between patient and doctor, or the doctor and his or her conscience. Painkillers may not be what a patient wants if they want a cure for the cause of their pain; painkillers may then be seen as 'fobbing them off'. For some people, the doctor will always be in the wrong.

Painkillers also have to be carefully titrated, and patients can be annoyed at the realisation that they have to take responsibility for finding out how much and when to take medication: patients' views of medicine may be very different from a more scientific one.

'He's supposed to be the expert; he should know how much she should take. I couldn't believe it, I went back and said it wasn't working, and he said,

Ok, double the dose! Why didn't he tell me that before? Then I did double the dose and she was so floppy I stopped giving it to her. I don't know what to do now. I don't want to go back to him again: it's such an effort getting us both there, and he's useless anyway!'

The doctor may have in mind a collaboration with a patient and his or her carers, but the carer or patient may not have understood this at all. When this does work, it can be very satisfying.

'Now I've got used to it, I like it that he asks me. I feel he treats me as an equal partner. He says I'm the expert on my pain, he's just making suggestions and it's for me to say if they help or not. I didn't like it at first that he didn't just know.'

Pain can cause problems in relationships with professionals when and if it cannot be controlled. Unfortunately, there are still pains which come into this category. The process of working through stronger and differently targeted forms of treatment for pain takes time and may not be fully understood by the patient. Information (and misinformation) from the internet can help, or can make things worse. A doctor may try a less-expensive drug first, and be reluctant to offer a more expensive one: if the patient knows this is happening they will interpret in terms of their own phantasies about how important they are, how hard the doctor is trying, what they 'deserve'. Side-effects and their trade-off with analgesia may not be properly explained or, if explained, understood. If they are understood, a more sophisticated patient may disagree with the doctor, not only over the prescription but also over the relative importance of different side-effects. It takes a long consultation to sort all this out, and a long consultation with an exhausted carer and/or patient (or overworked doctor) may not be possible.

Many people are afraid of offending their doctors, for example by being 'too demanding', or by 'not getting better'. Understanding the doctor through phantasies of parents can make it hard to 'make a fuss' or 'be a nuisance', even if the doctor themselves never intentionally gives the impression of interpreting patients' requests or questions in this way. Patients can fail to challenge even quite obvious cases of mismanagement or neglect for fear of upsetting or being abandoned or 'told off' by the doctor. Extreme, indignant anger can also be harder to allow expression than a more realistic level of irritation: much easier to say 'thank you doctor' and leave the surgery, to fume later. It is not only supportive, good doctors who are treated with kid gloves in this way. Ill-treatment or dismissal may be expected by anyone who experienced this as a child (or interpreted ordinary parenting as such).

Moreover, patients may not interpret the treatment as faulty, or 'work in progress', but see its failure as deserved, or 'natural' in some way, and take any blame (if they think there should be some – and they will) onto themselves.

> 'I've been in pain for months now; but it hurts too much to get to see the doctor. Getting into the car is just too painful. And when the pain goes for a while, I forget I have to make an appointment. Then it starts up again. Anyway, the pills he gave me didn't work. They just put me to sleep all day, and I can't do that, I've got small children.' 'Why haven't you gone back and told him?' 'It's too much effort, and I don't think they can do anything anyway.'

As with any treatment which fails, the patient has to decide whether to accept what is offered or to fight for more. Pain can make fighting seem impossible, though at other times it can add force or even rudeness to a distressed telephone call. When pain makes it hard to speak, polite words may be left out and a kind of 'telegraphese' be used which can be interpreted as rudeness. The phantasy that their pain is the responsibility of the doctor can also make patients sound angry on the telephone.

Professionals, like family members, do sometimes get angry or frustrated with patients who 'will not get better' or have unrealistic expectations, even when they think that professionals 'should not feel like this'. A patient with intractable pain can be seen as a source of irritation to their doctor, to be avoided or guiltily 'forgotten'. In addition to the doctor's own frustration at being unable to get rid of the pain, a sensitive doctor can also 'pick up' the patient's frustration and irritation, which the patient feels unable to express.

'ALTERNATIVE' FORMS OF TREATMENT

Pain can send people to seek help from many places other than the doctor, a pain clinic or a local chemist's. Acupuncture, physiotherapy, osteopathy, the Alexander Technique, Chinese medicine, herbal remedies, homeopathy, psychotherapy and many others may be considered. Some of these treatments involve the sustained and containing attention of a sensitive practitioner, which may help to locate emotional aspects of the pain and to contain and relieve them. Religious rituals may also be sought.

Mary asked for 'the laying on of hands' (an old Christian ritual) when her back had been hurting for several years, and her favourite cleric came and performed it for her. Afterwards she said her back was still hurting but she felt a bit better in herself.

Some of these treatments leave people feeling helped and supported. Some leave them feeling cheated of their money. Relatives can be exasperated when they see a member of the family 'wasting' their money on something they are sure will not help, or conversely, exasperated when their own particular recommendation is rejected.

PLACEBO EFFECT

The placebo effect is also important in pain management – the body can sometimes be persuaded to heal itself. Pain can also come and go for no apparent reason. There are many ways in which the placebo effect can be used, but unfortunately they are not compatible with the requirement that doctors tell patients the truth.

It would seem that a doctor could truthfully offer a placebo saying, 'This works for a proportion of patients; it could work for you. Let me know because, if it doesn't, there are other drugs to try.' Unfortunately, doctors fear that a patient who then found out that 'this' was a placebo (which they would the minute they looked it up on the internet) would feel cheated, and this would damage their relationship.

The placebo effect makes it hard to know if any form of treatment has 'really' worked or not. Belief may make a significant contribution to some aspects of pain relief. Interestingly, though, none of Ann's psychosomatic pains (see earlier) seemed to be cured by any obvious form of belief: not recognising them as psychosomatic, she had not expected psychotherapy to cure them and was taken by surprise at the pain disappearing in response to previously unrecognised feelings becoming conscious.

SUMMARY

How pain is understood varies from person to person, and the full implications of pain to any individual may not be consciously recognised by others or even by the self. Disagreements about how to live with a pain and how (or whether) to treat it can cause conflicts. Anxieties about other aspects of life, including the effect of painkillers in the long term, can also play a part. Emotional pain can increase physical pain; physical pain can for a time replace emotional pain. Relations with others can be significantly affected. Unconscious phantasies determine how children interpret their parents' and siblings' pain as well as their own; adults too perceive and interpret the pains of other members of the family, including their children, according to what is going on in their inner world.

Where the emotional meaning and significance of pain as well as the anxieties attached to it can be understood, some forms of pain can be relieved, if only partially.

CHAPTER 7

Grieving

INTRODUCTION

In the 1980s, when I started working with people with disabilities, I was told I shouldn't talk about losses: this was considered 'too negative'. 'Change' was allowed, but not loss. Thirty years on, I remember asking, at yet another enthusiastic announcement of reorganisation of the local NHS, whether losses had been considered as well as gains from the new proposals: I was greeted with a blank stare. Later I discovered that my job was about to be lost, but nobody had told me or the managers responsible.

A normal response to a significant loss is a massive 'Noooo!' When people have no faith in grieving processes, they cannot move on from this position. There are many ways of pretending a change is not happening, or has no significance (when it has), as I described in Chapter 1. This chapter spells out what happens once change and loss have been acknowledged. 'Acceptance' is a process; it does not happen overnight. Initially seen as 'giving up' or 'giving in', it has to transform slowly into 'finding out what can replace the loss' and 'whether I can live with the loss', without actually knowing if there is an answer. Clearly there are huge risks involved.

WHAT IS GRIEVING?

Grieving for a loss involves the painful giving up of a past view of the world and replacing it with a new one more appropriate to current reality.

It cannot begin until the loss has in some way been acknowledged: until the thought 'if I say it, it will be true' becomes (if only just) bearable. During grieving, each thought, belief, piece of behaviour or assumption (with accompanying feelings) which was linked in any way to the loss has to be reconfigured to take into account the change. Our whole view of the world and our place in it has to change. Any event, situation, person, assumption, hope, belief, ability – in fact, what I would call any phantasy – which brings to mind whatever was lost may be met with the realisation that it no longer applies. This triggers a new awareness of the loss, with accompanying pain. The pain brings it to consciousness, enabling (or forcing) a reorganisation and reprogramming of previously automatic processes so that they now include the fact of the loss. The next time this particular situation comes to consciousness it will have slightly different associations, changed to fit the new reality. Gradually the new version becomes automatic and the internal world has shifted to fit.

So, for example, being beside a river may remind me of the last time I was beside a river, getting into a boat. If I can no longer get into a boat I have to face this change, and it may hurt: considerably if it means I am getting old before my time, less if boating is not really of much importance in my life. Momentarily I have to grieve for the loss of my ability to get into a boat. But this means that the next time I am beside a river I remember not only getting into a boat but also my grief and my thoughts. I may have ended by thinking I need to ask my husband if he wants to go boating with someone else, or that I might be getting old but I can still walk, or I've got plenty of years left yet, or I need to do some exercises so I can keep more supple. I will also remember the outcome of these thoughts, and the pain of losing boating moves a bit to one side. Clearly, I have some control over the comfort these thoughts bring, but only to some extent; my husband might decide he needs a new wife who can get into a boat, in which case my grief would be extended in a new direction.

Once grieving has been completed, life is seen differently. No longer dominated by hiding losses or struggling with them, energy is released for new potentials to be appreciated. Being beside the river becomes appreciated for itself, with boating firmly in the past. A wheelchair, initially rejected as implying loss of status, of hopes of 'normality', perhaps still disliked, becomes valued for its ability to increase mobility. Other people with similar disabilities or illnesses, previously ignored as of no interest, become sources of information, entertainment, friendship, company. But this process cannot be hurried – it takes time and, often, hurts.

Finding oneself unable to undertake the more basic of daily activities – using a screwdriver, changing a light bulb or making a phone call, for example – can be utterly frustrating and may evoke fury. It is such frustrations that have to be tolerated in the early days of a loss. Thinking of the need for a screwdriver must now include thinking of someone else who must use it instead – and this may bring many discomforting feelings, including anger. There may be thoughts about the capacities of those around ('They're useless! They won't do it properly!') as well as thoughts about loss of role ('What am I good for now? I'm worthless if I can't do *that!*' or 'My wife will prefer the man who comes round with a screwdriver.'). Jealousy and envy are easily evoked during grieving; reassurance may not be easily accepted. The inner world already feels as if it is in pieces: external events may be taken as evidence that this is true.

If grieving does not take place, conscious and unconscious fantasies and thoughts belonging to the past are not updated; current situations are only experienced as if they belonged to the past; life cannot move on. We may avoid river-banks and screwdrivers entirely, without being able to say why – though our partners might know.

GRIEF FOR THE LOSSES INVOLVED IN ILLNESS OR DISABILITY

The losses involved in illness and disability are far-reaching. Abilities and capacities previously taken for granted may be replaced by slower or lesser abilities, or lost altogether. The grief thoughts evoked by such changes are not simple; because they are symbolic too, whole sections of one's inner world must be reworked. There may be loss of a perception of the self as healthy, capable or (in some way) 'normal'; 'able to protect my family'; 'not bad looking'.

Alice knew that her father only respected people who worked; for her, giving up work as a result of her illness involved reassessing her dead father's opinion of other people and of herself, as well as her own – and reducing the size of his pedestal in her mind.

Part of the fear of 'becoming disabled' for Mat was the knowledge that she had mocked, avoided and ignored disabled people herself when she was healthy. She had also resented the special privileges a disabled boss had been given, particularly because this boss had been much better off financially and in every other way than Mat herself. She was now ashamed of herself.

Unrealistic beliefs may also be lost: 'Those things don't happen to me', 'I thought I was invincible.' An image of the body as 'whole' may change to damaged, spoiled, crippled or broken, with 'bits missing' and implications of lost attractiveness or loss of place in a significant social hierarchy. Uncertainty is a characteristic of many of these losses, as it may not be clear at the outset exactly what will and must be lost and what can be saved. Coping with this uncertainty is part of the grief work.

Janice felt that 'strong women', in particular black ones, never asked for help; her illness required her to learn to ask for help and to change her classification both of herself and of 'strong women'. Neither of these was easy, and both involved a lot of emotional work. As she found ways of asking for help, Janice had to face other people's reactions too, which were not always kind and supportive. She had to struggle not to give up and revert to her previous defences of managing entirely on her own, as best she could, which by this time was not as well as before. All of this affected and was affected by her grieving for the loss of her previous self, and her previous self-image. Janice later said she was pleased with her new self, and she felt the process had represented some growth for her.

Ike's illness triggered memories of past experiences during a war, when he was a victim of 'friendly fire'. This in turn took him back to his father betraying him by leaving him and his siblings, and his mother abandoning them while she drank herself to oblivion. He had felt that the army was a reliable father which valued him. Recognising that he had been abandoned by the army, which tried to cover up the incident, felt like another abandonment, equally life-threatening. He felt he really must be quite worthless for this to happen yet again.

FIRST REACTIONS MODIFIED

Initially the feeling is often dramatic: 'I've lost everything!', 'My whole world has changed!', 'Things will never be the same again!' Talking or thinking may be needed before this changes to a more realistic 'I've lost *this*, but not *that*.' Associations move, too, to frightening childhood anxieties which may have to be challenged for the first time: 'I need to look after myself *totally*, nobody will love me now – but how can I?!' Grief thoughts often stop as frightening scenarios come to mind. It takes courage to move on from these thoughts; meanwhile, hopeless despair may take over for a while. Many people seek a friend or counsellor to help them sort out what it is they are anxious or distressed about. Their most anxiety-provoking fears may be more obvious to someone else than to the person themselves.

Anxieties and thoughts about a deteriorating future are part of the work of mourning which may take a long time to modify. In the case of a condition which causes gradual deterioration (such as arthritis or dementia in old age), remaining abilities may be used to comfort and defend against thoughts of a terrifying nature connected, for example, with the end of life. The gradual erosion of each of these abilities may mean that a new source of comfort and defence has to be sought: 'As long as I can drive, I am ok; even if my legs don't work properly I can still get out and get around.' Where this is an important source of comfort, loss of the ability to drive, if it comes, will require some emotionally painful work to find some other way of being 'ok'. Trying to understand what it would mean not to be 'ok' is an alternative strategy. If 'worst fears' can be acknowledged and worked through, there can be a sense of relief; keeping them at bay is hard work. Grieving for losses which do not evoke terrifying fears feels different from grieving for those which do. However, facing these anxieties, particularly alone, may be too difficult.

Just which changes are forced by a loss, and which by an unnecessary reaction to a loss, may be unclear at first. Giving up playing the guitar may be necessary; listening to music may be too painful at first but possible later. Someone who decides that their children need to be prepared to lose their mother by making them hate her has misunderstood grieving processes and increased the potential loss to the whole family. Loss of a mother's love for a small child is life-threatening, not only practically but also because this love is the basis for loving as an adult: for loving partners and children and being loved by them. One of the results of an effective grieving process is to reinstate in one's mind a sense of having loving and caring parents (and a Good Object), often temporarily lost in the fury and despair of grief. Holding loving parents at the back of the mind is nourishing and supportive throughout life, colouring everything that happens. Ending with bad relations also leaves a mark. Working through and improving 'bad' feelings towards parents, alive or dead, is one way in which counselling or psychotherapy can help to make people feel better about themselves and their world.

Initially it may be impossible to use a stick, a wheelchair or a diary to help with deteriorating balance or memory, not just out of pride or fear of losing an important self-image, but sometimes because they are too tied up with people in the mind. Someone whose grandfather used a stick may have to come to terms with *being like their grandfather* before they can use one. Someone who very much does *not* want to be a housewife *like their mother was* may find it particularly hard to accept losing their job and staying at home to look after children. Sorting out feelings about their mother and her role in the family may be necessary before they can be comfortable with their new role. (It is much harder trying to become a parent who is *not* like the ones you had, than it is to follow their footsteps.)

THE MOURNING PROCESS APPLIES TO EACH LOSS

With any condition that brings deteriorating health there are likely to be multiple losses, each of which requires its own grief work. It is not possible to grieve all in one go for all the losses represented by, for example, brain cancer, motor neurone disease or multiple sclerosis – or old age. Not only the diagnosis itself, but each small loss of function, as it arises, requires its own grieving process, with its own time span. Forewarned, however, is to some extent forearmed, and recognising the effect of previous losses and the time span over which they have lasted may help to make later ones slightly more bearable.

One loss following another rapidly, as a consequence of some newly diagnosed condition, may mean that high levels of distress seem to last for a very long time. It can feel as if this is how life will be from now on: that 'normal life' really has been lost for ever; that crying will never stop; that a normal, loving self, good tempered and able to think of other things and other people, will never return. Neither the person grieving nor other family members may realise that grieving is taking place consecutively, 'in series', one loss needing to be worked through after another. Recognising this process can be a relief, since it means that levels of anxiety belonging to a new, terrifying loss will reduce eventually, once enough grief work has been done.

Cher lost her mother shortly after she was diagnosed with multiple sclerosis as a result of balance problems which had recovered but were followed by a period of double vision. Later in the year she had a new MS symptom which lasted for a few weeks. She felt as if she had been weeping non-stop for more than a year and thought she was never going to stop.

In counselling she was able to think about each loss separately, and she realised that she now felt quite differently about her first symptoms even though they had not completely disappeared. Tracking her reactions to this first loss, she was able to recognise the way she dealt with losses. She was able to see that her recent spate of weeping was connected with all of the losses, but mainly with the most recent symptom. She recognised that she was beginning to come to terms with the loss of her mother and had made some realistic changes as a result. She gradually began to feel that she would be able to come to terms with her MS and its symptoms, and that she would not be crying for the rest of her life.

Locating an earlier loss, and considering both how it was dealt with and how feelings towards that loss have changed, can help to clarify how an individual has reacted to loss in the past, and to establish how they may expect to react to current or more recent losses. It may or may not be possible to shorten the process: it may only be possible to understand it and live through it, however painfully. Understanding it, however, sometimes brings a reduction in anxieties connected with loss of control. Some of the confusion and self-blame (or blame from others) for suffering grief may be reduced, leaving only the grief itself.

Some illnesses are too short for a grieving process to run its course in this way. Someone who is diagnosed with such an illness may not have time to fully come to terms with it. They may at times seem to recognise what is going on, and then appear to forget and not to know. Such lapses of memory may be misunderstood by those around to mean that the person does not want to know, and that a pretence should be kept up. They can also lead to quarrels between family members as one witnesses a period of 'forgetting' and another is there when there is clear knowledge of what is happening; each may interpret what they see as indicating how the person wants to be treated. (Perhaps, in fact, an internal conflict has been externalised; it is perfectly possible to be 'in two minds' about such knowledge.) Such differences in memory or knowledge may also reflect beliefs the ill person has about the capacity or desire of each visitor to bear truth or distressing knowledge; this too may change over time as their own grieving processes work on their perceptions of those around them.

TURNING TOWARDS OR AGAINST OTHER PEOPLE

People who are grieving are often bad-tempered, confused, inconsistent.

> *'I could cope with his falling over, or needing to use a wheelchair; what I can't cope with is his bad temper; the way he's behaving towards me. He wasn't like this before. I don't know if I can stand it.'*

Is he going to be like this for the rest of his life? Or is he going through a grieving process which will eventually end when he has accepted his physical problems? Families often make allowances for people in this situation, but they have to decide how much to put up with and when to fight back. Is the bad temper part of a grieving process, or is it a resistance to the pain of accepting the wheelchair? Or, most likely, both? Is it reasonable to say, 'Enough now, get on with it, it hurts us too'; or is it not? How long is it reasonable to allow him to be bad tempered? Do I threaten to leave, or will that make him worse? What does that mean about me, that I could think of leaving a man who can no longer walk? Do I just have to accept the bad temper? These questions are difficult if not impossible to answer and contribute to the sense that illness makes people feel 'bad' in many ways.

It can be problematic for everyone concerned when grief causes someone to change their feelings or behaviour towards particular members of the family. This can happen in identification with someone who has died.

Jennifer felt she was the only person who really cared when her father died. She found herself newly close to one of her brothers and distancing herself from the other. In counselling she realised this was how her father had been, and she had been quite different before.

Like the small boy who blamed his mother for his father's neurological illness, adults too can become confused about who is to blame for what. One or more adult children can be designated 'bad' while another is idealised as 'good' by an elderly, infirm parent; often, and most unfairly, nearer, more involved children are likely to be less idealised than those who are absent, a long way away. Reality keeps idealisation in check. Life-and-death anxieties can lead to splitting and blaming, perhaps for real faults, perhaps for phantasy ones, probably for faults which belong to other people entirely, perhaps long-dead.

On the other hand, changes may be in the opposite direction. How adult children are seen may improve with the mother's loss of health, for example. She may become more able to accept or respect or rely upon her children, regardless of their actual behaviour or feelings. In the mind, images of a daughter or son may become combined with images of a caring mother or father as the person becomes too ill to want to take care of themselves any more and feels the need for and the pleasure in having someone else to take over; the actual daughter or son may reap the benefits whether or not their own behaviour has to change.

Anxieties about loved people sometimes take on a huge importance.

'She couldn't manage without me.' (Expressed by a dying elderly man, about his fit and healthy daughter.)

This may be true, but it may also be a confusion about who cannot manage without whom; about who is actually dependent (and very frightened about 'not managing'). Two anxieties can be expressed at once, one hidden behind the other.

After her son died, Melanie Klein (Klein 1940) described how she found herself dreaming that her mother had lost a son; she awoke to feel horrified to recognise that, in her attempts to get rid of her own bereavement, she had inflicted it on her mother in her dream. In this process her mother, long dead, was for a while lost to her, increasing her sense of hopelessness, abandonment and despair. It was only after she had realised this that she was able to regain a sense of her mother as a comfort and support, sharing her loss.

Where there is a sense of life being under threat there may be anxieties of a kind which can be characterised as 'all or nothing', 'me or you', 'life or death'; these can lead to blame and attacks on others as well as the self. (I describe these as paranoid-schizoid mechanisms in Chapter 2.) After these have been worked through, a different kind of anxiety can take over, in which real concern for loved people takes priority. This shift may depend on very early experiences of being cared for adequately, which laid down patterns in which concern for others could be deep-rooted. Adults who, as children, were neglected in any way may have learnt that they needed to think of themselves in a way more-cared-for children never did. Those who were always looked after may assume that they will be looked after now. During grief for loss of abilities, which resonates with the dependence of childhood, early patterns, helpful and realistic or less in tune with current reality, may reassert themselves.

EMOTIONS

In tracking the feelings involved in a grieving process, it seems that the initial stages of grief generally involve a high level of anxiety and distress, which reduces over time in gradually decreasing waves. Some want others to suffer as they are suffering; others make enormous efforts to avoid causing distress to their nearest and dearest, though they may also end up making them suffer by misguided attempts to protect them. Some weep; others refuse to acknowledge any pain at all. Some throw themselves into life; others withdraw. Some focus on reality; others cut themselves off from it. Some try to take control; others give themselves up to passivity: 'Do with me what you will.' While some fight reality, others fight realistically. Many people fluctuate from one position to another, depending on the time of day, when they last ate, who they last spoke to, what is happening in the turmoil of their internal world.

Once the phantasies which govern and are linked with a particular issue connected with a loss (such as no longer being able to use a screwdriver) have been considered, modified and put away in a new form, some work has been done. The next time a screw is needed there is a new set of phantasies which are prepared and ready, which include the fact that the old capacities are gone. Frustration and anger are eventually replaced with regret and sadness, which after a time may drop out of awareness as a missing screw no longer triggers thoughts of a screwdriver. Thoughts of asking someone else for help may form a transitional stage, whereby responsibility is still taken for ensuring that screws are taken care of; eventually the need for a screw itself may be ignored and no longer evoke any emotion if it no longer requires action of any kind.

TIMING

Because each association to a loss evokes other associations, often including past losses (one funeral evokes memories of a previous one, for example), the grieving process can take a long time: generally much longer than people think it should.

The idea that grieving is a process of modifying unconscious phantasies, thoughts, beliefs and assumptions, one by one as they are triggered, and to adjust these to the new reality, allows us to understand both why it can take two years and why these two years may consist of periods of heightened grief and periods of forgetting or 'carrying on as normal', either as if the loss had not happened or as if it was no longer a problem. Over a period of two years it is likely that most links with the loss will have been evoked and modified, probably more than once, to include the new reality, however painful. Within this time there may be periods when every situation, every event, may require modification of automatic reactions, thoughts and feelings; and periods later on during which fewer situations evoke new links, new associations. Over time, more and more of the everyday assumptions are modified and the person is said to be 'coming to terms with' the new reality. However, within the first two years – or more in some cases – there are still likely to be new situations which bring unthinking links to a lost past reality unchanged in phantasy, which then give rise to a new awareness of the pain of loss.

It is usually not until two years after the event that emotions aroused by the loss have – for most of the time – reduced to a more normal level, and life has been reorganised to accommodate it.

> *'Why does she still not want sex? I can understand she's grieving for her father but he died six weeks ago and she didn't even like him! Surely she should be over it now?!'*

Well, actually, no. If she didn't like him she now has to work through all the lost hopes and disappointments of never being able to make it up with him. Her relationship with him was built up over more than six weeks, and it will take many more before she is in any sense 'over it'.

It is impossible to predict how long a grieving process will take for anyone, as so many factors are involved. The only predictions I have learnt to make are that the two weeks or so leading up to the first anniversary *are likely to* bring up painful feelings associated with the loss, and that after this anniversary there is often a lightening of mood; and that the two weeks before the second anniversary also bring up related feelings, but this anniversary *seems often (though not always)* to bring some kind of closure, with the person feeling quite differently about the loss now. The second anniversary is also the anniversary of having *survived* the first year. After two years, most assumptions about the world seem to have shifted to include the loss. However, these predictions are not hard and fast rules.

Rebecca Atkinson (2007) discussed her complex feelings about (possibly) being offered the chance to regain her sight, which had been gradually failing over a period of years. She described how her identity had been changed as she joined the community of visually impaired people; how she gained some friends and lost others. She described how congenital blindness can be felt by some to be part of their soul, their identity, like being black. However, she then asks:

What if your soul is sighted, and then you go blind?

You will cry and wonder why. You will hope and pray. You will wish it would all go away. But the longer your sight has been on the slide, the more it seeps into every crack of your psyche – until one day you are no longer the 'sighted person' who can't see any more. Somehow, strangely, in the dead of night, your identity has rolled over in bed and you wake up and get out the other side a 'visually impaired person' – and it feels like part of you.

It doesn't happen overnight, and perhaps it doesn't happen to all who sail the strange seas of sight loss with me. But for me there came a point when impending blindness was no longer my alien but my friend. I had had my time as a sighted person. I had seen the world through my eyes. Now it was time to touch it and smell it and hear it.

Grieving can result in benefits: it can bring new connections, a new sense of security if it is based on reassessment of less realistic phantasies about the self or the world which previously created a slightly unsafe, 'wobbly' feeling. However, this does not take away the fact that it can be extremely painful both at the time and in retrospect.

Ultimately there can be mixed feelings about whether the process has been a good one or, on balance, not worth the pain. In spite of the transformation, some of the painful feelings never go away – although they may become familiar, 'lived with' and, in this sense, different.

(Grief over the loss of a child, or attached to having a severely disabled child, has an added dimension. As the child's peers grow up there are repeated losses as the parents grieve the loss of the child in their imagination at each age, each birthday in particular. People say that their distress about the loss of a child does not go away but may, after ten years or so, 'move aside' as other concerns gradually begin to take centre place in their lives.)

PARTNERS

Partners go through their own grieving processes. As well as having their own, personal losses (which are often overlooked or forgotten for a while), they identify with their ill partner and suffer on their behalf too. Grieving processes can take place for each at different times, one sometimes waiting for the other to recover before allowing themselves to feel their own distress. Each may have different ideas about remembering the past. This is a point at which mutual understanding can be difficult, as each may think their own way of grieving is the only or the best way. New discoveries about the self may mean new discoveries about a relationship – and these may not be to the benefit of the partner. As well as grief for losses and changes there can be envy as well as pleasure in watching someone else develop new sides to their character, particularly, for example, if they involve a new assertiveness, or a new capacity to ask for what is needed.

Partners play a significant part in grieving processes. They may have to maintain everyday life while their other half is withdrawn from the world, either because they are ill or because they are in the early stages of grief. They may also be needed for reassurance, even though it may not work very well; they may have to cope with despair and hopelessness without going under. If their main source of emotional support has up to now been the ill person, they may indeed struggle to find alternatives. Who cared for whom within the relationship may for a while be reversed, and this has costs, though sometimes also benefits. Friends may be called upon, but surprisingly (and hurtfully) it often turns out that friends who previously *took* support cannot or do not want to *give* it. Supporting others requires different skills and perhaps different personality traits, which may not have been required in the friendship before.

Grief requires attention to the thoughts and fantasies which emerge; partners may be required to talk through some anxiety which requires their attention too. Partners are also able to help hold onto memories, including memories of 'how I was before'. There are many aspects of the grieving process where it is not clear if a partner is being asked to do something which will advance the work of grieving, or if they are being asked to help to distract from it, either to avoid the work or simply to provide temporary relief. This uncertainty can create conflicts.

COMFORT

Comfort can help at certain times in the grieving process; at other times it is unwelcome. There are times when, for good reason, the grieving person wishes to be allowed to feel the full extent of their misery and distress. At other times the person may wish to feel nothing, so comfort at this point may simply serve as a very unwelcome reminder that there is something to grieve for. Part of the difficulty for other people is that they may have no way of knowing what is going on at any particular time for the grieving person; and therefore no way of knowing how their attempts to offer comfort or distraction or even a listening ear may be received.

Comfort may come from inside, from memories of being comforted, from comforting thoughts, old or new, or from outside, from other people. Comfort allows difficult thoughts and feelings to be borne and processed. It may allow consolidation of ideas and phantasies sorted out during a period of high anxiety or concentrated thought. It may allow more healing feelings to be re-established: 'I still love you even if you can't cook any more', 'You're still the same person.' It provides a period of respite from more distressing feelings, and may enable the person to find the energy necessary to face yet another set of distressing feelings later. Without some comfort, many people would feel there was no point in carrying on, no sense in bothering with all the pain and distress needed to re-establish connections with a world which is irrevocably changed.

When the person is feeling punished, angry and punitive towards the world, towards themselves, towards a lost loved person, a lost past self, and/or, crucially, to an internal parent, a 'mother-in-the-head' (who failed to protect them from the loss, or may be blamed for causing it), they may not want to see anyone and comfort may be rejected. They may just want to accuse and punish other people out of bitterness. Self-isolation may be a strategy which is aimed at preventing friends from being irrevocably alienated, though it may also alienate them by evoking in them feelings of rejection and uselessness. Later, under the influence of more benign phantasies, comfort may be welcomed and allowed to offer some healing.

Jokes are another aspect of the grieving process which are acceptable and helpful at some times and in some circumstances – and quite definitely unacceptable at others. They can allow the problem to be named and acknowledged in a way which brings more pleasurable feelings, in particular feelings of 'rejoining society' or 'being part of the human race'. They may be unacceptable when people feel they are belittling a loss or being inappropriately disrespectful.

Frank said his mates at the pub would tease him unmercifully when he spilt his beer or lost his balance as a result of his neurological condition. He liked it; it meant he was still one of them, that nobody was pretending or patronising him. He knew they would laugh behind his back – he would have done the same himself – and he was glad they respected him enough not to feel they had to protect him. He could also joke about it himself.

About a week after the harrowing death of a 13-year-old nephew, Shula told her colleagues at work. A long conversation followed, in which various stories were told about dead and dying relatives. The stories became more and more surreal and eventually the whole office was laughing. Shula returned to her own work feeling comforted and supported, knowing she had the sympathy and understanding of her colleagues.

Less than 48 hours after the fall of the Twin Towers in New York, jokes referring to it began circulating. There was discussion on the internet about whether this was acceptable or not.

A stand-up comic with cerebral palsy began his routine by dropping his crutch and shouting at it for being 'too stupid' to stand up by itself. The audience found it very funny. Critics discussed whether he encouraged laughing 'at' or laughing 'with' him and his disabilities. Either way, he was naming and shaming a common misperception in a way which made it bearable to the audience.

Jokes and comfort both assert that life goes on, that it is worth living; that however terrible an event has been, not all pleasure has been lost. At the right moment this helps; at the wrong moment it seems like cruelty. Getting the moment wrong is one of the ways in which illness can make people feel bad – being too scared to risk getting it wrong (and cutting off the bereaved person entirely) is another.

REMEMBERING

Grief work requires naming and acknowledging what has been lost, as part of the process of sorting out what can be kept. Talking about memories or writing them down helps to reduce the threat that they, and the emotions they evoked, will be lost entirely. Someone who was once a pilot may find it necessary to talk through his or her past exploits in planes before feeling able to give it up and let it lie. 'I was beautiful, you know' may be an essential step in admitting that youthful beauty has now been lost. Both the pleasures and the pains of such beauty may need to be acknowledged before others can be allowed to see a lined or damaged face.

> *'She's always going on about the famous people she knew. She wants me to be impressed, but I don't know who most of them are. I'm sorry for her: it must be galling for her to be left with just me to talk to after being so important then.'*

People are often confused about memories, thinking that they should be avoided if they hurt, and imagining that any remembering of the past means someone is 'stuck in the past' and is unhealthy. It is not clear whether reminding someone of a loss will be welcomed or not.

> *'I feel bad talking about walking up mountains because you can't do it any more.' Partner: 'But I love it when you talk about being on the mountain: when you talk about it I'm up there with you!'*

> *'My husband hates talking about [our dead daughter]; I love it! It brings her back for a while; I want other people to remember her.'*

Memories of the past are significant in the mourning process. In the initial stages of grief there may be periods when a loss is momentarily forgotten. Although this brings relief from one kind of pain, it brings another pain which after a time can feel worse: loss of the memory can feel as if it means the lost situation or lost person/self is forgotten, and this can seem like a huge loss. Establishing memories of the lost person or situation (which may be 'me, before this happened, before I got old') seems to be an important part of a grieving process.

Too-painful memories, frozen in time, have ultimately to be replaced with memories which can 'live' again in the mind, in phantasy. 'I enjoyed that ten years ago', similarly to 'When she was alive my mother would have liked this', allows warm feelings to re-emerge in resonance with a happy moment in the past. Awareness of the fact of change has to become bearable for the memory to be bearable. Without this, any memories may 'have to' be blanked out, and it can feel as if nothing remains; they are 'gone as if they had never been'. Good memories, eventually, can be a comfort and can reconnect the individual with their own past, with a younger, lively self and with other people who belonged to that past.

In particular, it seems to be memories of loving and being loved which matter most, both for their significance in the past and the hopes they hold for the future.

LOSS OF OTHER CAPACITIES CAN AFFECT GRIEVING

There are many ways in which some loss of capacities can make grieving harder. Previous means of dealing with loss, as well as previous defences and previous sources of comfort, may no longer be available. Reading, listening to music, watching films or television, talking to other people, gardening – all may have played a part in coping with changes in reality, and any or all may be lost as a result of loss of physical function caused by an illness or an accident. Less obvious defences or sources of comfort may include cleaning, repairing the house, or any form of job which enabled someone to feel of some worth and in some way to address their own particular 'demons': their own anxiety-provoking phantasies; the 'people-in-their-head' who made demands, accused them or watched over them.

For Sally, cleaning meant fighting off both her mother's accusations in her head and her mother's depression. Having to watch someone else fail to do it properly upset her terribly.

Mary thought she would be all right when she got older because she could always 'sit in a corner and embroider'. When a stroke took this ability away from her she was furious with God, stopped going to church (which had been a large part of her life) and felt that life was no longer worth living.

Loss of function can also make people feel that it is not worth putting in the effort to go through another grieving process, perhaps after an experience of multiple losses. Somehow, the game has to be worth the candle; the pleasures to be expected from life have to be counted as potentially greater than the sum total of the misery to be gone through. Loss of certain (or all) capacities for pleasure, including the capacity to eat, to speak, to see or listen to others, to sleep, to enjoy normal bodily functions, may ultimately equate for some people (though not, it seems, all) to a sense that facing grief and losses is a waste of time since life is not worth living any more. It can be difficult to know, in extreme stages of neurological deterioration, whether someone is content with their life as it is or whether they are not, but sometimes relatives are sure they do know, whether they can demonstrate the evidence or not. Close observation may provide clues as to changing moods. When asked, some people in extreme states of paralysis communicate that they are content with their lives.

SUMMARY

Once a loss has been acknowledged, a grieving process can begin, if only with temporary stops and starts at first. Each association to the loss, each connected idea or thought or event, has to be allowed into consciousness, paid attention and worked through. Once this work has been done, the internal world is ready to greet the external one with a new set of assumptions and beliefs more appropriate to the new reality. The grieving process involves sorting out what has been lost, what has to be lost, what can be regained, and what can be salvaged. Immediate reactions to a new symptom can cause more losses than the original symptom itself; successful grief work can enable new possibilities to open up.

CHAPTER 8

Damage to Capacities to Think or Feel

INTRODUCTION

Changes in mental processes such as memory, or the ability to 'catch on' to what is going on in a conversation and to respond, or to find their way around, are for many people their 'worst nightmare'. Afraid of losing their minds, they may block all discussion about what is happening or they may seek support or help from the medical profession – which may or may not be forthcoming. However, talking about these issues in counselling can bring some comfort and some relief, partly by clarifying the facts. Loss of one capacity does not necessarily imply loss of another: affection and care may not be lost, for example. People often expect things to happen faster than they will. If losses are happening, it might be useful to talk about ways of reducing their effect, or to make plans and to begin the process of grieving for the future. It is possible to feel a little more in control of a process which ultimately may take away control; it is also possible to find ways of bearing the consequences.

If a partner is losing some mental capacities, the implications for the other partner may be serious – and, for some, difficult to discuss. Lack of insight, lack of consideration for a partner, depression, loss of memory and lack of motivation are all threats to relationships which may both affect and be evidence of an ongoing grieving process. Emotional blunting and consequent difficulty making decisions are similarly complex symptoms. Under the medical grouping 'cognitive or psychological or emotional dysfunctions', these are also among a group of problems which raise a difficult issue for families and professionals: namely, the question of whether they are caused by the condition itself, by a reaction to the condition, or by defences against the loss.

Families and professionals may have different explanations for the symptoms. Causes and explanations can be divided into different categories:

- 'neurological'/'physiological' explanations ('hard wiring'/they can't help it/it's the physical effect of the illness) and
- 'psychodynamic'/'psychological' explanations ('soft wiring'/they could/can help it), which can be subdivided into:
  o 'It's just them, they were always like that.'
  o 'It's a reaction to the illness/disability/injury, they weren't like this before.'
  o 'It's a reaction to the medication.'
  o 'It's their age/the stage in their lives.'

(People may know that emotions can be blunted by certain medications, particularly anti-depressants, as well as by some illnesses; they are less likely to know that heart and blood pressure problems may affect cognitive capacities. See Waldstein and Elias (2015, Chapter 4).)

Each of these explanations may call for different judgements from members of the family. Blaming or not blaming, tolerating or not tolerating, challenging or not challenging – all depend on people's interpretation of the causes of any of these behaviours. In fact all of the 'explanations' might play a role. Too much insistence on one may lead to or arise from insufficient understanding of the other. Decisions about how to react or what to do may have to take into account the fact that a definitive answer as to cause may not exist.

'WHAT?' VERSUS 'WHY?'

Sometimes just recognising more clearly 'what' is a problem can do away with the need for 'why'.

The fact that an ill husband appears no longer able to keep in mind his wife's appointments with the doctor may be more important than the reason why. His wife may see him as a bad person, 'being selfish', 'just like a man'. Thinking about it, she may acknowledge that this is a change. She may also suspect or know (and resent) the fact that he is going through a grieving process in which his own concerns take priority. He may be denying both his illness and her appointments for reasons to do with excessive anxiety, guilt or fear about his wife possibly being ill, or resentment at having to share the limelight. On the other hand, he may have lost the capacity to lay down memories (to pay attention) or to retrieve *this particular category* of memories on cue when they have been laid down. Confusingly, he may have no difficulty remembering his winnings at the bookies or some other facts or events which may be laid down in a different system of the brain, or which have different symbolic meaning. ('Wife' could just as well be replaced with 'husband', and vice versa, here.) Understanding, or just recognising that this is what is happening, can help a partner to decide how to behave in response, and can affect their feelings.

At first, because the implications are so frightening, questions about the role of the illness in such behaviour may be difficult to raise or even think about. In addition, knowledge is often limited and not passed on by those professionals who do know. 'Not wanting to worry someone unnecessarily' allows professionals to avoid alerting people to cognitive or emotional problems *possibly* associated with their diagnosis before they happen, so information may only be passed on when the effects of the condition have become serious enough to be noticed by the professionals – by which time the family may have found out about it on the internet and/or had serious problems as a result of their ignorance or misinformation from a wacky website.

Where information is lacking, someone may try many ways of making their partner 'wake up' or remember things which matter to them or to the rest of the family. Whether a husband or wife can do better if they are shouted at, or if their partner gets upset, hits them, ignores them, writes down appointments or 'to do lists' on a calendar and draws attention to it as he or she goes out, or whether none of these make any difference, may then provide information about the condition and its implications. It is only after the shouting has stopped that thoughtful discussion can begin. An outsider may be needed to hold the complex emotions being processed during such a discussion, which may end with a partner realising that at best they may have to learn how to manage without expecting the other to remember. Again, 'what?' questions may be more illuminating than 'why?', at least at first, partly because they can sidestep issues of blame.

Sandra was afraid her thinking was being affected by her neurological condition and by her anti-cancer drugs. She could not always follow television detective stories, and would watch them in the afternoon for a second or third time, so that she could join in conversations in the evening. She was very afraid she was getting the same kind of dementia as her father had, and was eventually relieved to discover that her problems were very different.

'What do you think is actually happening?' can throw up the realisation that a couple lack the words to talk about it. 'Losing your/my marbles', 'going doo-lally' or 'losing it' are more appropriate for insult than for sensible discussion. People are unclear what 'cognitive dysfunction' is, and have no idea that this may or may not include problems with *feeling* as well as *thinking*. Professionals' language may confuse rather than illuminate, but there is a real problem in choosing everyday words to describe what is happening when someone is losing one or more of a huge number of functions of the mind distinguished by psychologists. A lucky few may obtain an appointment with a neuropsychologist who can and will explain; most will not. Information on the internet may be helpful, but it can also be frightening and difficult to know what applies to whom.

'Why?' questions depend on interpretations. When someone begins to lose their mind there is a gradual disconnection between their view of the world and their partner's, which can be very distressing and can be resisted for a long time. This means that one may struggle to make or to verbalise the (perhaps obvious) link that 'you're losing your memory', or 'I'm losing my memory'; either or both may much prefer any explanation which avoids this conclusion. As one begins to realise it is happening, they may have to struggle with the other who is still rejecting it. Each is making their own interpretations based on their phantasies, which determine how they 'read' reality.

Whether or *how* a partner can tolerate living with the change is actually a separate matter, which may depend not only on how everyone interprets the behaviour, but also on the attitudes and past experiences of both.

EFFECT OF COGNITIVE AND EMOTIONAL PROBLEMS ON GRIEVING

Thinking

Difficulties in thinking can mean that grief work takes longer or is distorted, or losses fail to be assimilated. Thoughts do not 'update' to fit reality. This can be very frightening for the individual affected, who may gradually lose touch with those around. Ideas may become 'stuck'.

An old lady on the ward in a mental hospital grasped the arm of a young nurse as she went by. 'Where am I going, dear?' she asked anxiously. The nurse said cheerfully, 'You're not going anywhere, dear, you're staying here.' Five minutes later the old lady asked the same question of another nurse and was given a similar answer. They knew her well; she asked the same question over and over again, day in, day out, alternating occasionally with 'When am I going?' A student stopped and sat down. 'Are you wondering where you are going when you die?' she asked. The old lady looked her in the eye and snapped, in a perfectly sane manner, 'Of course I am!'

To think through the answer to such a question requires not only a competent brain, but also, perhaps, an interested listener.

Problems caused by direct onslaught on the brain, as in some neurological conditions, can slow thinking or distort it, causing 'holes' for example, which can lead to confabulation (where the person 'fills in' because they cannot actually remember what they were doing a few minutes or a few hours ago). Shame or terror of mental deterioration and its consequences may be a reason why they do not simply admit to having forgotten, but we do not know what phantasies lie behind it, and it may be an automatic process which 'just happens'. Thinking can also be affected by anxieties caused by an illness or its consequences. Hallucinations or dream-like states in which real and imaginary conversations become confused can also distort memories and affect thinking.

Indirect damage to thinking can be caused by lack of sleep, which might be a consequence of the illness or of pain, or of anxiety associated with the illness. Some drugs taken for pain, for tremor, for depression, for spasms or for bladder function, for example, can also affect feeling and thinking as well as sleep. Bladder problems themselves can disturb sleep. Some social consequences of an illness, such as losing one's home or being in hospital, can also affect the capacity to sleep, to feel safe, or to have sufficient peace and quiet, any of which can affect the capacity to think.

The ability to think can also be affected by others' 'protection' or 'keeping in cotton wool' which can prevent an ill or disabled person being kept up-to-date with information or knowledge, not only about family events, perhaps, but also about their own condition. Children in particular may be given a strong message that they are not supposed to talk to an ill parent about some possible loss, present, past or future, because the adults cannot bear the thought of it. A partner planning to leave, or unable to cope with an ill partner returning from hospital, may find it very difficult to admit to the hospital that this is the case, and may simply disappear or fail to turn up for agreed discharge meetings, all the while insisting that the partner *is* to return. In this situation, being given messages they suspect are lies, it is very difficult for the ill person to think about the future and prepare themselves for leaving hospital. Hope may continue to triumph over experience, and even when it becomes clear to everyone else that the partner is not going to be able to cope, the ill person may resist admitting the fact. On the other hand, the ill person may be the first to suspect, and have to struggle with hospital staff who cannot instantly accuse their partner of lying without more direct evidence.

Working through thoughts can be made harder by the fatigue which can accompany any neurological condition.

Temporary losses in consciousness may mean that 'the moment is lost' and a loss is not processed at the natural time. The delay may have an impact on the ability to recognise exactly what happened and what it meant. Loss of consciousness at the time of an accident, for example, means that awareness of what happened depends on others' reports – and these may or may not be forthcoming, truthful or complete. Much of the grieving after an accident involves working through the exact sequence of events, partly in order to sort out issues of responsibility, blame, guilt and control. Lack of information about this crucial time can have significant implications for the ability to complete the grieving process and for the way thoughts and feelings have to be handled in order to 'move on'. There is also something disturbing about having blanks in the memory, and people usually feel better when they have some reassurance about what went on while they were unconscious, or, even more, if they regain a sense of their own continuous history.

The capacity to think rationally and intelligently depends on a certain level of emotional equilibrium. People recovering from a devastating loss sometimes describe how they feel they went temporarily 'mad with grief'. These reactions usually disappear over time, but a neurological condition such as MS or Parkinson's, or a stroke, is not just one event, one loss, like a road traffic accident in which everything changes in a single moment. On first diagnosis, symptoms may be getting better: MS tantalises with its promises of remission, nobody knows how it will develop, when or if the next symptom will appear, what it will be, when or if it will go. After a stroke, too, there is a period in which improvement may be rapid regardless of what anyone does, to be followed by a much longer period in which improvement, if it happens, is much slower and depends on the behaviour not only of the person who had a stroke, but also of those around who help to motivate or support exercises. People often become very depressed in the aftermath of a stroke and may struggle to regain a lost equilibrium, a lost sense of life being worth living. Men may lose their erections and not realise that they will probably return. All of these effects may challenge the capacity to think in one way or another.

In the case of a deteriorating neurological condition such as MS or Parkinson's, each symptom, when it comes, may bring with it a new loss, which means a new struggle between grieving and denial. Grieving and defences against it may be a chronic or cyclical characteristic of someone with such a condition. And in some cases this may mean that 'mad' behaviour or feelings or inability to think clearly are chronic or cyclical characteristics too.

Thinking also requires a certain level of memory, sufficient to hold a train of thought.

Memory

Memory is essential for several aspects of grief, as well as for thinking. Memories and memory keep alive good, loving people-in-the-head. Constant calling to a partner may result from a fear of losing both the internal and the external partner. Memory problems can give rise to a fear of being abandoned to a leaky memory, even to forgetting who you are, being unable to hold onto memories of the self or other loved people as well as the fear of losing the people themselves, who may get too irritated or too frustrated to be able to cope. If you lose your memory you may forget that your partner is in the kitchen for a few minutes, and feel they have abandoned you. Being constantly followed around is something carers may find intolerable. It may result from devastating anxieties about abandonment; it may also involve some kind of projective identification whereby in phantasy a more lively self has been 'deposited' in the carer, which can lead to the carer feeling invaded or controlled and the person with memory loss feeling empty and at sea and desperate to keep the carer/self in view.

In the car, Maud, in her late eighties, constantly told her son and daughter-in-law which way to turn and where to park, although the journey had been taken many times before. Exasperated, her daughter-in-law exclaimed, 'Why do you do it? You know we know where to go!' Maud said simply, 'I do it because I can, I am checking I can still do it.'

Part of the work of grieving involves re-establishing internal people – in particular, the 'mother-in-the-head'. As well as providing a sense of being loved and supported perhaps (or, not uncommonly, disapproved of and undermined), she may also in unconscious phantasy 'have an opinion' or enter into a conversation about the illness, about its causes and consequences. Working through 'her' feelings and thoughts about the changes in the self requires some capacity for remembering thoughts as well as emotional work done. Equally, working through perhaps angry, guilty, disappointed, hurt or even furious thoughts and feelings towards her may require memory as well as thinking.

The hallucinations brought on by high temperatures or some drugs can affect not only thinking but also memory. Hallucinations which are almost plausible can cause distressing confusion.

Angie, 78, was afraid of returning to the hospital because she remembered overhearing a conversation in which a doctor was taking away a baby from the woman in the next bed as a punishment because the woman had been rude to him. She could not see that it must have been a dream or hallucination and firmly denied that it could have been a memory from many years ago.

Michael, 93, was certain the nurses had been 'fiddling with him' in the night when he was hospitalised with a broken hip after a fall. His daughter was only really convinced that this was (probably) not true when he insisted that a female visitor he could see was a Roman Catholic bishop come to rescue the poor orphan children on the ward with him. His daughter was not sympathetic and nor could she laugh at the time; she was angry that he did not believe her when she told him he was having hallucinations.

Sudden damage to cognitive capacity in people who previously were fine can make family members angry as they are faced with a new, unattractive version of a previously loved parent or partner. In addition to disliking the new suspiciousness or disbelief (or worse) demonstrated by their parent, an adult child may be secretly afraid they are being shown a vision of their own future.

Loss of capacity to communicate

Any threat to the ability to communicate, from a high temperature to loss of speech, deafness or blindness, can make it harder to access other people's minds. As well as increasing loneliness, this can reduce the impact other people can have on the grieving process. Their presence and capacity to offer comfort may still be available, or it too may be lost. Slow, quiet or halting speech means that listeners have to seek reserves of patience and effort – which they may or may not find. Family members do not always want to spend time 'just listening' and may not realise the importance of the consequent loss. Deafness disables both people in the conversation, and often irritates partners intensely, particularly if a hearing aid has been refused. Joking in particular, and the pleasures of light, surprising interactions, can become impossible.

Communicating with others is one way in which people sometimes find out what they think and feel; it can enhance communication with the self. Grieving requires discovering and perhaps analysing one's own reactions, 'picking up' one's own feelings, thoughts and beliefs; talking to others can be an important route to understanding the self.

Neurological fatigue can not only make it hard to think, to sort out ideas, to 'reprogramme' the mind, but it can also restrict contact with others, making any social event or even any potentially helpful conversation a huge effort which may have to be abandoned.

If ordinary conversation is no longer possible, there are other means of communicating feelings and connection with others. Singing together can be powerfully evocative of happier states of mind: songs may remain when much else has been forgotten. Songs and music in general can help in the capture and sharing of sad feelings about losing lovers – and all that they represent. Non-verbal communication (including washing, stroking, putting on nail polish or makeup, or oil or hand cream on the skin, for example) can be comforting and reassuring – if those concerned can access their comforting and reassuring natures. This may sometimes be possible. Losing patience in such situations can be a real sadness for all concerned: keeping it successfully can be a reassurance and source of some gratitude, happiness and pleasure which makes grieving more bearable.

Emotional/bodily awareness

Perception of other people's emotions depends on awareness of one's own bodily feelings and physical states, which can be affected by neurological damage. Loss of sensation in the feet, for example, can make a person feel their 'feet are not on the ground'; this can create a general feeling of unease or lack of contact with reality which is somehow experienced in both the body and mind. Stomach pains or tension in the body caused by an illness can be 'read' as anxiety, hunger or guilt, anger or emotional tension; and can create irritation and self-centredness, accusation or withdrawal. A feeling of 'wearing body armour' or 'scrambled egg in the head' may create specific forms of discomfort and awkwardness, not only in movement but also in relating to others. Temperature changes caused by an illness can have a direct effect on comfort and, again, this can affect the way someone reacts emotionally.

Any of these changes to the body will affect emotional states and emotional reactions and the ways people 'connect' to the world around them. Sometimes this can mean that either person in a conversation may 'disconnect' as a result.

Emotions also affect decision making (Bechara *et al.* 1997). Difficulty making decisions can be irritating for partners, creating an uncomfortable kind of dependency. In addition, when grief work requires decisive thoughts, these may not be forthcoming, making it harder to abandon ideas which should be discarded. Professionals trying to sort out new accommodation for someone whose disabilities are increasing may become irritated when their client constantly changes their mind and cannot settle for anything. Even though they know in theory that this is probably part of the illness, they can become frustrated as if the person were simply 'messing them about' – which is how it feels.

As described before, people normally 'pick up' other people's emotional states through a subtle mutual interaction. Each 'reads' the other's emotional state by an unconscious resonance process, and reacts to it. Blunting of emotions can prevent this process: the two parties to the conversation 'lose touch'; they become 'out of sync' and the conversation no longer becomes a sharing of minds.

Margot complained that recently her husband never noticed how she was feeling, though in the past he had. He had been diagnosed with MS about ten years earlier. The counsellor asked her husband if he thought it was because he could not feel 'for' her, or if he did not want to. Did he have feelings now as he used to? He said, rather sadly, that he had noticed that nothing excited him any more; he didn't feel either the 'highs' or the 'lows' and he wondered if he had stopped loving his family. Margot became sad herself, and there was a sense of a huge shared loss, which replaced the isolation and irritation.

In projective identification (from person A to person B), described in Chapter 2, massive denial of some emotional state (perhaps evoked by a conversation) takes place on the part of person A, with the result that person B feels the emotional state is theirs and theirs alone. If neurological processes cause the denial or the loss of resonance, person B can still feel they have a 'double dose' of some emotional state, and they cannot share this with person A because A does not feel it.

This process can contribute to a discomfort which some people can feel in the presence of people with certain kinds of neurological damage. There can be a sense of 'deadness' or unreality; there can also be an 'overload' of emotions experienced by the onlooker which can feel disturbing to some, though others are not bothered by it in the same way.

SUMMARY

In this chapter I have tried to gather together some of the ways in which cognitive or emotional disabilities can interfere with grieving processes and with relationships. Understanding how an illness or new disability affects a relationship may need to include exploration of these areas, including seeking new, correct names for various aspects of a very difficult problem, and finding ways of feeling less alone with the feelings aroused.

CHAPTER 9

Parents

INTRODUCTION

Illness and disability can challenge parents in different ways. There are vitally important practical concerns: holding onto or losing a job; moving house, perhaps; one parent having to take on responsibilities which previously were shared; a partner moving out because they cannot cope with the changed relationship, or because they are too afraid of the future. All of these take attention and effort, as well as bringing grief and sadness, leaving one or both parents more tired and often more irritable, busy and distracted. As well as worrying about the impact of the practical issues themselves, parents often worry about being preoccupied, permanently tired, or unable to take time to do more enjoyable things.

> 'What I'm most sad about is that we used to be able to go out together as a family. Now I sometimes take them go-cart racing, but she can't come. She says, "You take them!" She could come, but she doesn't like being seen in the wheelchair. It's not the same going on my own with them. I feel bad being away from her for too long, leaving her at home on her own.'

The effect of deteriorating health on the temper of one or both parents is often mentioned as a cause for concern with the children.

'I could cope if he wasn't so cross all the time. I don't think it's good for our son to see him like that. If it was me, I think I'd be more careful to find ways of coping. He just doesn't seem to want to bother. I think he's a bad role model for our son. And he used to be such a good one.'

'He's impossible. He sits there watching the news all day and he wants the children to be quiet. Even the baby! He shouts at them if they make a noise. I can't bear it. The house isn't big enough for us to escape from him.'

In this chapter I look at ways people react to these changes, and in particular, at ways they help their children.

PARENTS CAN HELP THEIR CHILDREN

Although guilt and other anxieties can temporarily overwhelm both parents when one is faced with a long-term or serious illness, illness does not necessarily destroy the capacity to be a good parent. Much of parenting involves 'being' (which may not change very much) rather than 'doing' (which might).

As well as providing sufficient physical care, when they are supported themselves parents do find time and space to think about their children. They can notice how the child thinks and feels about the illness and its consequences. Listening to the songs the child listens to; looking at the games or the social media used by the child; as well as seeing how the child spends their time, how a younger child plays, how they react if the parent asks for help or says they are tired or cannot do something – all of these give parents hints. Booklets or websites run by charities for children whose parents have a particular condition may provide opportunities to look together and ask, 'Do you sometimes feel like that? Or think that?' If a parent has cancer, Macmillan nurses provide an excellent service, including helping parents talk to their children about their illness. People with other conditions may be less well served.

Once they know what to look for and begin to ask questions, parents find ways of discovering what is going on in their children's minds – at which point they may be astonished not only at what the children are thinking and feeling, but also at the ease with which they can put a child straight, reassure them about facts which the child misunderstood, and reduce anxieties which were seriously disturbing the child. Parenting in this situation is not nearly as difficult as people sometimes imagine.

Once the initial step is taken, a benevolent circle can be set up. The parent discovers they can actually help their child. The child's behaviour improves as a result of their anxieties lessening, not only because of things their parents say and do, but also because they feel more secure in the knowledge that their parents have them in mind; they no longer need to worry about themselves in quite the same way. The parents' confidence increases and so does the child's confidence in the parent. With a greater sense of a confident and secure parent supporting them, the child's own feeling of confidence and security can increase, and bad behaviour can give way to behaviour which is more satisfying to everyone concerned. The child may even discover ways they can realistically and gratifyingly help their parents, without fearing collapse if they fail.

Sometimes partners or grandparents tell children 'not to trouble mummy' with their upsetting feelings 'because she is ill', although parents who are physically ill may be well able to help their children with sad or upsetting thoughts and feelings – and they may need to check what a child is being told behind their back. On the other hand, other people may be very slow to notice, take seriously and intervene if a single parent is losing the capacity to take care of themselves and their child. This raises one of the many problems with trying to help children of ill parents: there may be a real problem when adults strongly disagree about what kind of support a child needs.

(In Chapter 2 I look at why children behave badly when their parents are ill.)

PRIORITIES

For many parents who are faced with a new illness or increasing disability, anxieties about their children are high on their list of concerns. These anxieties may outweigh anxieties about paid employment.

'How can I be a parent when I can hardly look after myself?! How will my children cope without a fully functioning mother?'

Doctors and other health professionals have different priorities. Focusing on their patient's illness, they sometimes find it difficult to hold in mind the idea that these patients are parents, and may take no consideration even for very young babies if their mothers are ill. Parents in this situation may have to fight to clarify whether a hospital-based procedure is truly urgent, or whether it can wait until the baby is older and less likely to be traumatised by the mother's absence in hospital.

Within the family too, there can be a question about whose needs should take priority: an elderly mother, a partner, or children – or the self? Children's needs may regularly have to wait; at other times an adult will have to be patient – and it might be an adult whose ill-health or malfunctioning body is making them feel like a child. If the relationship is good, this may be managed, but it can still evoke jealousy, rivalry and accusations: 'You *always* put them first!' For a parent who is struggling to balance their attention and their physical capacities between the needs of unequally dependent family members, this can be hard to bear. It can also be read as a healthy protest from someone who has been patient for a long time and needs people to know this. How it *feels* in this situation is not necessarily how it *is*, and parents on a good day may be capable of discussing it kindly. However, a tired parent whose own needs are regularly totally ignored may snap and afterwards feel guilty, determine to discuss it later, and drop off to sleep before they can do so. (Illness makes people feel bad.) Covert accusations may be more disturbing than open ones; accusations from elderly parents may sting more than children's. Which is worse: to be a 'bad daughter' or a 'bad mother' or a 'bad wife'? Being a 'bad' son, husband or father has different connotations, though they may matter just as much. (The relative importance placed on these roles varies from family to family, and may be a source of friction even before illness comes into play.) In single-sex relationships there can be further anxieties: what does this mean for the couple's hopes about each other, themselves and their capacities to care for each other? And their relationships with each other's families? Who should come first?

Even adult children can be indignant when parents decide that a step-parent's or even biological parent's needs should come first, if only occasionally, but this may be the way it is. Important as children are to parents, parents have responsibilities to partners too, and they will have to live in future with the knowledge of how well they cared for each other.

Decisions about priority are often made without conscious thought. Discussion enables counter-arguments to be put forward, but the ability to argue sensibly and effectively may be lost at times of stress: 'Just because I can't tell you at this moment *why* you're wrong doesn't mean you are right', as I used to say to my teenage son.

In some families it can be very hard for a carer parent to put themselves first even briefly, which would be classed as being selfish; even if they are ill themselves, other members of the family may always take priority. Self-neglect by carers is not uncommon and can cause worry in other members of the family, whether they appear to notice or not. The argument that a carer parent needs to look after themselves may appear rational but carry no weight against internal parents or childhood strictures which say something like: 'You should always put yourself last (if Dad is going to approve of you)!' Work to uncover and challenge such ideas may be necessary before behaviour can change.

Some people feel that children are (or should be) there for parents, rather than the other way round. Some feel that children are simply a nuisance: in competition for someone else's attention. Many feel that their own or a partner's illness is the most important concern in the house for good reason, maybe financial or practical but maybe emotional. Some are secure in the knowledge that the other parent will manage without them.

'I get really angry with them. They don't help me like they should. They just quarrel all the time. They should know I need help now their father has left. How can I do everything when I'm in a wheelchair? The older one just goes out all the time, he won't do anything for me. The second one is much better, he helps sometimes. I want you to tell them to help me more.'

'My husband doesn't care that I'm ill. His own illness is the only thing that matters to him. I worry about the children, but he doesn't. I didn't realise the children were so worried though, until I asked them last week, after our conversation [in counselling]. The oldest said he was afraid I'm going to die. I thought they were ok.'

'My father likes me to massage his back when he feels bad. I have to do it for hours. I'm not allowed to stop; he doesn't care about my homework. He wants me to rub in this ointment.'

Some parents never had the experience of anyone paying attention and listening to them when they were small, and consequently have little idea of how to do this for their own children. Their own needs may always take priority as an adult because they never came first for anyone else as a child and had to learn to look after themselves.

Anna Freud observed that those children in her war-time nursery who had mothers would run out into the cold and have to be called back to put their coats on; those who had lost their mothers would put their own coats on carefully. (We do not know what kind of parents these children became, of course.)

Step-parents may struggle with feelings of competitiveness at the same time as truly caring about their partner's children while being unsure about how much they can 'interfere'. They may be in a good position to help the children even though they can also be the target of split-off bad feelings which have arisen in connection with the ill parent or their partner. It may feel to a child 'safer' to hate a step-parent than an ill parent; 'steps' and 'exes' are also both easy targets for blame which the child does not want to attribute to another, closer parent or to themselves. Being a step-parent is hard at the best of times, but illness in one or other parent can make this problem worse. On the other hand, an ill mother who trusts the partner of her children's father can (eventually, after a struggle with her own emotions, perhaps) be relieved that this person can care for her children in ways she cannot.

Step-parents can also dislike the children of their partners, which adds a whole level of distress to their situation and that of the parents, especially if one is ill. It is normal for parents to dislike their own children at times, perhaps at certain ages, perhaps because of certain temporary characteristics which pass, but for a step-parent the consequences can be much harder. Children can easily be blamed for not behaving as they should, as the step-parent believes they would behave if the child were theirs, or if they personally were the child. Understanding a child may be harder if it involves recognising unlovable aspects of a lover in their child, for example, and seeing little or nothing of the self or loved relatives. Children can become a battle-ground between parents and their new partners, in which 'either them or me' becomes the rule, rather than 'both, and'. When an illness tips the balance, the chances are that nobody wins, everyone loses.

ATTENDING TO CHILDREN

Self-centredness, memory and attention problems, lack of insight and some disinhibition can all be symptoms of neurological damage (although many people with neurological problems have none of these). These symptoms can also be personality characteristics of supposedly 'healthy' people and can affect the way people function as parents. They may not seem to worry enough, or realistically, about anything, including their children. Although they sound fine in superficial conversation, they are incapable of carrying through any action requiring sustained attention. The other parent may or may not realise how bad things are, and a child may not tell them in such a way that they are understood.

Parents who are grieving may also stop attending to children for a while as they focus their attention on their own losses. Children in this situation sometimes show problems to teachers, but again, may not be taken seriously unless and until they begin to behave noticeably badly.

Some parents simply do not see any reason to worry.

'Children are resilient; they will survive.'

'Children have their own lives, their own friends. They can forget about it; they should go off and play. They should go to school and leave all the unpleasantness of an illness behind.'

However, many parents are aware that this is not quite sufficient. Even if they work hard to protect their children from too much practical involvement in the illness, ensuring that their children do not become 'child carers' in any practical sense, they know that their children are in some way affected by their parent's illness. Many talk of their longing to enable their children to live a normal life, knowing that the illness makes life abnormal and uncomfortable in many ways. Some feel that the children *must* be affected (but aren't sure how); others that the children *should* be affected (but aren't behaving as they should be or would be if they were). Some are pleased with the way their children are, and do not want it any different.

'I don't think she notices, really.'

'My Gary [14] brings me cups of tea. He asks me what I want to eat and he always gets it for me. He'll go for fish and chips any time. He's a good boy.'

Others worry, but are not sure whether they should or not.

'He doesn't say anything. He just keeps himself to his room. But most boys of his age are like that aren't they? But he used to whistle around the house a lot and I've noticed he stopped when his father went to hospital last time.'

Some parents are reasonably confident in talking with their children about the way they feel and think about illness in the family. Well enough supported themselves, they can turn their attention to their children and explore and address the children's anxieties. Knowing or suspecting that their children would be more able to talk freely with someone outside the family, they may arrange this with a trusted teacher or school counsellor or other family member, providing information about the illness and trusting in the other adult's capacity to understand their child.

'When we lost a baby we didn't deal with it very well at all as a family. Eventually the doctor sent us to a bereavement counsellor and she helped us so much. So when my husband was diagnosed with MS we went straight back to the counsellor and she helped us talk with the children about it. We know now, you have to talk about these things. It doesn't help if you keep it to yourself, if you bottle it all up.'

Experience from parents' own childhood may or may not be helpful.

'One of our teachers tried to talk to a girl about her father dying. We were all listening. We nearly died of embarrassment. I can't talk to my daughter; she'd be embarrassed.'

'Nobody told us anything. I was in hospital when my mum died, and nobody told me. I was eight, I kept asking when she was coming to see me, and they just said she couldn't come. I hate it when people lie to me.'

If there were any illnesses around in a parent's past, the chances are that nobody talked about them at all. Until fairly recently, children's fears were usually left to fester and grow, unchecked, in secret. A parent whose own father or mother died may have been left with very unrealistic, upsetting and frightening fantasies about death.

'I used to imagine lying in a box with the earth falling on top of me and being unable to get out, nobody hearing me call.'

'When my father died abroad [when I was three] nobody talked about him. It was like he'd never existed. Nobody cared except me. I was furious with my mother: I blamed her for sending him away. He wouldn't have died if he'd stayed with us. I talk to my children all the time.'

Some feel that an illness has brought opportunities and benefits to the family as well as difficulties.

'The children are much more aware of other people than I was at their age. I think it's good for them, I don't think it does them any harm.'

SEPARATION

When a parent has to go into hospital, small children in particular may suffer from separation anxieties. As I described in the introduction, the 'good mummy' (or daddy) in a small child's mind can become a 'bad mummy' (or daddy) if the child becomes frightened of their anger towards her or him, for example. Melanie Klein's small son became afraid of being poisoned by a witch when she went for a 'cure'. Nightmares may represent a bad parent retaliating to the child's angry distress in the night. The child may be helped to keep the parent alive in their minds by people talking about them and by having a 'mummy-substitute' in the form of someone they are attached to (which might be an understanding father). Without this they may be afraid the parent has died or left them for ever, probably because of something the child did or felt or thought.

When the parent returns, the child may or may not recognise them as the same person who went away; this can be very distressing for a mother or father who has been longing to see their children again. Changes in appearance can make a big difference to children too: a small child can get upset when their mother has a new haircut or new glasses, or a father cuts off his beard. Afraid of 'bad mummy' (or daddy) lurking behind the scenes, a child may have to be quite sure that *this* mummy is not that one before he or she can trust her. Having an affectionate person who knows their likes and dislikes, their routines and their language, who can temporarily slip into the role of mother (and Good Object), helps the child, partly by keeping them from becoming furious with her and attacking her in their mind.

Older children may try to blot out the separation or its effects and assume they can make the same demands on their mother as before she went away. A mother may be torn between wanting them to notice differences and wanting things to go on just as before. Children can also be proud of or pleased with their new capacities or freedoms and not want to return to an earlier relationship. The parent may feel they are the only one grieving for a loss of a whole stage of the child's life. They may be just as upset with a partner who, having taken over many of 'their' household tasks during the hospital stay, now walks away from them once more. The partner may feel that the one who was ill has some catching up to do. Their own anger and distress at being left alone to cope with a whole household can be covered up and at the same time expressed 'innocently' in this way. The reality of the illness can easily be 'forgotten' or discounted, both by the person who was in hospital and their family – who wants to remember that a parent was ill, if they are now better? Why distress people by talking about it?

The denial, like any denial, may hold for a while, but the separation will have changed the inner world of each member of the family, and eventually this may show. Talking about it may help to prevent children (and partners) from totally detaching themselves, from totally giving up on parents surviving and loving them and continuing to care for them; from fearing that the whole hospital stay was their fault – and that they will have to pay.

LOSING A JOB

Losing a job may have financial and other practical consequences which may be devastating for a family, particularly if there is an emotional attachment or significance to the job (which there usually is). Symbolically as well as practically, work may be tied up with 'living', with 'being of value to anyone'.

The first year or 18 months may be the worst, when people have all the problems but have not yet worked out the solutions. This applies to new disabilities (when someone is unable to walk but has not yet accepted or obtained sticks or buggies or new living accommodation) and to jobs: nothing to do except cope with the illness or disability, partner still in the position they were when two incomes were available, not yet having worked out how to enjoy life with less money but perhaps, in some ways, new possibilities. Parents have to handle their own feelings about this transition period, but are also faced, perhaps, with unforgiving or unthinking children, or children who are behaving particularly badly (in order to distract from their own or their parents' anxieties). To their own anxieties will be added anxieties conveyed both wordlessly and directly by the children: 'Will we be poor?', 'Will we have to move house?', 'What about my school, friends, local area?' If the children are mute teenagers escaping to gaming worlds or the internet, there may be further anxieties about their isolation from the family and what this means, although also a silent relief that the parents can ignore them when they want to.

> 'I was forced to give up my job, but it's meant that I've got to know my daughter quite differently. When my son was born I was working a 14-hour day, I never saw him as a baby. But I did everything for my daughter, it makes me much closer to her. We miss the money, but my wife has a better job now.'

'Because I'm not working any more either we can go out a lot. His pension is enough and his Union is very helpful; they funded us to get a big Motability car. We get out at least once a week into the country. My son can push the wheelchair. Mind you, he tipped him out once. It was awful, the wheelchair was bigger than him, I think he was trying to race, his dad [in the chair] was encouraging him too. There are plenty of places you can take a big wheelchair. We might have to sit outside the pub, but now he's got a leg bag [for urine] he doesn't need a disabled loo any more.'

By two years after a job is lost, generally some solutions have been found and the (internal and external) world, including the family, has changed to accommodate it.

SINGLE PARENTS

For single parents of young children, a serious illness or disability can threaten them with the loss of their children – a devastating loss for all concerned. Although many people have thought about who would take their children if they were run over by a bus, for example, they may or may not be happy about the choices available. Single parents have generally been let down by at least one relationship, often more, in their lives, and the idea of someone other than themselves looking after their children can be amongst their worst fears. Particularly if they had problems growing up themselves, they may have realistic fears about what would happen if their children were sent to live with their own mother or sister or brother, or if someone came to live with them to help with the children. They may also fear the consequences of a child's other parent or their relatives taking a child. Children may be split up. Using foster parents and live-in carers can also be very difficult to manage, both emotionally and practically. For these parents, an illness can be massively threatening, particularly if it means a repetition of the parent's own childhood. In addition to the loss to themselves, they may fear enormous loss to their children.

Single parents may also have to negotiate relations with the other parent or parents of their children. If they become ill, an absent parent may have no idea of the real impact, or they may manipulate the situation to obtain some concession, or to add fuel to their grievances. Fighting between parents, if only over the telephone, adds a complication and a massive anxiety to the task of parenting. Illness can increase fights – but single parents may also fear the children being taken away if the extent of their difficulties are exposed. Children can be drawn into trying not to 'give away' secrets, but may let them slip – and suffer the consequences.

On the other hand, an absent parent who has a good relationship with their ex-partner may be in a position to help to understand a child, or to help the child to understand the illness. Not having to live with the illness, they may have a useful distance which could be used for the family's benefit if relationships allow – their own partners too may be a source of support. One of the problems here is telling the children's 'other family' enough for them to understand. There may be many reasons (such as pride or shame) for concealing difficulties, even if there is trust.

Single parents may depend on older children for help; my impression is that this is stressful for all concerned. The children may feel more unsupported and needy than the adults recognise: they can and do help, but it costs them a lot, and occasionally they may make the parent feel it. (Their internal Good Object may be shaky and in need of strong external support which an ill parent may not be able to give – see the discussion on internal parents in Chapter 2.) These children may be in a position to choose where to live, although none of the alternatives may be satisfactory and an adolescent may move back and forth from one house to another, constantly feeling unwanted, unhappy with their own (and their parents') incapacities, while disrupting the parents' lives as well as their own. Disabled or ill single parents in this situation may find themselves vulnerable to their children, who are in a position to exert real power over them, both practical and emotional. This is a situation which can be risky for all concerned. Even the best parents make adolescents angry, and a child may physically hurt their mother or father or a sibling who somehow stands for everything they hate about themselves or the world. Scared of their own reactions, they may retreat to their rooms or even leave home and put themselves at risk in order to avoid inflicting damage on an infuriating parent.

Single parents can also worry about adolescent and young adult children who are a real support and help to them. Will they feel able to leave home and make their own lives, have their own families? Some very much want their children to do this; others are ambivalent. Separating is always hard, particularly for single children of single parents, but an illness can complicate it further. For some parents, being looked after by a relative may seem obviously better than depending on paid help (if there is money) or social services (if available); for others, the child's own life may come first. Financial considerations may mean the child is forced to continue to live with the parent. The idea that the parent might find some other source of support is a mixed blessing for a child who has grown up with the experience of being 'alone together' with one parent; for the parent, help from outsiders brings new challenges. Separation can feel like betrayal, however much it is wanted by both. Some children in this situation leave the country for a while, but this may depend on there being siblings or some other family member who could take responsibility. Everyone seems to assume that elderly parents are their children's responsibility; if they have none, then nieces and nephews may be expected (by themselves as much as anyone) to step in.

EXPOSURE

An illness or disability may bring with it a new exposure to the outside world. Parenting may suddenly come under scrutiny – from carers, from health professionals or from social workers called in for other reasons. Ill or disabled parents may have to cope not only with their own anxieties about their own lives, both realistic and exaggerated, but also with other people observing and possibly judging them. Added to this distressing mix are issues of class, education, culture, religion, sexuality and background. All of these influence not only beliefs but also the way childhood and parenting are experienced. Differences in these areas can bring into conflict not only children and their parents, but also parents and professionals.

A grandmother, from a strict religious background in an Arab country, had to take over the care of her grandson. Her daughter, his mother, had left home and lived in England for many years before becoming ill, and he was at a local school amongst children who behaved very differently from the way the grandmother thought children should behave. The boy had many conflicts with his grandmother, fuelled not only by his own mother's very different approach to upbringing, but also by friends and teachers at school. His grandmother was very suspicious of attempts by teachers to offer support to the boy, being afraid they would bring him into contact with the wrong sort of young men.

Hierarchies of class and ethnic relationships can add to problems in this area. People who have experienced racism may be anxious about their family relations being exposed to members of a group who look down on them. Others fear being inspected by members of a group they consider beneath them, perhaps even dangerous. Health professionals may find themselves uncertain how to behave in a respectful manner when there is a serious conflict between their own convictions and the family's. These issues can become particularly fraught over issues of childrearing. 'Saving the life of a child' or 'abandoning a child' are emotive issues which may conflict with ideas of respecting others' cultures.

In addition, family members may be in conflict amongst themselves and with the children. Illness can also take away power from a parent. Professionals may find themselves co-opted into family conflicts in which they have an obligation to get involved, but little conviction that the outcome would be in the child's interests. In addition, unfortunately, the best interests of the parent and the best interests of their children may not always coincide. A mother would be devastated to have her child taken away, but the child may be seriously threatening both their lives. Everyone may struggle to know what, if anything, to do.

WHAT TO TELL THE CHILDREN

Telling children about a parent's illness is not easy. Parents may not be clear themselves what is wrong with them, and often their opinion or view is different from the medical version. Children may end up with highly distorted versions of the truth.

Claire grew up knowing that her father had had a six-week mental breakdown when she was very small because he had taken a new drug against malaria. She also believed, because she knew her mother believed, that her father had had a mental breakdown because he was clever, and clever people went mad.

Doctors or nurses can be asked to tell the children, but they may not be able to explain at the best level for the child's understanding.

Much of 'telling the children' actually happens 'on the hoof', in throw-away remarks.

'I told my son you said that children often blame themselves when their father gets ill or goes into hospital, and he didn't say anything, but I did notice he's started whistling again, and he was back to punching his father on the arm. I hadn't noticed he'd stopped that too.'

Often children find things out without being told – and what they find out is often mistaken. (One girl was sure her mother was a drug addict because she found her drugs and had not been told she was ill.) They may not be told that an illness was their fault, but may well work it out for themselves. If 'it started when you were born' the child can feel they were responsible: even parents can be confused about whose responsibility it is that a child was born. Parents have also been known to tell the children 'I'm ill because of the stress your father/mother put me under', regardless of the effect this will have on the child's relation with the other parent – and on their internal parents and their whole sense of security. Not to mention the child's anxiety about causing stress themselves, which can actually increase the chance that they would misbehave. (Too much fear of stress would also be very limiting in later life: having any job, having children or having a partner can all cause stress, and an adult who avoided them all would miss out on much of life's richness.)

Children are sometimes told by well-meaning relatives that they have to look after a parent who is ill or replace one who is in hospital. The child needs to know they can still be a child, that they will still be looked after by the adults, not forced into an adult role they cannot sustain. A parent can correct this – if they know it has happened.

Parents may be only too glad of the assistance of religion in encouraging the children to behave well and may not realise what a strain this can put on the child. Whatever parents believe, children may decide for themselves that God could cure their parent if He wanted to, perhaps if the child prayed hard enough or was 'good' enough. If the parent themselves is struggling to reconcile their beliefs about their God with their current situation, they may (perhaps unwittingly) encourage children's anxieties that it is the child's bad behaviour which makes their parent ill (because God is not pleased with them). This adds a huge new dimension to a child's anxieties: having to answer to God may feel even worse than having to answer to a parent. A parent may or may not realise they need to address the child's (mis)understanding of their religious beliefs. Religion can also add to the parent's anxieties if they are unsure how to deal with their children's difficult questions about the relationship between their religion and illness or disability; in avoiding these questions, they may miss opportunities to talk about simpler questions.

Part of the difficulty is the uncertainties: do we ever know the full reasons why someone becomes ill in the way they do? Almost certainly not, but we fill in the gaps and our children fill in the gaps too. This is why talking is a good idea; at least some of the misconceptions can be sorted out, though others may remain.

Clearly, in an ideal world, children would be given correct information at the right level for their understanding, in such a way that they can ask questions and say what they have understood by it, so the adult can correct misperceptions and misunderstandings. Because children interpret what they see, hear and feel differently at different ages, adults would check what they are thinking about a parent's illness as they grow up. Sadly, the world is far from ideal, and this seldom happens. This can become yet another source of parental guilt feelings and illness making people feel bad. When Hannah's mother (see Chapter 10) read what she had written, she felt guilty that she had not done more, earlier – though it is not clear what she could have done, nor whether Hannah would have allowed it.

What children also need is a sense of an adult in charge; in particular, respect and understanding for both the child's parents, including the ill one, is of enormous importance for a child's sense of security and long-term development. Children identify with both parents: if they are at war, a child has to deal with a war inside itself as well as in the outside world; if one is despised or put down, the child has to deal with a despised self too. They need to know they are not solely responsible for an ill parent, but that there is at least one other adult around to take responsibility. They need to know who they could turn to if anything happened to a 'carer' parent, and that the 'carer' parent is taking care of themselves. Particularly if they live alone with an ill parent, they need to know that they need and have someone they can talk to.

Many of these needs will not be met. Being a parent always involves the sorry realisation that *being human* means *not being perfect*. From the screaming baby to the accusing teenager, their children will tell them – if the parent has not already worked it out for themselves.

PUTTING IDEAS IN THEIR HEADS

Adults often worry about putting disturbing ideas in the heads of their children. This can, of course, happen. (A mother said to her son that his new adult teeth were like a monster's: he ruminated on this and worried about whether he was becoming a monster.) However, ideas about illness are often in a child's head, preformed, and much more disturbing than anything a parent would tell them. They may indeed be the object of projective identification, in which case the child itself is keeping the parent from mentioning the idea, because they are already terrified of it. Children read signs of the parent's symptoms – and may misread them. They see what happens to their friends and can be afraid their own parents will break up or get cancer like their friends' parents did.

In counselling it becomes very clear that if a child can share their frightening ideas with an adult, (most) adults will be able to reassure the child, rejecting them convincingly or modifying them into more realistic ideas. They may become a reason for grief, which can be hard for both child and adult, but they are no longer a reason for terror.

People tend to put off doing and saying things they know will distress others: distressing others, particularly children, distresses the adult too, and may make bad news seem more real and force real fears to be confronted. So we do not tell children before going for tests at the hospital – it can wait. Perhaps it's nothing and everyone can laugh about the fears afterwards.

However, there are two important results of this. One is that if there is 'something', the children have had no warning, no chance to think through 'What if...', while this can truthfully be followed by 'But it's ok, it's probably nothing.' A 'what if' in this situation can range more freely and be followed through more easily than one in more threatening circumstances. In addition, preparatory grieving does help. Some of the questions which might need addressing can be thought about in advance, and alternatives worked through.

There can be a risk. The idea that a parent or partner might die in the near future is a powerful shock to the system. Children as well as partners can react very badly, withdrawing affection, turning to themselves and away from the world, or towards more risky friendships. I wrote 'Flirting with death' (Segal 2009) because I had come across several people who reacted as if their partner, on the edge of dying of a serious illness, had had an affair with death. Marital troubles can start at this time: the partner is afraid of being abandoned and unconsciously begins the search for a replacement. However, if this can be recognised, and the recovered partner makes an attempt to really understand what it was like for the one who had to sit by the hospital bed, not knowing if they would wake up the next day suddenly on their own or a single parent, the relationships too can recover. It takes an effort of imagination for a mother to understand what it was like for her child to not know if she would be alive in the morning, and after recovery nobody may feel like doing this – until the child shows mysterious signs of serious disturbance many months later.

LOSS OF ENJOYMENT

Illness can threaten many of the pleasures of parenting, and some people feel this as a huge loss. Like any other loss, they must grieve for it or deny it; and different parents choose different paths.

> 'There are things I can't do for them, but I do what I can. It does mean I'm home when she comes in from school. I think that's important for kids. I didn't like going out to work and leaving her with a childminder.'

> 'I'm a useless mother, I can't do anything.' 'What can't you do?' 'What do you mean? I can't cook, I can't clean…' 'What do you think the Queen did for her children? I don't suppose she did the cooking or cleaning? What do children really need from their mothers?' 'I think they need them to listen

to them, to be there. Mmm... The Queen went on a tour when Charles was quite small. So I'm a better mother than the Queen?!'

A social worker described a mother who was severely disabled by MS who said she wanted to make her children hate her so they wouldn't mind when she died.

Father: 'It's hard watching them play football and not being able to join in.'
Mother: 'I'm never sure if I should take them to play. I know it hurts you to see them, I'm never sure if it would be better not to let you know where they are going, or if they didn't go.'
Father: 'No! I'd rather suffer the pain of watching than think they weren't doing it because of me.'

Both children and adults are at risk of feeling guilty for enjoying themselves if someone they love is sick or ill or unhappy. Particularly in a long-term illness, parents may struggle to counter this idea and to restore a sense that happiness, enjoyment and pleasure are good and important, and that the ill parent and the carer parent both want this for their children too – assuming they do.

SHAME

Parents sometimes say their children are ashamed to be seen out with an obviously ill parent. They may be correct; however, sometimes it is the parent who is ashamed, or whose own anxieties and distress are attributed to the child. Parents can also (intentionally or unintentionally; knowingly or unknowingly) evoke shame in their children.

Many parents feel desperately ashamed at being ill. It is not entirely clear why this should be, but it is clear that it often is so. Shame is to do with being 'in the wrong' (when you want to be *right*), and an illness or disability can make people feel 'wrong' a lot of the time. Difficulties at maintaining previous roles may be interpreted as signs of blameworthy incompetence rather than a more neutral, to-be-grieved-for incapacity (like the incapacity to grow one's own wings). Many people believe that, obviously, they *should* be just like everyone else, and if they are not, they must be not just sad, but at fault. The sense of letting one's children down can be painful, and when this is exposed, people can feel ashamed. It is as if the body is felt to be a reflection of the inner soul; that a flaw in the body signifies a flaw in the self, and this is a sign of badness in some way.

> 'I knew a lady whose MS got really bad. She was always complaining. I'm strong, I wouldn't be like her [so my MS won't get bad]. I think she was just a weak person.'

> 'I feel terrible. I told my daughter I would never need a wheelchair, and now I might.'

Many people believe they have more control over their bodies than they do in reality. They often think they could cure their own illnesses, for example by controlling their thinking or certain aspects of their behaviour – by 'mind over matter'.

> 'If I had MS I wouldn't let it affect me. I'd do yoga, I'd go to therapy... I'm a positive kind of person. I'm like my mother.'

> 'I know I've got arthritis, I know it hurts to walk, but I am not going to get to the point where I can't walk upstairs. My father played tennis with a totally destroyed hip joint [if he could do it so can I]. I will be able to go on walking... You won't have to look after me when I'm old.'

These rather omnipotent, magical thoughts may or may not diminish with age and experience, but they are particularly characteristic of late adolescence and early adulthood. At some point in their adult life people may realise that there are things which they cannot control – in particular, some illnesses and some changes to their bodies. Shame can be attached to these changes if the adult feels they should have been able to control them. In other words, shame can arise when feelings of helplessness and lack of control cannot be fully acknowledged, perhaps because they are too frightening.

For one mother, shame seemed to be related to a sense that she had been (and still was) very angry with her own parents for 'letting her down' by not being *good enough when she was small. Now, as an adult, she felt her own daughter would be similarly accusatory towards her, and she felt helpless to do anything about it.*

Young adults can look on their own parents' infirmities with condescension or scorn; they may feel they 'know better' than to let these things happen. Shame can also be attached to a later realisation that parents perhaps were not just 'weak' or 'lacking in will power' but perhaps were misjudged by a younger self, more ignorant of the world. The misjudgement itself can feel shameful in someone who prides themselves on their ability to see the world as it is.

> *'I didn't realise how bad it was for my mum when my father got ill. I'm a bit ashamed really, I thought she was just selfish. I thought she should have stayed at home and looked after him. I see now why she carried on going out.'*

Shame can be attached to an illness understood as coming from the devil, or as a punishment for past sins.

> *'God was going to heal me but He hasn't.'*

If a parent's shame is unrecognised, it may be evoked in the child; if it is known, it may be expressed openly to the child. Either way, the child may simply pick it up as a truth, or work out for him or herself, that illness or increasing disability is something to be ashamed of.

People who have grown up with a disability, for whom it is already normal, may be less likely to feel ashamed; however, many do, either openly or secretly. In particular, those whose parents felt ashamed of them may have to struggle against such feelings. Parents can feel terribly ashamed of an ill or disabled child, as if the child is a reflection on them, on the goodness or badness of their own 'insides', their sexuality, their own essential self. This can make it very hard for their children to feel comfortable with their own different bodies or minds. The company of other people, in particular those who have developed a political awareness related to disabilities which enables them to stand up for themselves and for others with disabilities, helps some, though not others.

> *'I hate people pretending that a disability is the best thing that ever happened to them. It's not the best thing that happened to me!'*

Acknowledging and exploring the shame which accompanies any difference from the mainstream can be more helpful in the long term than denial of its existence. The temptation otherwise can be simply to export the (denied) shame onto others.

> *'I'm all right, I'm just blind, I wish people didn't see me as stupid. I'm not brain damaged!'*

People who have brain damage are not 'stupid' either, though this may be one of their (and their children's) biggest fears.

GUILT

As well as feeling shame, many parents feel guilty about being ill. They feel they have betrayed their children, that they are letting them down. Guilt may be attached to the illness itself if they feel responsible for having it, whether realistically or not.

If their own parents are still healthy or just beginning to become frail, an ill or disabled younger parent can feel terribly guilty and distressed at seeing themselves as no better, or in some ways actually worse, than their own parents, as well as guilty that they will not be able to care for their parents in old age. 'No better' or 'worse' here often implies for the parent (unconsciously) not only physically, but also mentally and morally, 'no better': a galling pain for a grown child whose life may have been spent still trying to demonstrate they *were* better than one or both parents. The struggle to win, to beat, to do better than an internal parent may then be carried over into a struggle to do better than a child. Guilt mixes with rivalry: a partner watching a father determined to beat his son may be puzzled about the excessive effort he puts in.

Distressing guilt about the child's future in connection with the illness can also make it very hard to talk to a child.

'Someone I worked with recently said jokingly that it's quite a good way to reduce the size of your clinics if you talk to people about disclosing [AIDS] to their children, because they don't come back for months as they're so terrified.' (Guardian 2006)

'How can I tell him it's hereditary and he will get it too? I'm not going to tell him until I have to.'

'We could have had IVF to make sure the children wouldn't have [my genetically inherited illness] but we didn't want to go through all that. We just took a chance.'

DIFFICULTY OBSERVING THE ILLNESS-RELATED ANXIETIES OF ONE'S OWN CHILDREN

Some fears are so great that they are simply denied. If a parent fears that the child's life will be totally ruined, this may be unbearable and become unmentionable. For some, the only defence they have is denial: they simply block it out and resort to one of the many reassurances which are ready for them.

'All the while they keep treating me, I know it's ok. [My children] will be ok. I was three when my mum died; [my daughter]'s six already. She'll be fine. (A mother, expecting to die within a year.)

When an ill parent denies that they are worried, partners may be left to worry alone; and the children too. Anxieties about how to talk to children without upsetting them, anxieties about causing and facing children's realistic distress, and acute anxieties about how to handle their distress, particularly if the parent who is ill was the one who took care of these things before, can mean that the partner really does not know where to start in helping his or her children to cope with their other parent's illness. If the parent is not dying, the easy way out is not to talk at all, and this is a route taken by many desperate parents.

Other exaggerations can make things hard too. Afraid *all* their children's troubles are caused by the illness, felt to be shameful or 'their fault' in some way, too-guilty parents cannot bear to find out what is actually going on in the child's mind – which may be something quite different.

Parents can be blinded too by other aspects of their own current experience. Illness can make them feel like distressed and angry children themselves, without space or capacity in their minds to be a parent. (Ill or 'carer' parents sometimes say counselling helped put them back in touch with being an adult and a parent again.) Losing the support of a husband or wife who was 'a rock', a defence, perhaps against less secure internal parents, can leave a mother or father feeling unsafe themselves. Identifying with a suddenly shaky, unbalanced partner, or with one whose ability to think or to feel has been damaged, can make a mother or father feel shaky and unbalanced themselves. They may want to see their child as capable of replacing the ill parent emotionally, whether or not they want the child to take over practical household tasks.

Many parents, ill or healthy, seem to relate to a 'child-in-their-head' which is influenced more by their own past (and their own parents) than by their real child 'out there' in the real world. They often find it difficult to recognise that their children have independent minds and assume they think the same way the parents do. It is easy to do this with children, particularly when they do not speak much to contradict the parent's view.

Lack of knowledge also plays a part. For example, if parents believe that young children cannot feel guilt or loss or anger they will not recognise these in their child. If they believe that children cannot understand or think or imagine things for themselves, they may make no attempt to help them understand, or to help them to sort out their thoughts and their imaginings. Many people do not recognise how much small children understand of adult conversation, particularly before they are old enough to speak themselves; at this age, of course, they may easily mis-hear and misunderstand things which adults could explain if they tried. Even before they understand words, babies as well as children pick up adult emotions: their reactions to distressing conversations may be strong but totally confusing and easily misinterpreted by a parent. In particular, a small child may listen out for information about absent parents. Adding to this (as I've said before), children do hide really disturbing thoughts and anxieties.

DIFFICULTY SEPARATING CHILDREN'S CONCERNS

When there is more than one child in the family, they may be 'lumped together' in the parent's mind. Sometimes parents seem to assume that if the oldest child has been told something, a younger one will know it too. It is only when asked specifically that they realise that this may not be true.

> 'They know you don't die of MS.'
> 'Both of them?'
> 'Yes, we talked about it when I was first diagnosed.'
> 'That was a long time ago. Are you sure the little one was listening?'
> 'Oh. No... Perhaps he was too small then.'

One consequence of parents identifying with their children is that parents may assume that, if they are not worried, their children will not be worried either. Unfortunately this is not always true. They also assume that their children are taken in by adult attempts to pretend that they are not worried. This may also not turn out to be true.

A good aspect of this is that children are not always worried about the same things the parents are worried about, or which the parents think the children will be worried about.

> Mother: 'I'm really sorry his dad can't play football with him like the other fathers can.'
> Son: 'I don't like football anyway. What I mind is that he doesn't laugh at my jokes any more like he used to.'

> Mother: 'I am really upset, I promised her I wouldn't use a stick, and now I have to. I'm afraid she must be embarrassed.'

Daughter: 'No I'm not.' (With some prompting, she was then able to describe quite different, more serious, concerns which her mother was able to settle satisfactorily.)

TAKING A CHILD FOR PROFESSIONAL HELP

It is not easy to take a child for professional help, besides the difficulty in finding someone appropriate. Parents can be afraid of what the counsellor or therapist will find; of showing themselves up as bad parents; of raising problems in the child's mind which were not there before. It is painful to have to see your child in distress, even if you know that, like a vaccination, it will save more distress later. They can also be afraid of adding to the child's distress, which they know is there though hidden, by showing their own. But sometimes it is clear to parents that their child is not telling them something, and they do seek help. As a counsellor for people with multiple sclerosis I was asked at times to talk with the children of clients about the illness and its effects on the family, and it was clear that having a knowledgeable adult in the room allowed children to say things that they never said at home. I could also sometimes guess what might be wrong, when it was unspoken.

One boy told me he was going to buy his father a low sports car when he came out of the nursing home, because you could drive it when your legs didn't work. I said gently how hard it was to know that he would not be coming out of hospital, and that he was going to die. The next day I had a phone call:

'I just rang to tell you my son cried for the first time with me last night.'
'Oh dear...'
'No, it was good. He hadn't let me comfort him before. He seems much better this morning, less uptight somehow. I hadn't realised how anxious he was, I knew he was horrible to me all the time, but I didn't know it was because he blamed me. He's different now, more relaxed. Thank you.'

When children blame one parent for the illness of the other, they may have lost both parents – and be unable to find a way back on their own.

PARENTS NEED TO BE SUPPORTED THEMSELVES

Parents need to be supported themselves. Being a parent at the same time as being a carer is an enormous task, and one which requires help and support from at least one other adult if any kind of mental equilibrium is to be maintained. Without this it is easy for totally unrealistic judgements, self-accusations and perhaps even self-neglect to take over. Equally, being an ill parent requires support of an emotional and psychological kind as well as physical. Illness undermines people and makes them feel bad, but support from an understanding adult can help counteract some of this.

With such support, parents may be well able to support their children too.

Parents may not be able to support their child if their only source of support is a partner who is too ill, or if they have no partner and no family or professional backup. Their ill partner's needs and/or their own needs may have to take priority and there may be insufficient time or energy left to pay attention to a child's unspoken anxieties. Someone may be neglected. In this situation parents may simply be grateful if their children can hide their own feelings and their own needs, and if they can avoid making demands. (Some of the longer-term consequences of this are discussed in the next chapter.) Where parents are not sufficiently supported themselves, anyone who suggests their child might need something else may simply be dismissed. After a while, the child or children themselves may be unable to avoid making their anxieties known, though they may do it by evoking anxieties or other feelings in others, and the signs they give may be unclear.

Support for parents needs to include permission to think, rather than simply to distract themselves. 'You go away and let me take over today' may help more if the parent has somewhere to go where they can talk about their and their children's needs. Children need parents who can and do look after themselves as well as each other: ill parents need healthy carers. Having a carer parent who wears themselves to a frazzle does not help children, nor either parent. Nor does it ultimately appease a cruel conscience or accusing 'mother/father-in-the-head'.

SUMMARY

Parents who are ill or struggling with a new disability may find it hard to think about their children, particularly if they feel guilty about the disruption their health causes in the family. However, counselling or other similar support for parents may help them think more clearly about their children and their needs. Where it succeeds in reducing parents' own anxieties it can help children indirectly. Parents who are supported, confident and not feeling too guilty or ashamed can often help their children themselves.

However, there is surprisingly little help for parents who are ill but coping, or 'just a bit worried' and in need of advice or information. Charities or support groups for any particular condition (such as MS societies) can sometimes provide information for a parent to read with a child. School counsellors may be helpful. My own co-authored book *Helping Children with Ill or Disabled Parents* (Segal and Simkins 1996), aimed mostly at professionals, was originally published for parents as *My Mum Needs Me* (Segal and Simkins 1993), and both are still available.

CHAPTER 10

Children

A parent's illness can have many effects on their children, not only while the children are small, but also when the children grow up.

This is not a popular idea. It can be resisted not only by parents (who may feel they are being accused) but also by the children themselves, who may insist that they had a good childhood, and that their parents' illness did not affect them at all. I would not disagree with such children: I would only say that even those who had a good childhood *may* have been affected by a parent's illness – perhaps in 'good' ways, perhaps in ways which affect their morality, which make them 'better people'. Illness can make children as well as adults feel bad, and they have to find ways of dealing with this.

I am very grateful to Hannah Barnard for allowing me to use her testimony here.

PROLOGUE: HANNAH

'Growing up with a disabled father was normal life for me. I was eight years old when my dad had a stroke; one that badly affected his language and left him with total paralysis of his right-hand side.

'I can't speak for my brother and sister but until I was 21 I didn't know what a huge effect Dad's stroke had had on me. I was obviously aware that life for our family was different than for most people, but that didn't

consciously affect my emotions. My dad was still my dad and our family were still strong. It took me many years to acknowledge that what had happened to my dad was horrible, unfair and hard to live with.

'People who don't have personal experience of similar situations often don't realise that a stroke does not just affect the day it happens, or the short time following that, but it affects people for life. Most people who know me will not know that it took me more than 13 years to express the anger/sadness that I felt about my dad having a stroke.

'I guess that as a child, I didn't think about the huge impact that it had on me. I just got on with life and enjoyed it. I have many happy memories of being a young person and think that I had a great up-bringing and a good childhood. There were times when I thought "I wish Dad hadn't had a stroke" but they were fairly rare. My childhood was a good one, so why wish for it to be different?

'When I left school I did a Psychology degree. Part of the course focused on stroke and I found this particularly hard. I already knew a lot about the science of strokes and obviously had experience of the effects, but hearing lecturers talk about it so coldly/scientifically was hard for me. I kept wanting to shout out "These are real people you're talking about!"

'It was at this stage of my life that I really allowed myself to express any real emotion towards my dad and the situation our family were thrown into all those years ago. For a long time I kept it bottled up and felt stupid for allowing myself to be affected by it so long after the event, but then, as I said earlier, the stroke itself isn't the hard thing, its living with the consequences and coming to terms with the effects that is really difficult. I felt angry and upset. I felt jealousy towards friends of mine whose parents had good health. I felt anger towards my dad, even though I knew it wasn't his fault. I felt I had been robbed of a "normal" childhood, even though at the time of growing up I was happy. I felt a big mix of emotions, all of which were negative.

'One thing that particularly upset me was that I had no memories of Dad from before the stroke. Even though I was eight when it happened and I have memories from when I was younger than that, I cannot remember Dad. My brother and sister and our family and friends can all remember Dad from before he had the stroke. I think it's really unfair that I can't. He's my

dad and I should know what he was like. People tell me stories about him from before the stroke but it's not the same as having my own memories. Having said that, he is still my dad and I do have memories which include him and he's still a part of my life today.

'Once I allowed myself to express these negative emotions I found it much easier to accept what had happened and it made my relationship with Dad a better one (even though before this I was unaware that it needed to change). It was still some time before I talked about these feelings with anyone else. Knowing that someone else knew my feelings helped. It was great to be told that it was ok to have these feelings, even though I had already lived with the situation for 13 years. I have never had any counselling about this and the only way I have worked through it is to talk to my family and a few close friends about my feelings. But just being able to talk to someone helped.

'It feels to me that Tuesday May 8th 1990 was the day I lost one Dad and gained another. He's still the same person but at the same time he's a different person. The stroke has limited what he can do and how much he can support me and my family both practically and emotionally. As a child I never grieved for the loss of my dad because he was still there. It's only recently, as a young adult, that I have come to acknowledge just how much was taken from me when my dad had a stroke. It is important to understand that illness/disability of a parent or close family member has a huge effect on the individual family members. It's ok to be upset and angry about what happens and it's ok to grieve for the loss of someone even if they are still alive.

'Now, aged 23, I feel I have finally come to terms with what happened to our family. I am sure there will be times in the future when I am upset by the situation, but I now know that it's ok to feel these emotions, and being honest about such feelings makes them easier to live with.'

INTRODUCTION

In this chapter I look at parents' illness from the point of view of children. In the 1980s I counselled around 30 children whose parents had multiple sclerosis, and I draw on this work, as well as other sources. I co-wrote a book called *My Mum Needs Me* (Segal and Simkins 1993), reprinted for professionals as *Helping Children with Ill or Disabled Parents* (Segal and Simkins 1996), and a paper (Segal 1998) about it. I have also worked with many adults whose parents were ill when they were small. When children are dependent on adults to take care of them, their view of the world, their responsibilities and their resources are very different from those of adults. Adults, particularly those who did not have an ill parent themselves, are often surprised at children's views. Those who did have an ill or vulnerable parent when they were small may find some recognition of their own ways of being. Although most of the children I have worked with had parents who had multiple sclerosis, their concerns resonate with those whose parents had other illnesses.

There are many ways of responding to illness in a parent, and a short chapter cannot possibly do justice to the full range. In my books I look in more detail at some of the issues raised here. It is interesting how little this topic has arisen in the past in literature and poetry, though there are some books dealing with the final illnesses of elderly parents (for example, Barnes 2008; Barthes 1981; Rieff 2008). I suspect it may be because the topic is painful in many ways – illness makes people feel bad, and people are often ashamed of their treatment of and feelings towards their elderly parents, however much they loved them.

I begin by looking at what children told me directly; I then look at what I learnt from adults who had ill parents when they were small.

WHAT CHILDREN HAVE TOLD ME…

Lack of awareness

Like Hannah, children themselves may not see their parents' illness as a problem at all. When children have talked to me as a counsellor about their parents' illness, most of them began by telling me that everything was fine, there was no problem. It was only during the course of a one-hour session, in response to gentle exploration, that they seemed to realise that they did have worries, and they could talk about them.

Their main concerns seemed to be (both) their parents' health and (sometimes) their own 'bad' behaviour, or their inability to live up to their own standards.

Worries about their parents' health and their own behaviour

'I think my father should let me stay at home and not go to boarding school; I could look after my mother. He doesn't understand, he thinks I should go away and not worry. How can I not worry? It's worse when I can't see her, see she's ok.'

'I do worry sometimes. My mother called me and I didn't come. I heard her calling several times but I sort of pretended I hadn't. She was on the floor, she'd pulled the cupboard over on top of her. I couldn't get it off her. I had to get the man next door to come round. I should have gone when she called me.'

'I think mummy went to hospital [two years earlier] because I was playing tag with my brother...and she was "home".'
(Pause, while the counsellor tried to work out what she meant.) 'You mean, you had to hit her?'
Wordless nod.
'And you thought that was why she went to hospital while you were at school the next day?'
Wordless nod. (By which time both mother and counsellor were nearly in tears themselves.)

'I think my mum is going to die. My gran says it's my fault she's like this.'

Cognitive problems in mothers seemed to cause serious anxiety for children, who worried, sometimes realistically, that their mothers were not able to look after themselves and put themselves in danger. They also worried about their mother's relations with other members of the family; there was an awareness that they needed another adult to help to control the mother's behaviour. They did not mention their own need for mothering. However, they did have normal adolescent worries about their own bodies or relationships at school, some of which a mother would almost certainly have dealt with if she had been functioning better.

Many children have expressed fears of burdening their parents and making them worse in one way or another.

Megan, 9: 'I'm scared when I make the tea for you. I'm afraid I'll spill the water on my hand.'
Mother: 'Why didn't you tell me? I thought you liked being a big girl.'
Megan: 'I thought I had to do it for you, you can't do it.'

Counsellor: 'Sometimes children blame themselves for their mum being ill. I wonder if you ever do?'
Child (whispering): 'I know she wasn't ill before I was born, I think it was my fault.'
Counsellor: 'You mean, because she had you?'
Child (nodding): 'Yes.'

Children often made it clear to me that they felt their parents to be very vulnerable.

Girl, 12: 'When I stayed with my friend I was homesick and I cried; I didn't tell my mum because granny said I shouldn't worry her.'

Many children decide that they cannot tell the parent their worries.

'I couldn't tell my mother I was being bullied, she's not well, she's got enough troubles.'

Rivka Yahav and colleagues (Yahav, Vosburgh and Miller 2005) interviewed 56 children and adolescents, aged 10–18, who each had one parent diagnosed with MS six months or more before the beginning of the study. They found that many children felt they had to hide their personal problems, so as not to impose a burden on their parents.

It's not me who...

Some of their worries were attributed by children to someone else.

'I have to get home, I can't stay after school, I can't leave my mother alone too long. She likes me there, she gets worried if I'm not home. She likes me to watch TV with her.'

This child's mother probably did worry about being left, but her daughter also had worries about it which she found it harder to admit. Attributing the child's own worries to their sick mother was not unusual.

> Becca, 15: 'Nobody at school understands how I feel. I really hate my mother, not because she's ill, it's other stuff, but I can't tell my friends, they're like, "How can you hate your mother? She's ill!" It's so unfair.'

Becca hated having conflicting feelings about her mother's illness; conflicts with friends, distressing as they were, may have been preferable. Her insistence that she was not angry with her mother 'for being ill' suggests that she too thought this would be beyond the pale, and that she might have redirected any unbidden anger about that to 'other stuff'. This kind of redirection increases the sense of being misunderstood, because it is hard to reach the root of her anger without getting back to the (for Becca, unspeakable) anger with her mother 'for being ill'. Becca re-created at school the feelings of being misunderstood: her difficulties with friends would also mirror her difficulties with her mother and possibly also on some level feel like a justified punishment for having such bad feelings in the first place. Friends would indeed have found it hard to understand. Young teenagers can be very unforgiving about those who fail to live up to their high moral standards, untested by time and age.

Nicky, aged eight, had been upset at school because a boy had insulted his father, saying he was 'mental'. Nicky had fought the boy. Talking about it with the counsellor, it became clear that he had no other words for his father's cognitive problems, which were caused by his MS. He was very frightened, not only that his father was 'mental', whatever this meant to him, but also that it meant that he himself would also 'go mental' when he grew up. Fighting the other boy perhaps enabled him symbolically to fight this fear too. He seemed to be helped by some information, including a discussion of what he saw of his father's 'mental' problems; a clear explanation of the way MS affected his father's brain; more accurate words to describe it; and a discussion of the real possibility that he might develop MS himself. He was encouraged to talk about how he thought he would deal with it if he did get it, as well as what it meant that he had a 'one in a hundred chance' of getting it. His mother also told him that she hoped that there would be a cure by the time he was old enough to get it.

Worries about the health of the other parent

Some children made it clear, with or without saying so, that they were afraid that their other parent was going to die or get ill. It seems as if the fact of one parent becoming ill alerted them to the realisation that their world was not as safe as they thought it was, and they were not clear where the threat ended.

> *Sid, 12; his father had MS and was able to walk but not to work: 'My dad ought to help my mum more. He doesn't do anything, he just expects her to do everything.' (This boy, along with several other children in similar circumstances, did not believe his father was really ill; his father suffered from invisible symptoms, including neurological fatigue.)*

> *'I'm afraid Mum can't cope. I may have to stay here, not to go to university, to help with Dad (who was very disabled). She gets terrible headaches sometimes.'*

> *Emily, 11; her mother had MS, unable to walk but was working part-time: 'I'm fine. It's ok, my mum having MS. My dad looks after her, I don't really have to do anything. Well, yes, I sometimes worry what would happen to Mum if anything happened to Dad. I don't think I could look after her myself.'*

In fact, Emily lived almost next door to her mother's brother and his family, and in counselling she realised that they would take over if anything did happen to her father. A worry of many years was taken away immediately once she had been enabled to express it aloud.

I also picked up that many children were angry with their fathers for being ill because they were concerned about their mother's health – even if she was healthy. Children are very concerned, I think, about their need for a father *to look after their mother.*

Misunderstandings

Children were also confused about their parents' health. Not knowing enough about the illness seemed to allow their minds to roam freely.

'I think my father got his MS by potholing.'

Many children (and adults too) often failed to distinguish between symptoms and character. Was constant irritability or tiredness or bad driving caused by the parent's health condition, or was it caused by working too hard; or was it 'just Dad' or 'just Mum'? Was the child justified in complaining about it or was it simply something which the family had to put up with? On the whole it seems to be more natural for children to think these are characteristics of the parent; seeing them as invisible symptoms of an illness requires some work and some understanding which family members, including the ill person themselves, often lack.

Resentment can feed into misunderstanding too.

Becca, 15: 'My mother is just an attention-seeker. There was nothing wrong with her until that doctor saw her limping a bit, then she suddenly got so much worse! I don't believe she's that bad. I think she just wants my father's attention. And she likes us to wait on her, to do things for her all the time. She's jealous because me and my sister are getting to be teenagers and he likes us better than her.'

It was difficult to imagine what Becca's mother could do to convince her daughter that her symptoms were real rather than imaginary. Everything she did was interpreted by her daughter in her own way.

The resentment may also be shared with (or originate from) the other parent. A mother who considers her husband 'useless' may not object very strongly when her son expresses this sentiment. Under pressure of her husband's illness (which might well include impotence or loss of another kind of strength or function), she might not be aware that she is subtly encouraging her son to do this – until she has to seek help for the child's 'difficult' behaviour.

'Falling over means they are going to die'

Several of the children I counselled told me that they were very worried when their parents fell over. It became clear that when a parent fell over they were afraid the parent was going to die.

This leads to an important issue. I think that some older children were afraid in a similar way to an adult: falling over meant the parent could not walk, or balance, or could not take care of themselves; someone who cannot do these things is not well, and may die. (Even when they know that people with MS are likely to live a long time, both adults and children can make these associations.) But I think that, for many children, there is something much more significant about a parent falling over.

When a parent falls over, the child's whole world may be turned upside down. Reality is no longer what it was. For many adults, parents, like home, *represent* security and stability; for a child, the feeling can be more that parents *are* stability, security, in charge, taking care of children. When parents fall over, children look *down* on them when they should be looking *up* – with all that these phrases imply. It feels deeply and disturbingly wrong – practically, socially, morally and emotionally. Nobody puts these feelings into words, and a child may end up feeling that he or she is in the wrong – the discomfort of feeling that a parent is in the wrong can be much greater for a small child than taking the blame themselves. And the idea that neither parent nor child is in the wrong seems to be unimaginable for a very small child (and many adults too). The parent may also feel a similar sense of 'wrongness' and respond with embarrassment and shame. Not infrequently, a parent who falls may get angry and shout at anyone around, including a child.

'You shouldn't have spoken to me! You know I lose my balance when I'm distracted!'

'Get away! Don't come near me!' (For the parent this may not be meant to imply that the child is at fault, or caused the fall, but a child may interpret it as such.)

The child's confused feelings may be not only ignored but exaggerated or reinforced by the parents' own confusion and anxiety. Instead of the child having a chance to think about what they thought, felt or feared, they may be convinced that it is far better not to know. Fears and anxieties resulting from such situations can be hidden from the child's own awareness as well as from the adults around.

Later an adult may apologise to their partner: 'I'm sorry, it's me I was angry with, not you.' But whether they apologise to their child, or how the child feels when they do, is another matter. An apologetic parent may be of little comfort to a small child who would much prefer a parent to be strong and invincible and never to make mistakes in the first place. There are many aspects of reality which children and their parents dislike intensely.

Making a parent better

'I thought that if I prayed hard enough, God would make daddy better.'

'We need to help mummy more, then she'd get better.'
'You think that if you helped more, her MS would go away?'
'Yes. Daddy said so.'
'Oh dear. I think what daddy means is that mummy would feel better. It is very hard, but you can't make her MS go away, however good you are. You can't make her worse, by being naughty either, though you can make her feel worse, if she's tired or something. You thought she was ill because of you?'
Nod. (And the father looked shamefaced.)
(The counsellor has to be careful to restore the father's position of respect in the child's eyes before leaving the session: he has brought the child, and undermining parents is not helpful to anyone; recognising and forgiving mistakes, particularly those commonly made by parents, is another matter.)

Parents sometimes want their children to be told to offer more help. The counsellor, on the other hand, may feel it is more important to help the children to understand the reality of the illness: this may need to be clarified before the children are brought in. Where parents are using blame as a tool to manipulate their children into helping more around the house, the counsellor may see this as potentially an extremely risky strategy. Eventually a child may feel they have been conned; alternatively, they may continue to believe all their lives that they were responsible for a parent's illness. Either seems not only wrong, in the sense both of unrealistic and bad, but also cruel and unfair on the children, with the potential to cause all kinds of future problems.

Parents may be totally unaware of this point of view and many will immediately respond with new awareness of their children's position. However, it has to be recognised that not all parents are interested in their children's welfare, being more committed to their own. The children may, quite rationally, agree with their priorities – a parent's well-being is of vital importance to a child, and if it requires that a child be prepared to believe two untruths before breakfast every day, a child may well choose to do this for as long as they can.

Children often try to help their parents by maintaining even obviously unrealistic views of the world, rather than challenge (and possibly weaken) parents who already feel (to the child) extremely vulnerable. The problem is compounded by the fact that children may see their own (child's) vulnerability in their parents at the same time as they take on or take over their parents' parenting capacities. The child then feels 'I'm the strong one; you're the weak one', which has obvious advantages in the short term. This is the problem of a 'parentified' child. In the long term it leaves the child feeling extremely unsafe and vulnerable, without strong parents to depend on. The parents 'out there' may of course be far less vulnerable than the child believes or assumes.

Children, particularly very young children, can feel responsible for family welfare in a way which astonishes adults.

John was eight when his mother left the new baby outside a shop and went home without her. He said he decided at that point that he had to take charge of the family, that clearly his parents were useless.

They often feel they have to protect parents, in particular from their own bad feelings and behaviour; their desire to make their parents better may have roots in a feeling that it was their bad feelings and behaviour which caused the illness in the first place. The enormity of the task is also almost unimaginable to an adult. Since parents to a small child make up the largest part of their world, anything wrong with the parents means that something is wrong with the world, and the child may feel this inside themselves, in a level of nagging anxiety or gut-wrenching stress which is constant; something like the need to 'save the planet'.

In the child's mind *both* parents may be in need of the child's help. An illness may prevent either of them feeling to the child like a source of internal and external strength – and the child may not feel strong enough to put them back together. To a small child, having a vulnerable parent may feel like living in a collapsed world or a crumbling house. The desire to make it all better may well be accompanied by feelings of hopelessness or despair.

WHAT CHILDREN HAVE SHOWN ME...

As Hannah makes clear in her testimony earlier, children are not always aware of their own feelings or thoughts or reactions to a parent's illness. Sometimes adults have to guess from their behaviour. In this section I describe observations I have made, rather than things children have openly said.

Blaming the other parent or a sibling

Martin, aged 12, who is described in more detail in *Helping Children with Ill or Disabled Parents* (Segal and Simkins 1996) and *My Mum Needs Me* (Segal and Simkins 1993), made it clear that he blamed his father for his mother's illness, though he did not say so directly. This seemed to be a way of deflecting his own blame of himself. Perhaps partly because he did not want to say this, he found it hard to speak to his father at all. When his father shouted at his mother, Martin was afraid it would make his mother worse. He was also afraid he would have to look after her himself, and was very afraid he was not old enough to do so, though he insisted he was and he could, or should be able to. He misunderstood his father's attempts to protect him from his mother's illness, and just thought his father wanted to send him to boarding school to get him out of the way.

Other children seemed to blame a brother or sister, rather than the other parent. Such blame is very destructive of relationships. It not only undermines potential sources of real support for the child at the time, but it may sour relationships in adult life. In order to enable the child to stop blaming their parent or their sibling, they have to understand that they are not to blame themselves either.

One of the most distressing (and enlightening, never-forgotten) moments of my working life arose when a family came to see me because the father had multiple sclerosis and was at the end of his life. After a lot of discussion it became clear that everyone in the room, including me, believed at that moment that the father was going to die because the mother did not love him enough, and, against considerable internal resistance, I said this was what they were telling me. It took quite a few heartbeats before I was able to say that this was of course not true; that he would die because he had had multiple sclerosis for a very long time. The phantasy that 'love can cure all' was still, I suspect, strong in myself.

Helping – or being paralysed by anxiety

Anxieties about their parents sometimes translated into children offering help; but if the anxiety was too great, despair could take over. Too much anxiety can lead to feelings of hopelessness and uselessness. Being overwhelmed by the enormity of a self-imposed, impossible task (of making the parent better) can lead to a child becoming paralysed themselves and unable to function. They can also, like Becca, deny any anxiety at all, and refuse to help on the grounds that the whole illness is a plot directed at making their life uncomfortable.

Fear that the second parent will die may simply lead to behaviour calculated (unconsciously) to make one or both parents feel threatened or frightened of their world collapsing, as the child fears. A child can determine to do without their parents and to rely entirely on themselves, which may mean cutting themselves off from family life as much as possible. Avoiding contact with an ill parent (or with both parents) is one way of avoiding distress when it all seems too much and the child feels too hopeless about making anything better, but children of single parents may only feel they have this option if they have brothers or sisters to take on a caring role towards the parent. Children in general seem to discount the role of friends (and other relatives) of their parents as potential carers or supporters. Parents may value their friends more highly, and trust more in their support, than children do. (The children may of course be jealous of the friends and their relationship with the parents.)

In several families, one child was the 'helper' and the other took on the role of the 'escaper', who was allowed or encouraged to avoid helping or even acknowledging the illness. Several children who stayed at home expressed a resentment towards an older child who 'escaped'; evidence from adults suggests that this can sometimes last into adulthood. One who left can also envy the relationship between the parents and one who stayed, though parents do not always prefer the child who stays. Parents' greater affection for the one who left, and who is seen only occasionally, can seem most unfair to a 'carer' child left behind. In young adulthood, children who leave may find replacement parents, sometimes in in-laws or an employer.

SHANE; INSIDES FALLING OUT

Shane, aged seven, seemed very competent and helpful. He was a tremendous support to his single mother, who was affected by MS not only physically (her legs were paralysed), but also emotionally and cognitively: she relied on her son not only to cook and to clean but also to remember appointments. After meeting an MS Research Counsellor the boy insisted on returning at intervals, and made sure they turned up on time. A year later, his mother reported, apparently unconcerned, that he was dirtying himself at school. With the counsellor, he drew a house and a tree, both without a baseline; a week later he drew in the centre of the page two eyes, a nose and mouth with no line around them; below them he drew a 'Mr Strong' with big legs and no arms; beside the facial features he drew disconnected arms, and then, above them all, a train which he called 'number 2'. The counsellor thought he was showing her how it felt to feel he had no bottom, no base; and that things were not properly held together in the right places, not supported, however hard he tried in his body to be Mr Strong.

After this, he collapsed in the chair in the counsellor's consulting room. For 35 minutes he was silent, looking exactly as if all the stuffing had been taken out of him; his head and arms flopping over the sides of the chair, his tongue hanging out and dribbling, his tongue playing with the zip of his coat, looking as if nothing was holding him together. The counsellor watching him felt very disturbed, rather revolted and distressed, and talked to him about what she saw. At the end of the session he pulled himself together and left the room as bouncy and cheerful as he had come in.

This child was in serious trouble, but his difficulties had not been fully recognised even when he began dirtying himself at school. (Perhaps his teachers felt this was 'normal' for a child in his situation, or did not want to have to talk to his mother, who was not an easy person to address, being loud, confident and a bit aggressive in her wheelchair?) He was good at hiding his anxieties and presenting himself as extremely competent. However, he was able to show the counsellor that he did not feel securely held together. It seemed, too, that when he was away from his mother he could not hold his insides in; perhaps he felt then he could at last 'let go'. (He was eventually picked up by social services as a result of the counsellor's forceful referral.)

While this illustrates something of the meaning a collapsed mother can have for a child, this particular child's situation was compounded by his mother's own past experience of sexual abuse, which probably left her uncertain about her own boundaries. Physical illness of a parent can in some circumstances leave children vulnerable to abuse, and it can force children to 'grow up' superficially, but experience from other parents suggests that the cognitive and emotional disabilities of parents can be more undermining of the child's state of mind.

Although Shane's experience was extreme, it illustrates the way in which parental instability may lead to feelings of instability in a child. It is not that the child thinks 'my mum is unstable'; Shane was very attached to his mother and would have defended her against all comers. It is rather that parents' feelings and experience of life are conveyed to their children in a 'whole-body' fashion; the child somehow absorbs the atmosphere of the home, picks up anxieties, senses parental troubles, and experiences them as aspects of his or her own reality. If thought is brought to bear on them at any time, the child may well misunderstand what is happening, (mis)interpreting the sensations in its body in terms of the child's own level of understanding and knowledge.

Identification processes

Children (of any age) can fear that their own body will become like their parent's, particularly if they are of the same sex or if they bear a close resemblance. They can fear that they will inherit a disease or symptoms. Parents can fear this too, and can find it very difficult to address realistically with the child. Not wanting to worry the child, they may not realise that the child has developed his or her own worries already, and, unlikely as this feels to the parent, anything an adult says may feel reassuring.

Matthew, aged five, sat swinging his legs throughout a family counselling session. The counsellor asked him if he was sometimes afraid his legs would stop working like his father's had. She wondered if he felt he had to keep moving them to make sure they still worked. He might have thought that his father's legs stopped working because he kept them still, rather than the other way round.

Suicidal impulses are not uncommon in teenagers, particularly of the low-level risk-taking variety, where they neglect to take care of themselves. They may be particularly at risk if their parent seems to the child to be no longer taking care of themselves; or if the parent has suicidal impulses themselves. Identification processes can struggle with desires for a separate existence. Becca was insisting on her separateness. Toby, aged 19, was more closely identified with a father who was suffering from depression after his MS made him lose his job:

'What's the point of going to college? I'll only get ill like my dad. He's had to give up his work, what's the point of studying for years? I might as well enjoy myself now.'

Toby, unfortunately, was not capable of enjoying his self-imposed exile from education and life with his peers.

Need for support

When I began counselling children of ill parents, including children who were now adult, I became aware that as I came out of the first session I would be in a particular heightened emotional state. Desperately searching for a colleague to 'unload' onto, I wanted to tell them that I could not do this work; that I was overwhelmed and about to collapse myself. I wanted to pass these clients on to someone else who would be more capable than I was. Using Klein's concept of projective identification, I began to suspect that this is what these children were (or had been) suffering from at the time of their parents' illness. When I was able to raise with a child the question of whether they felt overwhelmed by the discrepancy between their need to care and their ability to do so, I was often shocked by the vehemence with which the child responded. These children did not look overwhelmed; they looked perfectly normal, if somewhat reserved and self-contained. Clearly I was not seeing how stressed and frightened they actually felt: I would never have guessed, had I not disregarded the evidence of my eyes and recognised that my own feelings were resonating with something I could not see. However, once I had recognised the child's high level of anxiety, I no longer felt so useless. The children were enabled to access real help, whether from a parent or from another adult who was now able to acknowledge how anxious they were and knew how to handle it.

WHAT ADULTS HAVE TOLD ME, REMEMBERING THEIR PARENTS WERE ILL...

While counselling people who have been ill themselves, and members of their families, over many years, I have met many who have talked with me about their own childhood experience of their parents being ill. For some, it meant vulnerability and lack of supervision or support or a defender, which led indirectly to very bad experiences with other adults, related or unrelated. Some feared being taken away from a parent who might have been seen as 'not coping'; some *were* taken away and suffered appalling treatment in foster-homes or children's homes. Some, like Sally,

Nisa and Moira below, could be seen to have suffered enormously in some ways, but they also reported times of happiness. Some lived with other family members who clearly wanted and loved them, perhaps more than they felt their parents did. One woman of 50, in care all of her life, described having a wonderful time when as a child she was sent to stay during the school holidays on a ward of elderly people who competed for her affections. Later in life she gravitated towards older people, and was eventually happily married to a man many years older than herself. However, other aspects of her life were not so happy, and she never fully understood why her (ill and disabled single) mother could not look after her.

It is always impossible to be certain what has caused what: whether an illness in a parent was the prime cause of a problem; whether it could have been better handled; whether an illness turned a parent to drink or drugs or even violence, which then affected the children; whether it was simply the social and emotional milieu of the time which led to the child becoming an adult who had difficulties of one kind or another. The links I make in my work and below, in the vignettes, are links which seemed to me and to the client to make sense – but readers are allowed to be sceptical. Other people's experience is never as convincing as one's own. However, the connections I make may encourage readers to make links about their own or others' experiences.

SALLY

'My mother liked having me around; I was the youngest and she was quite old when I was born. She was quite disabled by the time I was a teenager. She didn't always make me go to school. The school used to let me off my homework too, they were always very sympathetic: "Her mother is very ill, you know." But it meant I ended up with no exams, unlike my older sisters who went to university. I think my parents both sort of forgot about me. I've always been someone other people depend on. I seem to have a very powerful sense of responsibility. Even as an adult, people don't take care of me, I end up taking care of them.'

NISA

Nisa was a very independent woman who hated relying on others. She always felt that she kept her distance from her children and husband. She also had difficulty breathing from her diaphragm. When she was one year old her mother was ill and she had been taken from her parents and brought up by a loving grandmother, aunts and uncles. Her counsellor wondered if she had learnt then to 'hold' her chest, not to let it relax, in order not to cry. She also wondered if this had contributed to Nisa keeping her distance from her children, whom she loved dearly. As adults, she and her mother got on well.

FERGAL

'My dad said we shouldn't tell anyone our business, the Social might come and take us away. Mum had TB; he struggled to look after us, but he did it well. We used to come home and clean up before he got in, but he always made sure he was there in the evening to do the cooking. We couldn't tell anyone or they'd have taken us away from him. You couldn't talk to him, he was always busy, and he wasn't that sort of person. I suppose I've always kept myself to myself.'

ALISON: 'YOU'LL KILL MUM!'

Alison remembered worrying about the way she shouted at her younger brother and sister. As a child, she always thought she should be a better Christian and not get so angry. She remembered feeling shocked at her own gut-wrenching fury with her younger brothers when they fought with each other; she knew she had gone 'over the top' when she hissed at them, 'That's how Hitler began!' Remembering this in counselling many years later, she recognised that she had been terrified their bad behaviour would literally kill their mother, who was suffering from severe (but by no means life-threatening) back pain at the time.

DEBBIE, 23

'We were always afraid our father would die. He was always ill throughout our childhood. We wouldn't let [our younger brother] Sam tell him he [Sam] was ill, it might have killed him [our father].'

Debbie was still battling with her younger brother on the basis that his bad behaviour could kill their father.

FRED

Fred sent his children to boarding school when he was diagnosed with a neurological disease because he had overheard someone say that his mother had died when he was a teenager 'because she had been worn out by too many sons'. He was afraid children caused stress, and stress would kill him like it killed his mother. (She had actually died of cancer.)

C.S. Lewis and J.R.R. Tolkien: mother-worlds

C.S. Lewis and J.R.R. Tolkien both created worlds in which anxieties about life and death, about the role of children and hobbits (representing children with adult capacities) in fighting for the survival of a magical, beloved world, could be played out, to the eventual great satisfaction of millions of readers and viewers. Both Lewis's country of Narnia and Tolkien's Middle Earth can be seen as representing a basic phantasy of a mother. I suggest that both were accessing the feelings and emotions evoked by the loss of their mothers when they were children. They both convey a powerful sense of a wonderful world in which magic is possible, which is under threat and which can be lost. Such a country or world can represent the 'mother-in-the-head' (or, better, perhaps, in-the-body) which originates at a very early age. It represents a mother who does not come and go, but is always there, holding and containing not only the child but the whole of life.

Both authors convey to the reader, by the threat to their magical lands, something of the way a child can feel when a parent's life is threatened. Both deal with betrayal, with hobbits or children who must fight to rescue a land which is at risk of disappearing for ever. Both evoke, too, the powerlessness of children in the face of such threats, and their need for help from someone much larger and stronger and more knowledgeable than themselves (Aslan the lion, and Gandalf the wizard) who is *not always there* when he is wanted.

Guilt

Lewis also describes more directly the desperation and hopes of a child with an ill mother in the volume which relates the origin of the land of Narnia. Digby, the main character in *The Magician's Nephew* (Lewis 1955), escapes from his mother's illness into a magical series of worlds, and returns with an apple which restores her to health. On the way he also has to cope with the threat of betrayal on several levels, and he wins his mother's health by resisting the temptation to cheat. The idea that a mother can suffer death (or, as Aslan explains, an even worse fate) if a child does the wrong thing is very powerful in this story. The other side of this is the idea that the child *can* make his mother better and save her life if only he can find the magic apple, the right ring, the key to health, but only with the help of a magical father. A child may become aware that he or she does not have the key to health, without at the same time truly recognising that their own misbehaviour is not going to be the cause of death.

Lewis's first children's book, *The Lion, the Witch and the Wardrobe* (Lewis 1950), includes Peter, who behaves heroically, and his younger brother Edmund, who betrays both his siblings and the beloved country of Narnia by his greed and small-mindedness. Children often feel they have a constant struggle with these two sides of their nature; if they have an ill parent, the life or death of the parent may seem to depend on the outcome of this internal war. Parents have a role in aiding this struggle, and in Lewis's book, Aslan the lion comes to the rescue.

Joanne (J.K.) Rowling's mother had multiple sclerosis. Rowling too created a magical world in which the hero manages without parents, with help from a powerful adult who, after a time, leaves the child hero to manage without his support. Harry Potter also rescues his world from the brink of destruction (for example, Rowling 1997), to the great pleasure of millions of fans, both child and adult.

We do not need to have actually lost parents to enjoy these 'saving the mother-world' sagas. Under the influence of ordinary anxieties, children play out these scenarios in their minds before they happen, preparing themselves for something which may never come. (The 'bad', dangerous characters can be read as terrifyingly aggressive, monstrous aspects of a phantasy child-self combined with equally terrifying parents: the stories reassure us that our good impulses, combined with good parents, are stronger than our dangerous ones.)

Moira remembered being too scared (at the age of eight) to go to the shop for her mother's medication when her mother was dying of cancer. She had always feared it was this which killed her mother. She also felt she had failed her father, who died two years later, by not loving him as much as he deserved. As an adult, Moira, a model housekeeper, wife and mother, lived with an abusive husband she could not leave. After she broke down in her forties she worked over several years with clinical psychologists and with a counsellor and was able to make some changes; however, at depth she continued to believe that she deserved all her husband's ill-treatment.

Moira demonstrates something of the intransigent nature of childhood fantasies. Her conviction that it was her fault her mother had died seemed really impossible to change in adulthood. This is an example of a belief which is formed in childhood, related to issues of life and death, and which becomes so fixed that it is to all intents and purposes immovable. (Long-term psychoanalysis might help but was not an option for Moira.)

Bodily effects of early life-and-death phantasies

Nisa's breathing difficulties, and possibly also her over-eating, are examples of a different kind of effect. Before a child can talk, fantasies and emotions may become fixed in physical parts of the body, affecting basic functioning such as breathing or eating. The relation with the mother is so closely bound up with living, breathing and eating when a child is a baby that disturbances at a very early age may show up in difficulties in any of these areas. Claire felt anxiety as a gnawing pain in her stomach, though she did not recognise it as such until she was in her thirties and in therapy. She had been aged two when her father became frighteningly ill and she had lost her home suddenly for the second time.

Long-term development

All of the people mentioned in this section had lives which in many ways were well functioning, though Fergal had remained a loner all his life.

Many children of ill parents I have met as adults were working professionals, or running successful businesses and successful families. Those who had turned to alcohol or drugs or a life of crime or prostitution made up, I think, no more than would be expected amongst the general population, though as far as I know, nobody has looked at these figures. My own suspicion (based on more than 600 counselling clients over 35 years) is that actual *loss* of a parent is more of a problem for later development than the *illness* of a parent which allows later modification of early fantasies. However, so many factors are involved that it is difficult to be certain how much effect such a loss itself has, as distinct from the effect of social or other consequences, of *ways of dealing with it* or even whatever *caused* the loss in the first place.

The illness of a parent may cause problems, but it can also be a spur to development, to seeking understanding, to writing, creating and to making new relationships. Some of these relationships can, like C.S. Lewis's marriage to a woman who was ill with cancer, be seen as an attempt to put things right this time round with someone whose presence resonates with that of an ill parent.

CHOICE OF OCCUPATION

There is another way in which the illness of a parent can influence people, and that is in their choice of occupation.

'I'm going to be a doctor when I grow up, so I can cure people.'

'My daughter is a nurse in the USA. I think she wanted to be able to look after people like me, but not me: I think that would be too much for her. I'm glad, I suppose, though I would like her to be here, I wouldn't want her to feel she has to look after me.'

'When I grow up I will become a priest so I can say prayers for you so you never have to go through purgatory.'

'I'm going to be a chemist so I can find a cure for MS.'

'My mother was depressed when I was small, but I could always make her smile when I danced. So I became a dancer.'

There are more subtle links, which may be less conscious (discussed in Chapter 2), such as a link between a desire to be an architect or builder or furniture-maker and feelings about an ill mother which belong to a time when a child is very small and sees the mother as part of the landscape, as 'home', or as part of the furniture. Pleasure in work can be influenced by resonances with early fantasies, in particular fantasies of repairing damage done by a primitive level of frightening anger with parents; and illness in a parent can make a child very angry indeed. Melanie Klein talked about 'reparation' as a powerful motivator; she was referring to primitive phantasies in which children feel they destroy the mother's body, and then desperately want to repair it and make it whole again. She described it without linking it to illness in parents – she thought it was a normal part of childhood development. (The popularity of the 'saving the mother-land' stories perhaps attests to this.) As I have tried to show, parental illness can affect these phantasies on many levels.

CHOICE OF PARTNER

C.S. Lewis chose a partner who was ill, like his mother was when he was growing up. Perhaps this was a coincidence, but perhaps not. Relationship counselling over many years has led me to think that people do often choose people who 'fit' into the 'place' in their minds which was created by one or both parent-figures; a partner who resembles some aspect of the 'parents-in-the-head' (however much or little this internal parent resembles the external parents). This resemblance may include some element of a parent's illness or disability, some aspect of their mental state, as well as some aspect of their appearance, of their occupation, the issues they consider important. There is evidence that people do favour others with whom they share some genes (Saxton *et al.* 2009, for example). Sometimes the influence seems to work in the opposite direction, where a partner will be chosen apparently because he or she seems precisely *different from* a problematical parent, though sometimes in counselling it turns out that, over time, the differences became less evident than the similarities.

Marjorie was surprised and happy that her new boyfriend was sympathetic when she cried, which she did, often. This was a contrast with the irritation her parents tended to express. After several years' marriage, during which she continued to cry easily, he began to show signs of irritation.

SUPPORTING CHILDREN WITH ILL PARENTS: CHILDREN'S POINT OF VIEW

Resisting support

Like Hannah from earlier, many children do not see the need for support when they have an ill parent. For them, life seems normal. They do not know that everybody doesn't have a permanent knot in their stomach. How should the child know that their 'bad' feelings aren't just a sign of their guilty conscience, that they should try harder, help their ill mother more, be a really 'good' girl or boy? How should a child know that their magical attempts to control things aren't a better way of dealing with a reality which others deal with worse? The child may in all sincerity think they are 'fine' because they have no idea that others feel or think differently from them. Or, detecting a difference, they may put it down to inferiority or superiority, weakness of character, bravery or cleverness. Or all of these at different times. A friend said she only discovered at the age of 29 that everyone didn't carry suicide pills around with them, 'just in case'. Her father had been seriously ill when she was three and she had expected him to commit suicide ever since.

Children are often more concerned to hide their feelings, their anxieties, their worries (about themselves or about their parents) than to ask for help. They may be afraid of being blamed or accused, as they already blame and accuse themselves, or as they are already blamed and accused by adults around them. They may be afraid of being 'taken into care', or being humiliated or shamed or found wanting in some other way they hadn't thought of yet. (Identification with a parent who is some way 'lacking', like Nicky's view of his 'mental' father, can increase the risk of feeling that exposure would bring only shame.) They often feel they ought to be able to cope, and that there is no other way of doing it. They do not know what it is they do not know, and what it is they need to know. Sometimes they know they do not have sufficient information, and sometimes they complain that they are expected to care for their parents without being treated sufficiently like an adult to be given the resources. Mostly, in my experience, they try to pretend (and actually believe) that nothing is wrong.

Perhaps for these reasons, children seldom seem to tell their friends much about their ill parents. Sometimes they have tried and been disappointed at the friends' reactions; more often they seem to decide to 'keep themselves to themselves' at least insofar as their parent's health is concerned.

Their anxieties about betraying the family, or being exposed themselves, can make it difficult to help them. If an adult decides that a child should be taken to a school counsellor or to a group for Young Carers, for example, to discuss the way they feel about their parent's illness, the child may be reluctant to go. The adult's own uncertainties may mean they do not persevere.

Once they get there, however, and get past the point when they have said they are 'fine, no problems', children and young people do often find not only that they have worries, but that these worries can be dealt with in a better way. Rather than just pushing them out of mind, they can often be actually solved in some way or other. There may be more help available than the child realised. Sharing their experiences with others (in a safe setting) helps to normalise them and can make the child feel less bad about their own feelings as well as their own experiences.

Simply knowing that others know how you feel, as Hannah described at the beginning of this chapter, can itself help. Worries can be handed over to adults; adults can be properly in charge again. Feeling understood is important and reduces various forms of anxiety and tension; ultimately it can also allow freer thought, better problem solving as well as a more realistic view of the world.

Of equal importance, perhaps, is that counselling or support groups challenge the child's belief that it is better to cut oneself off from others and simply to try to solve all life's problems single-handedly. Discovering that talking is more effective can have lasting effects throughout adult life. It may make the difference between, on the one hand, resorting to drugs or alcohol, and on the other, seeking company and conversation. If the support enables the child to feel that there are people in the world who can be safely depended upon, this is a lesson which may affect their adult relationships and their chances of finding a good, supportive partner.

Support from other children

It may be obvious that a child whose parent is ill may find it extremely hard to talk to friends, if they have any, about what is going on at home. They may lack the words; if nobody talks about it at home, how can they begin to talk about it? Like Becca earlier in this chapter, they may be deeply confused and uncertain, perhaps ashamed of their own feelings and reactions and of those of their parents. How can these be shared with people they want to impress, or with anyone who may turn on them and attack them? School friends cannot always be trusted. Children may take their cue from adults and try – even successfully – to forget what is going on at home while they are at school. Other children generally know better than to enquire about things their friends don't want to talk about. Blanking out an elephant in the room is not difficult, particularly if it is limping and looking reproachful or liable to burst into tears of rage or bitter sorrow; a new computer game or a television soap is much more entertaining and much, much safer. And other children have their own worries, their own concerns, which they may be too busy hiding to think about anyone else's.

If better support is not available, or the child too distressed themselves to make use of it, young adolescents in particular can find themselves seeking a 'partner-in-crime' who is covering up equivalent anxieties and is concerned to distract themselves and to deny problems.

Distraction

There are different kinds of distraction, and it is important to distinguish between them. Work can be a distraction from worries or anxieties, but it can also help a young person to deal with them. Kicking a football, playing music, art and writing help children to join with others and express feelings, anxieties or concerns that need expression. Some of these may help a child to feel that their experiences have found a safe place to be held, and then, through whatever medium, to change. A sense of mastery or control in an uncontrollable world can be restored by learning how to control a ball, a team, a paintbrush or an instrument. For this to help, a child needs sufficient trust in the adults around to learn from them and to cope with the frustrations of learning. Believing that every mistake is a sign of being 'useless' (or 'crap' or whatever insult is in use locally) is not conducive to learning or becoming good at anything.

More anti-authority forms of distraction, such as graffiti, street fighting, mugging or 'bunking off' school, may make a statement about existence, about making a mark on the world, about being noticed, together with a challenge, with aggression, anger or violence. These may be used by children whose families are too preoccupied, perhaps with an illness, to notice a boy of a certain age except insofar as they want him to help them. Drugs, of course, allow feelings to be extinguished as far as possible. The distraction value of a fight can be considerable; unfortunately, it may create more problems and have to be repeated. Winning a fight, however reassuring at the time, can lead to anxieties that the loser will demand a return match which may produce the opposite result. Real anxieties involving despair about life, existence, care and value may be evoked by fighting, but never fully overcome.

I am not sure what role the internet plays here. Clearly it can be used to make other people feel under threat, disturbed and distressed. It can also provide some companionship of a particular kind. Computer games can allow a child feelings of mastery and pleasure; they may or may not lead to real social interaction. Troubled children are particularly at risk from internet predators who may present themselves as able to 'fill a gap' left by absent or distressed or ill parents: the predators' warnings 'not to tell' resonate with such children's fears about worrying their parents.

Some of these forms of distraction at times will simply cover up distressed feelings; some will allow them to be expressed and worked through. Some will create bad feelings in others, with an outcome which depends on society's response. Some, perhaps by alerting the attention of someone who can help, will allow bad feelings to be owned, acknowledged, recognised and reduced. Some can bring a troubled child into conflict with authority figures who oblige by behaving like a bad, dangerous father-figure against whom the child can fight. There can be reassurance for a child in discovering there are limits to how much damage they are allowed and able to do.

Distraction techniques, particularly those that result in a fight or in serious risk-taking, can also be used to hide suicidal feelings. Internet gaming can be used in this way too. A child who fears a parent is going to die may be particularly at risk of dangerous behaviour in real life, as well as in imagination. They may eventually be picked up and helped by some agency, but they are more likely to be blamed and threatened for 'disturbing the peace' of those around them.

If a child has a good internal parent-figure who encourages and supports their endeavours, they may find pleasures in life and work which help them and bring good meaning and significance into their lives. For these children, distractions (such as a game of football, or a playdate) may indeed give them temporary respite from troubles at home. If their external or internal parents are less encouraging, less supportive, ordinary distractions may not be sufficient: they may seek more exciting (and therefore more dangerous) ones. Teachers or other relatives, friends of the family or the families of friends, or club leaders can play a significant part in creating or sustaining a good internal parent-figure. Therapy and counselling can sometimes help put people back into contact with a previous good parent-in-the-head.

Society, however, often fails to provide help and support to children who are vulnerable. Many adults felt they 'had to' suppress their own dependent, vulnerable selves when they were small, and they may turn on children who fail to conceal this aspect of themselves in a punitive way, as they turned on themselves when they were small. Punishment rather than understanding may be the best the child can hope for – at least punishment means the child has been noticed and attended to, their existence acknowledged.

Sexual relations with other teenagers

Relations with other teenagers, in which one becomes a confidant or involved in intense relationships, including or not including sex, may serve to distract a teenager from their own anxieties. They may also offer a real opportunity to unburden, to learn from another family's ways, or simply to feel an alternative source of love and affection in which family anxieties can reduce in importance or be put on one side for a while. Choice of partner at this stage may express good feelings about the self, or bad ones. A partner who is chosen mainly as an escape from parents or from loneliness, under the influence of too much anger or of too great unfilled dependency needs, may be a real help in the short term but prove less satisfactory in the long term. However, teenage love is real and can develop into something supportive and lasting.

The risk is that these relationships may become a means of expressing and passing on feelings stirred up by a parent's illness which are related to control, helplessness, cruelty, guilt, betrayal and fear of dying or of losing everything.

Again, what may matter is the quality of the 'parents-in-the-head', which will be determined not only by current family life, but by the whole, life-long relationship with the parents, real and imaginary. It is also influenced by the child's own character and resources, both internal and external. Good, life-enhancing internal parents may enable a young person to find good relationships, whether sexual or not; threatening or damaging or cruel internal parents may lead to a young person finding a partner who on some level reflects the risk of damage and cruelty. A parent who survives an illness may provide a basis for a better internal parent-figure than one who disappears. When the real parent is not there, the child's own emotions, judgements, beliefs and anxieties, unmodified by the real, living parent, can form the basis of many internal versions of the missing parent; and it is these (conscious or unconscious) fantasy figures which may govern choice of partner.

CHILDREN SUPPORTING ADULTS

Children may also be called upon to be a confidant to a parent or step-parent who is deeply anxious about the loss of their partner and apparently unaware of the child's own anxieties. From the child's point of view, this may seem at first perfectly fine: it can be flattering to be considered worthy of confidences; it can make the child feel grown up and responsible and proud of themselves. However, after a time, or when the child grows into an adult and realises the cost to their childhood, it may feel more of a burden.

> *'How could she put all her problems onto me?! I was only a child! She treated me as if I was her therapist! It wasn't fair! I used to end up worrying about her all the time.'*

> *'I never knew what she'd be like when I came home from school. I used to dread walking in the front door. She could be completely fine, or she could be in floods of tears and I'd have to sit with her for hours. It was worst when she talked of killing herself. I had to watch her pills.'*

> *'When I was about 12 my sister-in-law used to talk to me about my brother, about how awful he was. When I grew up I wanted to talk to her about my problems, but she didn't want to know. I don't speak to her now.'*

Children can be very worried about vulnerable parents, and feel that their support of the parent is a matter of life or death. The level of anxiety the child is asked to bear can be enormous. The adults may be totally unaware of what they are doing to the child.

> *'I feel my childhood was taken away. I had to look after her. Nobody looked after me.'*

Children who become 'parentified' can lose touch with their own childishness and appear more grown up than they are. They can also give the impression of a 'false self'; scared to show their own vulnerable and dependent self, they cannot be 'real'. Others detect this, and while some will be attracted, others will be made uncomfortable.

'I'm no good!'

Hidden underneath a competent exterior, a child of ill parents may secretly feel they are no good. This can be partly because of their own lack of ability to make the parent better, partly in identification with a parent they secretly feel is lacking something. Unable to confess such feelings, for fear of hurting their parents or of having the feelings confirmed, these thoughts may remain exaggerated.

'You are/I am no good to anyone!'

'I'm/You're useless!'

'Nobody likes you/me!'

'Nobody likes me' may be an expression of a shameful belief that 'I think my behaviour/my soul/my secret self stinks and everyone knows it!' Adults remember some of their 'stinking' thoughts on being told a parent was about to die, or in reaction to their illness.

> *'When they told me my mother was dying, I thought, I will get her jewellery box! I felt so ashamed afterwards that I refused to take it, I didn't want it.'*

> *'Sometimes I wished she would die. I still feel terrible about that.'*

> *'I should behave better, then she'd be ok.'*

> *'It's my fault he's in hospital.'*

> *'I should give up my life for her. I don't want to. If I was a good child I would...so I'm bad.'*

> *'I hate the smell in her room, I don't want to go in. How can I feel like that about my own mother?'*

> *'I don't like being left alone with her. She might die.'*

Dependency needs

Awareness of dependency needs may not be comfortable for a child who is being exhorted to 'grow up' and become 'more independent', to go on holiday with the school, to stay overnight at friends in order to give a stressed parent a break. Other children their age may be more comfortable with leaving their parents overnight; they are perhaps less frightened that they will return to a disaster, to hospitalisation or to a new symptom or new deterioration. The child may not dare leave their mother overnight for fear she may die or become more ill; however unrealistically, children can feel that they are more in control if they are there, somehow, perhaps magically, to prevent the disaster. How can they confess such fears? Even though this fear actually implies that the child is feeling more like a parent, to the child or to others it might look like being 'babyish'. The thought that the child might want a parent's comforting presence at times, or want to tell them something interesting, funny or upsetting, might itself be distressing if the child is afraid the parent is too ill to be told.

Children sometimes cling to parents when they are secretly very angry with them; afraid that their explosive anger could actually kill them, they may need to keep a close eye on their parents to ensure they have survived. Melanie Klein wrote about such a child (Richard) in *Narrative of a Child Analysis* (Klein 1975); I look at this in more detail in a paper called 'The role of a parent's illness in the emotional experience of a child' (Segal 1998). Richard's mother had been in a road accident when he was two, and he told Klein about it in his first session with her, when he was 10 years old. His enormous anxieties about his aggression were symbolised by his worry that the earth and Jupiter would be destroyed by the sun. His clinging irritated both his parents.

Adults may know they will miss a mother or father when they lose them; young people may not want to think about such things. Consciously, young people may be more preoccupied with getting away and 'living their own lives'. To be forced to recognise how much such plans depend on parents (and not only 'in-their-heads') is not comfortable and may feel shameful. To leave a functioning parent behind is not the same as leaving a parent who says 'How can I manage without you?' Almost as hard may be the conflict if the parent says 'You go' when the child knows or believes that the consequences for the parent's care will be considerable – perhaps even life-or-death.

Difficulties separating from an ill parent, both practically and emotionally, may mean that career choices are governed by the need to stay at home or nearby, or to sacrifice some aspect of the child's life or career in order to take responsibility for an ill parent. The parent may not want this, but children do not always ask the parent, relying on their knowledge of the needs and desires of the parent-in-their-head, who may be less resourceful than the real one.

Need for help with the ill parent

When a child feels they have to care for a parent who cannot manage, they may feel too small, too weak, not knowledgeable enough, and may desperately want to unload the job onto an adult who could do it better. (Rowling's Harry Potter, Tolkien's Frodo Baggins, and Peter, the oldest boy in *The Lion, the Witch and the Wardrobe*, all express this feeling very powerfully, if symbolically, as they try to save a mother-world.) Unlike an adult novelist, a child may be quite unable to verbalise this feeling and may only know how to pass the feeling itself on to another person, adult or child. Relations between siblings in this situation are not always supportive: they may include forms of bullying which make a sibling feel too small, too weak, not knowledgeable enough, and in desperate need of an adult who is not there. While bullying in this way, the bully themselves, for a moment, may feel in control, strong and powerful – though later they may feel bad about what they have done. These episodes may then contribute to feelings of being bad and in need of adult help and control – or to a decision to get away from home as soon as possible.

Steven, aged 14, mugged a younger child. The counsellor asked him what he thought the child would have felt and he said 'frightened'. The counsellor then asked if he ever felt frightened, and he burst out furiously that he was frightened when his mother drove the car last year; he had needed to hold the steering wheel because she was going too fast towards some parked cars, and he had been terrified. She had just laughed at him. Nobody had believed him that there was anything wrong with her. His aunt, listening, paled and said it was true, she hadn't known it was so bad.

As the child grows into an adult, uncertainty about their own goodness, their own capacity and strength, may remain, undermining their self-confidence, even when a child does well by external measures. No longer related to anything obvious in the outside world, these feelings of being useless, weak and, often, bad lurk in children's minds as they grow up, influencing their relationships with partners, employers, friends and with their own children, as well as with their work and their leisure activities. The reason for the feeling is long forgotten but the low self-esteem remains.

Effective support

Children with ill parents can be helped, often by their own parents. In Chapter 9 I looked at the support parents may need in order to be able to provide understanding to their children. Reduction in the parents' own (unrealistic and exaggerated) sense of guilt is often sufficient. Relations with adults who can support them and help them think can mitigate some of a child's anxieties. There are many ways in which they can be helped to express, examine and share their fears, about their parents, about their situation and about themselves, in a sufficiently safe environment. Once adult support has been provided, children's own growth processes can take over.

SUMMARY

As a competitor for parents' attention and time, illness may be far worse than the birth of a new sibling. It is noteworthy, perhaps, that the amount of time and effort spent helping children to prepare themselves for a new sibling is seldom mirrored in a similar amount of time and effort spent helping children to cope with parental illness. Mostly, children seem to be left to 'get on with it' on their own.

Even when parents try to think about the impact on their children, they may not know how to help their children without upsetting them, and nobody wants to upset children without being very certain that it is the right thing to do.

Although many children claim that they can manage perfectly well without their parents (and children's fiction is full of examples of children doing just that), the absence of a parent and their attention does count.

Children who 'bring themselves up', or 'find their own solutions', or even 'parent their parents', are likely to have different outlooks on the world, on themselves and on relationships from those who could draw more freely on adult knowledge, adult understanding and (for the lucky few) even adult attention to distressing feelings. A few children may benefit from withdrawal of parental attention (for example, if it was excessive or intrusive or even abusive attention); but many will struggle throughout their lives as a result of decisions made with insufficient knowledge and false, uncorrected beliefs. Some may be left with the conviction that the only way to deal with their own most powerful emotions is by denial, which in adulthood is likely to be assisted by alcohol, drugs, physical or mental illnesses, crime and various forms of risk-taking behaviour. In this they are, I suspect, in much the same position as a large segment of the population. Parental illness is by no means the only reason why people feel their emotions have to be denied.

However, many children of ill parents can, like their peers, find creative and life-affirming ways of dealing with the anxieties aroused by the uncertainties of their childhood. As described earlier, Hannah studied psychology, which helped her to work through some of her childhood feelings: many counsellors and therapists of one kind or another come from such backgrounds. Anxieties which are too strong can lead to despair, denial and destructiveness, but anxieties which are bearable (for example, as a result of real understanding and support from somebody, perhaps much later in life) can be a spur and motivation for achievement and creativity.

CHAPTER 11

Relations with Professionals

'My GP doesn't know much about it, not many people have my condition. The trouble is, I don't really have a GP any more, only a group, and it depends which one I get.'

'They never send the same person [as a professional carer] so you have to tell them from the beginning each time. By the time I've told them, I might as well have done it myself. I've asked but they take no notice.'

'My GP is really good now; he asks about me first and I can tell him. The other one never asked about me, he just wanted to know how my husband [seriously ill and disabled with a long-term chronic disease] was.'

'I couldn't see anything to suggest which she wasn't already doing. So I gave her a couple of addresses. But she didn't want me to come again. I think she felt I was criticising her, and I suppose I was looking for something to criticise in order to be of help to her. If she was doing everything already there wasn't anything I could offer. And I did want to offer her something. I felt so sorry for her, sort of overwhelmed myself, really, at how much she was doing for her daughter.'
'Did you tell her you thought she was doing a good job?'
'Oh. No, I didn't. I don't know why I didn't. I suppose I couldn't quite believe it was true, it all looked too perfect. And she was up from six in the morning until late at night taking care of her daughter. She didn't take any time out for herself at all. I sort of felt it wasn't healthy.'

'They scream at each other all the time. It's really uncomfortable going in there.'

'She told me to get out: I was just upsetting her. She had spent the last half hour telling me she couldn't walk any more and I said perhaps we should think about ways she could manage without walking. She was furious.'

INTRODUCTION

Illness and new disabilities create new relationships involving professionals. As with any relationship, they may seem irrelevant, of little interest as long as they deliver whatever is required, or they can be life-affirming and a source of pleasure. Particularly if an illness goes on for a long period, relations with professionals may become a significant part of everyday life, and losing the relationship can, for some, be almost as distressing as a divorce. On the other hand, sometimes these relationships can be painful for all concerned. Little choice may be involved. For patients, choosing or changing doctors or other professionals may not be easy, and the new one might be worse. Professionals may have no choice over which patients they see: they have to deal not only with their clients or patients, but also the expectations put upon them by their employers, who may not be directly their clients. The interests of all three may conflict.

I described before how, working as a counsellor with adults who as children felt they had to look after ill parents, I found myself coming out of sessions feeling I wasn't up to my job: I really needed someone else to take over; I was lacking competence, strength and knowledge, and needed help. After a time I recognised that this was something like these clients had felt when they were looking after their parent: too small, in need of an adult who would know more and do more. When I took it back into the session, these clients were able to talk about how helpless they had felt as children, and how unable to talk about it for fear of losing *both* their parents – the ill one because they needed more looking after than the child could give, and the other parent because the child saw them as not coping. I now suspect that, however much this was true, the child's own feelings of not coping were attributed to the carer parent while the child 'had to be strong'. These were grown-up, 'parentified' children whose feelings of being too small for their task were still affecting both them and those around them, including me, as a professional counsellor.

In their training, professionals are encouraged to think about their patients' point of view, less often about carers, and even less to think about their own feelings. Patients and carers, on the other hand, may sometimes be encouraged to think about their own feelings but be totally unaware of what is going on for a professional. This chapter raises issues about the relationship between them and the way this impacts upon each.

WHO ARE THE PROFESSIONALS?

In this chapter I am thinking in the widest sense of those who are paid for caring for people who are not family members: doctors, nurses, physiotherapists, occupational therapists, counsellors, dieticians – anyone working in a team for people with neurological or other illnesses, or amputations or other physical disabilities; also paid carers. Teachers and other people working in schools with children of ill parents may also become involved as 'professionals'.

WHY WOULD ANYONE WANT TO WORK WITH ILL PEOPLE?

As I have repeatedly said, illness makes people feel bad, and this is true for professionals too. So why would someone want to spend their life with ill people? In Chapter 2 I described how in childhood we have phantasies in which we have caused damage to our Good Object, the mother-in-our-head, which we want to repair. It seems that many people are drawn to the work (or stay in it) because they want to mend damage which was 'confirmed' by some significant (and probably relevant) experience in childhood; for example, by having an ill parent. (Choice of profession affects the particular phantasies which are evoked and which may be satisfied.) Although illness makes professionals feel bad, this is outweighed by the highly significant reassurance which can be obtained by seeing people getting better, even if their illness remains. Seeing we can make others feel better in some way reassures us that we are not bad people; whatever we feared in our secret phantasies, we do not simply make other people's lives worse. Economic and other more external, social reasons also play an important part, of course.

Many health professionals depend for their work satisfaction on cures: for others it is sufficient that their client should feel better about themselves, be better able to live with their condition. Those specialising in working with people with neurological conditions have (or learn) a tolerance of people failing to get better.

> 'You work hard with someone to get their walking back, then they go and have a relapse and all your work is undone! You can't help feeling irritated, a bit demoralised; you don't want to give up on them, but when it's happened before it's hard not to. It's easier working with stroke: people get better. With MS you never know if someone is going to get worse again tomorrow or not.'

There is also pleasure in simply being someone who knows and understands. Knowledge and understanding are what primarily distinguish childhood from adulthood: although both are blamed for the fall of Adam and Eve, even in their story, 'real', working adult life, as distinct from total dependence on everything being provided, begins with knowing and understanding. 'Knowing in the biblical sense' means having had sex, and in phantasy the two are strongly linked; there is some kind of deep, whole-body, life-giving satisfaction connected with knowing, which includes much wider 'knowledge of the world' – another euphemism. Working with ill people means that a professional's knowledge and understanding is reassuringly valued and confirmed by clients on a daily basis.

Tolerating 'not knowing' is essential, but can be a struggle for students to learn, partly because *knowing* is so much better. They may have to teach it to their clients and their families too. But again, ultimately there can be satisfaction in the increase in security of understanding when 'not knowing' is admissible.

There is also pleasure in being someone who can be relied upon for someone else's daily existence – for life itself – and being recognised by being paid for such work, although professional carers have a problem in being paid far below their value.

With these motivations, professionals can be quite vulnerable if their work is not good enough. The stakes are high: not only may a patient's life actually be at risk, but both for patient and professional, the phantasies involved include highly significant ones about their place in the world, their 'goodness', their ability to keep alive internal parents as well as their own families – not only in the external world but in their internal world too.

WHY WOULD ANYONE WANT TO SEE A PROFESSIONAL?

Clearly, on a rational basis patients may want to see a professional in order to be made better or to have some help of some kind, or simply to know what is going on with their body or mind. However, there are barriers to overcome.

Any new symptom may be for a long time ignored – 'It's probably nothing', 'It will go away on its own' – before eventually some action is taken. The internet may be a first port of call, or a neighbour, where there is less commitment to taking action if the answer is 'bad'. Professionals may only be called in if a problem has become so bad that it can no longer be hidden from family members, and then only to appease them. People can go to enormous lengths to hide their problems from 'interfering' family members. There may be massive fears, realistic or unrealistic, about what will happen once the professionals do get involved. Not only may the doctor dismiss the patient: 'It's nothing', 'It's because you're a woman' (according to my mother's experience of doctors); or, possibly worse, decide the problem is cancer, not 'nothing'. And everyone has heard of the person who had the wrong leg cut off, or the wrong kidney taken out. Much safer, runs the story, to keep away from doctors and their ilk!

Some people are happy to visit their doctor or to see a healthcare worker who has already been tested out, and who they know will see things 'their way'. Some have other agendas which are nothing to do with symptoms.

A reluctance to 'bother' the doctor can lead to questions being unanswered, to incorrect information being held, to misunderstandings about the nature of the condition, about the way to take medicine, about what can and cannot be done. People develop the most outlandish explanations for their illnesses, and resistance to seeing the doctor can mean that there is no chance to clarify, explore and correct understanding. The chance may not be taken either, if either patient or doctor wants or needs to get away in a hurry (perhaps suspecting that one question too many might lead to a whole lot of cats being let out of the bag), or if either relies too much on their assumptions about how much the other understands.

CONFLICTS

It is clear why there might be conflicts between professionals and clients and their families. Any kind of diagnosis or test can evoke conflicting feelings in the client: all the desire to find out more may be attributed to the professional, with client and family reluctantly agreeing or actively opposing – until the doctor stops trying, at which point the family or client may suddenly discover they *do* want to know, and they want to know why the doctor has not yet found out. It is not at all clear who a disease 'belongs to' in phantasy; somehow not just responsibility but the actual disease itself may be 'handed over'. For a time this can allow the patient to get on with their life, knowing that someone else, not themselves, is taking care of the illness for them. Conflicts may also arise when this no longer works and the patient is forced for some reason to take back ownership and, perhaps, responsibility for symptoms or illness or a disability.

Conflicts may seem to be solved if a patient gets better for any reason; however, in chronic conditions this does not happen.

> 'He still thinks he is going to walk. He's had it explained to him over and over again that he won't, but he won't take it. He won't listen when we tell him how to move himself safely, either, he's fallen so many times. He doesn't remember that he went into hospital because he had a relapse which took him off his feet completely. He couldn't really walk for six months before, but he's forgotten.'

This kind of scenario is painful for professionals as well as for the patient and their family. Even when it is clear that the patient is suffering from thinking, memory and judgement problems arising from their condition, nobody enjoys refusing a request for help. A professional may find it very painful to see how unrealistic the patient is, and dislike becoming the 'baddie' who has to say no. These situations hurt the more when they tap into the professional's own desire to make things better, not to give up. They may sense in the patient an enormous anxiety about being abandoned to the ravages of a destructive disease. Particularly when the patient is around the same age as the professional, or otherwise easy to identify with, professionals may find these situations very uncomfortable. They may respond by sympathising and attempting to evoke a realistic side to the client which can acknowledge loss and grief; some respond by irritation, which may be expressed to the client or may be hidden; some by refusing to answer telephone calls and just waiting until they stop. None of these are entirely satisfactory, for patient or for professional. Such conflicts are part of the trouble with certain illnesses, for certain patients.

It may be when other professionals have given up that professional carers are brought in. They are not expected to cure but they have to watch people living their lives, perhaps in ways which seem quite wrong to them. They may also have to struggle to obtain proper recognition and payment for work which, like that of mothers and those who offer childcare, has undeservedly low status. They have to learn to keep their distance, to be allowed some intimacies and not others; to cope with family carers as well as the client themselves. Their own desires to be someone who knows, or can cure or give advice or solve the client's problems, have to be put on one side, perhaps at the cost of internal conflicts, in order to avoid external conflicts. Particularly experienced, competent professional carers can be enormously valued; so too can inexperienced carers who are happy to learn from their clients. Representing in another way an internal mother-carer, like actual mothers, professional carers can be welcomed with gratitude and hope or be derided, despised and put down.

Where matters of life and death are involved, relationships with professionals can be experienced in a heightened way and they can be extremely rewarding or feel extremely destructive. Internal conflicts involving high stakes can easily slip into external conflicts: one group of professionals set against another; one family member conflicting with another; family against professional, professional against family; the client siding with each alternately, perhaps. It can feel wonderful for a while, to be 'the only one who understands the patient': until the situation changes and the patient suddenly changes sides, or it becomes clear that this understanding is seriously mistaken.

> *'As a first-year student my friends and I picked up a lot of "anti-psychiatry" attitudes, and when one of us became ill and seemed confused and a bit mad we thought she was better off keeping away from doctors. Several of us looked after her ourselves for a few days until she eventually spoke on the telephone to her mother, who fetched her home, took her to the GP and obtained a diagnosis of paratyphoid.'*

PROFESSIONAL ANXIETIES

It may be helpful to distinguish two sources of anxieties for professionals: the physical aspects of an illness, and the psychological. Those who are comfortable dealing with physical aspects sometimes say they don't know what to say to some clients, particularly those who are not going to get better. These professionals, I think, underestimate the value of their understanding and the part they can play in being knowledgeable, supporting grieving, and recognising and acknowledging reality, including realistic hopes and fears.

Psychotherapists and counsellors on the other hand may worry about how to deal with the more physical side of a disability: what to do if a client has a choking fit or an epileptic fit; whether or how to offer help taking off their coat, for example. (In my practice, if a client appears to be struggling to change chairs, to take their coat off or shut the door, I may say, 'I don't know whether you want me to offer to help you or not.' This has the advantage of being true and focusing attention on what is often a significant issue for these clients, which is their relation with others who do not have the same disabilities, the need for assistance and what this means to them and to those around them. This is work they have brought into the room.)

It is clear that an illness can push people into working in areas which are beyond their training and have the potential for unexpected social difficulties – but an illness or disability does this to the person who has it too. If they recognise this, professional and client may be able to share their understanding.

PLANS VERSUS REALITY

For the professional

A physiotherapist, occupational therapist or other member of a rehabilitation team diagnoses a problem, discusses what the patient can do about it and makes suggestions or sets exercises or tasks; knowing what needs to be done, it may be easy to give instructions, and relatively easy to obtain what seems like agreement that the client will comply. A consultant makes recommendations, prescribes medication. A homecare manager is invited to discuss the needs of the patient with their family, and agrees a care package. A counsellor or psychologist agrees to a series of exploratory appointments.

However, as any professional knows, this may be only the beginning of the work. Some patients will do as they are told religiously and may even see some dramatic improvements; they will be appropriately grateful and perhaps even bring a box of chocolates to the department. Many others will not do what they have agreed to do, and this sets a problem. Does the professional chase up the 'failure' of their recommendations? Do they simply say 'It's the patient's responsibility, not mine' and leave it at that? Do they try to find out why the patient did not do what they said they would? Usually there is a requirement for a certain amount of following up, but it may be limited when the problems are complex. In particular, there may or may not be encouragement to ask questions about whether the problem arises from the patient's attitudes or from something in the way the professional made their suggestions.

There are many questions which could be asked. Are the exercises or the changes to behaviour painful or difficult in some other way which the patient hasn't managed to explain? Were the instructions written in a language they could understand? Does the patient prefer to remain the way they are for some reason? Does a client need someone else there while doing exercises? Are they dependent on someone who is ambivalent about taking them for appointments? Do they want more professional time than they are allocated? Is the patient refusing or unable to comply? Is the medication wrong, or does the patient have difficulty taking any medication? Are they being truthful about what they are doing? What is the professional's job here? Where does it stop?

When a patient has neurological problems there is an added level of difficulty for the professional. What about the patient's cognitive capacity? Are they unable to hold instructions, to listen, to remember? Are they depressed? If so, would anti-depressants help or make things worse? Is the patient afraid of losing control of their bladder or bowels while exercising? What is the effect of painkillers or other medication, and the time of day when they are taken? It may be hard to keep all these in mind: easier to allow management to insist 'One missed appointment and you have to go for a new referral', which puts the problem off for another six months. A patient with any of these problems is not going to obtain a new referral immediately, if at all.

To this I would add further questions which many healthcare professionals would also recognise, though they might use different language. Is the patient trying to put off a grieving process by denial, or are they grieving and finding recognition of their disability just now too painful? Will they be better able to face it next week? If they are in denial, *what* is it exactly that they are denying? What needs to change to enable the person to take help from me? Families are often faced with difficulties trying to persuade a reluctant relative to accept help from a carer.

Professionals are supposed to ignore the fact that the person of the therapist is significant: it is not supposed to matter if the therapist changes. But actually, of course, people relate to a person as much as to their profession. Someone who likes his or her therapist may be more keen to 'do their homework' for someone who has slipped into ready-made phantasies derived from parents or teachers who were liked and whose encouragement was helpful. Judging as much from their own inner worlds as the professional's behaviour, patients may feel that a professional *wants* them to get better.

Most people enjoy satisfying others, particularly if it means doing something good for themselves too. For a few, however, this will be enough to make them want the opposite. For these people, the professional is being seen through phantasies derived from hated teachers or parents, and the patient wants to see them fail. Unpalatable as it seems, many of us can remember something like these thoughts in our worst childhood moments. This means, of course, that we have these phantasies ready to understand – and misunderstand – other people's motivation. However, the therapist may unjustly attribute this to the patient, overlooking another explanation, such as a continence problem which has not been disclosed out of embarrassment. There are also people who cannot bear caring and, like alcoholics, may go out of their way, perhaps successfully, to 'prove' that nobody cares for them. These patients may have a greater effect than their numbers should warrant.

> 'When I'm not busy I think about all the people I've seen recently, and I always remember the ones I've failed with. I hate it when there is no-one in the waiting room.' (It was a GP who said this to me.)

Professionals may also be on the lookout for patients who do not want to get better because they are lonely, or are valuing the support of a predictable relationship, or are just attached to the professional for some other reason which is not in the job description.

On the other hand, patients often fail to keep appointments, and professionals are left with only their own thoughts about why this might be. Phantasies that they have somehow failed the patient, or failed to deal well enough with their condition, can create anxieties; a simple defence is to blame the patient, or 'transport' (which did not arrive on time), or a carer who was more ambivalent or too busy. A culture of 'blame the patient' may loudly assert the value of the professional and their time, in order to deny or distract from an implied low valuation on the service placed by others, including the patient. Neurological services are sometimes considered 'Cinderella services', easily deprived of money, and nobody wants to think too hard about what they can and cannot offer, largely because many neurological conditions cannot be cured but have to be lived with, reproachfully and expensively.

Counsellors and psychotherapists have different ways of dealing with missed appointments. Normally, failure of a client to turn up may be interpreted as 'resistance' to the work: the therapist will recognise how difficult it is for clients to face their own demons in therapy, and they work with this. They expect a certain number of first appointments to be broken. Failure to turn up later on in the contract might imply that the client is not finding it helpful, but it might also mean that the work is 'getting close to the bone' in a client who is ambivalent about wanting change or true recognition of their situation. If the client returned for the next appointment, this would become part of the work, perhaps bringing it to an agreed end; if not, the therapist may be left not knowing what 'went wrong'. They too may have anxieties that their service is actually not as helpful as they would like it to be, which may be increased by a client failing to turn up, when in fact there might be many other reasons. There is a further anxiety which can threaten psychotherapists working with people with physical illnesses if they are new to this work, and that is the feeling that someone who is ill should not be asked to deal with emotional difficulties. A therapist may have to challenge their own assumptions before they can whole-heartedly encourage someone with a serious long-term physical health condition to attend for psychological therapy. 'Counselling', with the implication that it is the person's *situation* rather than *themselves* which will be examined, may feel less threatening.

A psychotherapist, counsellor or psychologist working with one or two people who have chronic conditions may also struggle at first to know exactly how much weight to place on practical reasons clients give for missing appointments. There may indeed be difficulties: an illness may flare up; transport does give problems. But in my experience understanding the realities of these difficulties may throw up relationship or other problems which are actually highly relevant for the work, and clients may find they can arrange to come more regularly as they work on these issues. Even so, they may miss more appointments than other clients and this has to be managed, perhaps with a policy which is different for these clients. Deciding to treat them the same as other clients has important implications which have to be thought through. We find it hard to greet 'ill' people with the same expectations as 'healthy' ones, and yet this is one of the complaints I have often heard: 'I want to be treated just like anyone else!' Chronic illnesses are not the same as flu.

Sexual undertones can complicate relations with carers and other professionals for patients of any age or sexual orientation, and it may be difficult to put these into words if they are a problem. Professionals may have dealt with situations where disinhibition (whether brought on by an illness or as a character trait) brought sexual feelings into the open uncomfortably; they may be sensitised to these and avoid any risk of repetition, or they may feel confident in their ability to recognise and handle any problems. Carers or partners may be afraid 'their' patient will fall in love with their physiotherapist or nurse, but hope they can rely on professionalism to prevent this causing problems. Nurses, of course, represent aspects of an early mother-phantasy, and enter into many conscious fantasies, in childhood or later, supported and underpinned by numerous television series and the occasional real-life example.

Michael was a difficult, very egocentric man diagnosed with a neurological disease in his early twenties. He was told he had only a few months to live. His girlfriend at the time felt she could not leave him in this situation and, under various external pressures, agreed to marry. He continued to live for many years, making increasing demands on his wife. Eventually he fell in love with one of his nurses, and his wife felt able to divorce him with a clear conscience. She lived alone, nearby, and kept an eye on him and on the relationship from a distance.

Death being the other 'unmentionable', it is perhaps worth mentioning the difficulty that many professional health workers have with acknowledging its imminence. In the UK, issues of death and dying in the Health Service (note the name!) have been split off into palliative care teams and Macmillan nurses. Even General Practitioners may have difficulty talking to a patient or carer about the fact that the end is in sight. There is always some intervention which will 'help', which will stave off the end.

'It was obvious he was dying, but nobody would admit it. They kept saying he would get better. They made me feel I was bad even to think it.'

'It wasn't until she went into the Hospice that I found anyone who would talk to me about the possibility of her actually dying.'

'We didn't call the doctor because we thought he would want to take our father into hospital instead of letting him die at home. I now wonder if it would have been easier for us all if we had: he was very agitated, calling out for help; the doctor could perhaps have given him a sedative. The problem is, you don't know which doctor is coming, and what they will do. He didn't ask for a doctor.'

For the patient

For the patient, an appointment may have quite complex implications. It may indeed mean facing up to something very distressing, and it may take several attempts before this is possible. A patient may find it hard to prioritise their own health, or a particular symptom, particularly, for example, if they care for someone else such as a small child or an ageing, demanding parent. Some may place a low value on the service, on the grounds that anything which is free is worthless; others value the service highly and find it difficult to accept they have a right to it. Particularly before attending for the first time, the patient may be far from convinced that the appointment is worth their time and the effort involved in getting there or being there. (Seeing almost anyone else may make a person feel better than seeing the dentist; it is perhaps not surprising that dentists were the first to charge for missed appointments.) Some people see physiotherapists as representing sports teachers from school, and dread being made to feel incompetent, unhealthy, not dynamic enough, too fat. They may be afraid of being bullied or confronted with uncomfortable questions about their diet or their habits, their drinking or smoking or exercising. Any professional may be expected to offer a 'telling off', or instructions which cannot be complied with or which cost money or time. Later appointments may be dreaded or avoided because of exercises not done, or guilt and distress about disappointing the professional – or because of anger towards a professional who was rude or unhelpful or whose suggestions were 'useless' or only marginally effective.

Added to all this, of course, may be many practical difficulties. People with young children may have difficulty arranging childcare, particularly for multiple appointments. The timing of the appointment may not have been made in consultation with the patient. Transport can be a real difficulty; dependence upon others for accompaniment may be real or provide a convincing excuse.

'They took my crutches away when I went into hospital; I was walking when I went in, but when they sent me home I couldn't walk any more. If they'd only give me back my crutches I'd be fine. I just need someone to help me up, then I'm sure I could walk.'

For the patient there are other problems, many of which have been flagged already in previous chapters. Any exercises intended to improve matters involve at the outset recognition of a deficit; this means that some form of grieving process for the loss needs to have begun before remedies can be started. There also needs to be some level of hope. Whether someone will put in a huge effort will depend on their personal levels of optimism, which may be modified by interaction with professionals (or others) or may be too firmly entrenched to shift either way.

Deteriorating neurological conditions may require considerable input. People may need support with thinking about their condition, about themselves, about their children and their partners or families or their living arrangements. They may need help with decision-making, for example about medication. They may need regular physiotherapy exercises which might involve another person or equipment: perhaps nursing, perhaps a bed which will prevent pressure sores, or wheelchairs or crutches, for example. There may be new accommodation issues which take time to sort out. All of this is expensive, and even with the NHS it is not unlimited; while private health insurance does not normally pay out for 'pre-existing conditions', which means anything diagnosed more than a year ago. In other countries there can be enormous problems of finance.

People can feel guilty for using free services provided for them, particularly when newspapers have exploited sensational stories of misuse, exaggerating and extrapolating from one miserable case. They can feel guilty that they are on benefits and at risk of being labelled, by themselves at any rate, as 'scroungers'. It is surprisingly easy to 'forget' that it is an illness which is stopping you working, on the days when you have become so used to your symptoms that you do not think about them. On these days, however few they are, fantasies of returning to work feed guilt about taking benefits. The fact that symptoms regularly return can be temporarily forgotten.

Patients, carers, family members, professionals and financial considerations come into conflict when decisions have to be made about when to end treatment or stop medication if there has not been a full recovery. Patients and their families can feel abandoned; the point at which a rehabilitation team withdraws is the point at which a family may have to recognise that there will be limits to the improvement in the patient. Understandably, they may resist this, and somebody may have to deal with their reactions. The patient or their family may be angry that the free or insurance-paid service has been taken away. The idea that further improvement might be possible, but judged too slow or too unlikely, may be read as 'You are not worth it', or 'Your mother/ father is not worth it', with all the implications this has for the family's internal worlds.

At this point, perhaps worse conflicts can arise between family members who want the family to pay for more support and those who want to hold onto the money. Families then interpret each other's willingness or reluctance to pay themselves or to use someone else's money to pay with: readiness to pay reflects the value put on the person's rehabilitation; the hopes that the treatment will be effective; the desire to prove or demonstrate care for the ill person; the anxiety that someone does not care enough; the desire to demonstrate that someone else does or does not care enough – the list goes on.

Decisions about medication raise similar questions. When the earliest medications for MS came on the market they seemed to me singularly ineffective, offering far more unrealistic hope than change in disability. In the USA, some of the huge churches were funding this medication for members of their congregation, although the members of the church were amongst the lowest paid of the community. The main beneficiaries, to my mind, were the investors in drug companies, although I am sure the givers were also very happy to give and the recipients enormously happy to feel and be so supported and loved. There are risks to exaggerating the value of a drug, but it seems companies are prepared to take the risk. However, new medications for MS seem more effective, though there may still be complex questions about cost and who should pay.

(I am for some reason reminded of Magritte's painting of a pipe, titled 'Ceci n'est pas une pipe' ('This is not a pipe'). Is a foot just a foot, or a leg just a leg? I suspect not. A damaged foot is a sign of a damaged person. A foot may stand for a penis, for power, for life-as-we-know-it, for the capacity to create and enjoy life. Bodies have sexual symbolism which extends far beyond the genitals. Unlikely as it might seem, I think decisions about whether to continue treatment are coloured by such symbolism, and not only when money comes into the equation.)

For the organisation

Working in the NHS until 2008 I was struck by many aspects of organisational denial towards the effects of long-term neurological conditions. For example, I worked for a 'rehabilitation' team, when many of my clients were never going to get back to work; what they needed was long-term support living with a deteriorating chronic illness. They did not require 'independent living', but a mature adult dependence on good services. Supporting someone who is physically deteriorating but not going to die in the near future is expensive, and once financial considerations come into play, neurological patients are a massive problem for an organisation. During a reorganisation in my last years in the NHS I constantly reminded the managers that the needs of neurological patients were being ignored; that, for example, a requirement that someone 'showed measurable improvement' meant making ineligible those whose disabilities were simply being helped to remain stable rather than get worse. I was told that these patients would be considered 'later'; ten years later, these patients are still waiting.

Cognitive problems were also an issue – some patients had serious memory problems. Officially, this could not be taken into consideration. Patients 'had to' be sent back to their GPs if they missed two appointments, later even one, regardless of the difficulties neurological patients had in accessing their GPs: difficulties involving making telephone calls (problems with their hands, or with speech, with the presence of a carer affecting times they could make calls), requiring assistance to move outside the house, or remembering what they were supposed to be doing, as well as suffering the disruptive effects of neurological fatigue or depression.

Even on a practical level there was denial. A window had to be replaced in the front door of the MS clinic, and I was not allowed to insist that it was replaced at a level which would allow people in wheelchairs to open the door themselves; it was put in for the convenience and safety only of people who could walk.

Later, when staff were forced to write their notes in their cars instead of returning to the office after seeing patients at home, there was massive denial of the importance of talking to colleagues, for ensuring good teamwork, for maintaining morale in the face of often depressing experiences and for mutual support.

When work is closely controlled and systematised, perhaps 'for financial reasons', some of the less obvious aspects of the job which make it enjoyable, or even just bearable, may be lost. Time 'chatting' is seldom valued. 'Chatting' allows information to be passed on, other people's experiences to be used and dissected for use in the future. It can build trust and allow people to assess others' levels of responsibility, reliability and judgement. Some large organisations nowadays build in opportunities for staff to bump into one another and to chat, recognising that this can encourage new ideas and innovation. My suspicion is that healthcare organisations do not currently give this any priority, seeing chat as simply a distraction from work or a hindrance to getting a task done (which it might also be, of course, at times). Perhaps because levels of anxiety are high, paranoid-schizoid processes may come into play, involving high levels of control. This does not make for good relations within work, and unfortunately, good relations with patients, and good care for patients, depend on staff feeling well supported and cared for by the hierarchy above them.

Isabel Menzies-Lyth wrote about organisational denial in hospitals in her ground-breaking paper 'Social systems as a defence against anxiety' (1960).

WHAT DO PROFESSIONALS DO FOR CLIENTS? COVERT ASPECTS OF THE RELATIONSHIP

Relations between professionals and clients involve both overt and covert elements. On the surface, the physiotherapist, occupational therapist and speech therapist, or whoever, is there to perform some task. They may be expected to set a goal and to work with the client until that goal is achieved. They are then expected to discharge the client and move on to another. However, other aspects of the relationship may be in fact very important. These may actually determine how many appointments are made and kept; how much of the overt work is achieved. Significant work which is not part of the goal may actually take place too. (I remember early on in my work a client telling me that since she had been coming for counselling she had given up smoking. I had not known she smoked.) These aspects of the professional relationship may be acknowledged or ignored. Managers of services may or may not know about these aspects of the relationship and may or may not value them.

Containing anxieties: the importance of being there

By representing and evoking unconscious phantasies of a mother-in-the-head or father-in-the-head, a therapist may awaken in the client memories or feelings attached to being cared for and being safe. This feeling itself can be prized; it can feel a relief from otherwise semi-permanent anxieties or loneliness. This formulation makes it clear that people who have had bad experiences in the past with care-givers may react differently to therapists from those who have had good ones. For those who had very bad experiences as small children, an initial idealisation may not quite ring true and may turn into a denigration.

Just as a small child is more able to take their first steps when in the company of someone who knows and loves them, so an adult who finds difficulty walking may feel safer in the presence of a physiotherapist. In the presence of my singing teacher I sing better than I do alone. The simple presence of the therapist may enable someone to feel empowered and actually to be more capable than they would on their own. 'You don't need to worry, I'll catch you if you fall' works on many levels. Bad thoughts too may also be tolerated if someone is there to hear them. There may be a real sense of 'handing over' a worry, of the worry being 'held' by the other person, which can free up the capacity to think more clearly about other issues. Verbalising 'I'm a bad mother' may be a first step towards realising that there is more to motherhood than cooking and cleaning and fetching from school; until it has been verbalised to someone else it may remain an unquestioned conviction. Anxieties can be *contained*, in the sense that they gain boundaries; they lose some of the paranoid-schizoid 'going-on-for-ever' characteristic. When someone else says 'You're afraid you're going to lose everything, your whole life', the fear loses some of its force. When someone else can name and 'hold' anxieties, space may be found in the mind for new thoughts such as 'How are we going to deal with this?'

Familiarity

Whereas illness and disability are new to the client, they are old news to the experienced therapist. The therapist accepts them in the client as part of everyday life; they are not shocked or surprised or taken off guard or off balance, as the client may be from moment to moment. There is a reassurance in being in the presence of someone who can recognise the condition, even if they do not fully understand it. 'There's a lot of it about' or 'Oh yes, that's your Parkinson's' may be reassuring, though on a rational level people may not understand quite how this works. I think it represents a sense that the professional has a picture of the condition in their mind, and a picture of the person who has it too, and that these pictures are acceptable, recognisable, normal, tolerable; whereas in the client's mind (and in the minds of others they meet) this picture of themselves and their symptoms has been unacceptable, unrecognisable, abnormal, intolerable. In the presence of the experienced professional the client's picture of themselves can take on a different emotional colouring, a different value. (This is an example of the 'containing' function which I described in Chapter 2. The therapist's capacity to accept the condition or situation without panic is 'taken in' by the client, who then feels differently about it.)

Familiarity means that a carer may already know the kinds of things which irritate people with disabilities; they may know how to offer help without sounding patronising or implying that someone doing something for themselves, slowly, should be hurried. They may even know that everyone reacts differently to being offered help; that everyone wants their tea or coffee slightly differently, the way *they* want it, not the way the carer would drink it. Familiarity probably means that the carer has been 'burnt' in the past by upsetting clients or families, and is aware of how to avoid repeating the same mistakes. (Like anyone else, however, they may well make new ones.)

Professional carers who specialise in working with people who have particular conditions can develop familiarity with these conditions, even if they do not have technical knowledge, and this can contribute to their presence being comforting and a real help.

Understanding

Understanding goes further than familiarity, and professional health workers often, in my experience, undervalue their contribution to the clients' welfare by the fact of their understanding. Clients are far more likely to value a professional's understanding than to take note of advice. Understanding offers a sense of being in control, even if the condition cannot be controlled. A professional who (in the client's head at least) has some true, reliable knowledge, awareness and understanding of what is going on currently, and of what the future holds, is someone to hold onto while the client feels 'at sea'; a buoyancy aid, who might even steer the boat into a safe harbour or at least hold it together while it rides out the storm. A sense of someone understanding links with early feelings towards a Good Object and can evoke calm and peace. It may feel possible either to hand over responsibility, or to think sensibly, sharing responsibility with an understanding person.

When a professional understands, or gives the impression of understanding, even in a limited way, a client can be less afraid of their own ignorance. Both of these states, understanding and ignorance, may, in the client's mind, be exaggerated by their fears.

Professionals can also misunderstand and offer information which a doctor would not endorse. Even this can at times make a client feel better, by offering a sense of containment of anxieties: 'I'm going to start taking these homeopathic pills my carer recommended – they can't do any harm'; 'If I can solve my problems by going to the gym, I will start now. Well, perhaps tomorrow. But now it's up to me, *I'm* in control...' Religious beliefs help some.

Patience said she didn't know how she would have survived without her church and her religion. 'I know I am in God's hands, I do not need to worry.'

Problems arise when the client has strongly opposing beliefs, or if the sense of control makes them feel more guilty, for example, or if the 'cure' requires money to be spent which the patient does not have: 'Of course I'm still ill, but it's my fault because I don't make the effort/I don't believe enough/I need to buy more medicines off the internet...'

'I have asked them not to send Mary again; she kept praying over me and singing hymns all the time. I told her I didn't believe in God and didn't like it, but she just said God would forgive me. I wanted to hit her.'

Reliability

An unreliable body evokes feelings of instability, anxiety about movement, a need to hold still: if the body is unpredictable, the world itself can feel as if it is suddenly unreliable and unpredictable. When a therapist turns up at the expected time for an appointment, or does what they say they will, this may restore a sense that the world itself is reliable, not so changed. At this point, awareness that it is the person's own body which is unreliable may be more bearable in the knowledge that the containing world is safe after all. A safer world may also be trusted to help in a process of making things better and can support the struggle against the desire to give up.

An unreliable therapist, on the other hand, or one who says s/he has done something which has not been done, may tend to confirm anxieties about the rest of the world and make it harder for the patient to recognise the original location of their problems. Much energy may then be spent fighting the external world. This fight may be both correctly directed and at the same time exaggerated, driven by a desire to rid the self of bad feelings arising from the illness or disability as much as or more than a recognition of the real failings of services. Professionals may be drawn into using this exaggeration to deny their own or their service's actual failures.

Professionals may not recognise the significance to the patient of their own reliability; or may pretend not to in order to minimise their own (perhaps phantasy-driven, exaggerated) guilt.

Confidence

When the world feels unsafe, there may be a temptation, a need, a desire, to hold on tight, both physically and metaphorically. A desperate attempt to prevent further bad change can prevent movement – including movement which might bring *good* change. Holding onto an adult's hand may save a child's life – but if the child could never let go, that life would never develop. Holding onto an idea of being young and beautiful and physically perfect may be good when this is true, but being unable to let it go may condemn the person to an existence like Miss Havisham's, locked in a room with a decaying wedding banquet, torturing those around her, totally unable to build a new life based on more substantial pleasures. Faced with the need to learn to walk on an artificial leg, or to live with a life-threatening illness, an illusion of being whole and perfect has to give way.

A helping hand at this time can provide confidence in the new self – someone else who believes that it is possible may enable the person to 'move on' in a way they cannot on their own.

Hope

The presence of a reliable therapist offers, above all, hope. Further appointments mean the client knows that they need not 'give up'; they 'haven't been given up on'. Somebody still cares. They may feel anxious about satisfying the therapist, but even these anxieties may be preferable to a feeling of certainty that nobody cares any longer what happens to them.

The hope that a therapist offers is not just the realistic 'If you do what I say you will feel better' kind. Unconsciously it can involve far more infantile phantasies in which the whole world will be restored: 'Everything will be just as it was before.' The therapist can slip into paranoid-schizoid idealisations, becoming an 'angel' – which can easily flip into a 'devil', perhaps to be replaced by a new 'angel'. The hope may be that 'The therapist will make me better without me having to do any work!', but behind an idealisation there is always a persecuting fear: in this case there may be many, such as 'The therapist will make me worse!', 'I will never be as good again!', 'The therapist will make me do loads of work and it won't help at all!', 'I'd be much better off if they just didn't touch me, if they left me to myself.' There are real possibilities that some kinds of therapy, including medicines, can make people feel worse, or develop pains or other, worse symptoms: these contribute to anxieties which have a more primitive base, where 'good' and 'worse' include moral as well as physical concerns. A good therapist, or successful therapy, may help a client to disentangle these anxieties or to move towards a more, rather than less, encouraging phantasy.

Anxieties about therapy making people worse often underlie placatory attitudes from clients, a too-quick agreement, which is going to be followed by ignoring the advice offered. The sense that hope will be taken away has both realistic and unrealistic aspects: unrealistic hopes are under threat when a professional comes in; more realistic hopes may be rejected because they are not hopeful enough. The fact that illness makes people feel bad means that recognising the extent and limits of the illness may include many bad feelings. When grieving processes are not understood or recognised, or where some kind of projective identification is going on, both therapist and client may fear that these bad feelings will last for ever; however, the therapist's awareness that people do learn to cope with their condition can help mitigate the client's fears.

Many people have learnt over their lifetime that reality is preferable to living in cloud-cuckoo land, and when a therapist has to take away unrealistic hopes a client may respond with relief at giving up a losing battle. It is unlikely that such an idea truly comes 'out of the blue'. Most people will have played with ideas such as: things might get worse, nobody lives for ever, disabilities or illness could happen to me; at least I'm alive, and I'm going to enjoy life until I die! Some have been expecting to be told they are dangerously ill all their lives.

Negotiating the change from unrealistic to more realistic hopes is part of a therapist's task which may be recognised overtly, depending on the quality of the contract between therapist and their employer.

Chat

Professional carers assisting an elderly or young disabled person with daily life may be told whether their job includes 'chatting', perhaps by another name, or whether it is to be considered a waste of time or a distraction from the task. Chatting keeps people up to date and involves them in the lives of others; it allows them to feel they belong to the world and make up part of it. It also 'takes them out of themselves', bringing to an end, if only for a while, unhelpful ruminations about themselves, their lives or their bodies. Loneliness is a risk factor for dying earlier; social contact keeps people alive (Holt-Lunstad *et al.* 2015).

Some clients enjoy chatting; others resist it, or are very choosy about who they will chat to. Social hierarchies play a part. Being 'forced' to talk to someone they would never have met in their previous lives can imply 'social death' one way or the other; chatting can involve a relationship in which there is jockeying for place in an imaginary power-play. It offers opportunities to compare oneself and one's life with that of others; it can be enormously pleasurable but it can also be disturbing and distressing, particularly if long-held defences are threatened.

Chat can be a valuable pleasure for both professional and client, but it can be put under threat by certain (iniquitous) contracts which insist, for example, that travel time is not included for professional carers, who are thereby forced to pay for their own or to cut time with clients.

'She makes me feel important; she's always got time for me.'

'She wants to talk about her family; I don't mind, I enjoy hearing about it. I sometimes wish she'd do a bit more cleaning though.'

'He's always pleased to see me; he wants to show me his model trains. I just can't get him to do his exercises.'

'I like working with Ann, she's always ready for me; she won't take phone calls when I'm there, she says "My therapist is here, I'll call you back." She really appreciates the work we do.'

'I'm never quite sure he knows what I've come for. He'll ask me to do little jobs for him before I go and I don't like to refuse.'

In a private healthcare setting, 'bedside manner' (which may involve chatting) is known to be important: it may actually affect income by determining whether a client is willing to continue paying for the service or not. In a setting where payment depends on someone else other than the client, bedside manner may be valued less and the capacity to tick a box which says 'task done' may be more valued.

Counsellors and psychotherapists with psychodynamic (or certain other) backgrounds do not 'chat' with clients (though they need supportive conversations from colleagues sometimes). With clients they work tightly within the time they are given, and consider any supposed 'chat' from the client as part of the information the client is bringing to the session. (So, for example, someone who arrives saying they are 'exhausted', or 'how cold it is today', may find their therapist takes these as saying something symbolically about how the client is feeling in themselves.)

Receiving projections

One of the things which real-world parents do for their children is to stand for their internal objects. We need representatives in the external world of people and things in our inner world in order to reassure ourselves about what is happening in both. Other people can for a time take over aspects of the self which are difficult to bear: adults represent children's phantasies of their own power, their own aggression and their own potency to make things better ('The power of Grayskull!' as one television cartoon called it). Making the adult represent this aspect of the child allows the child to see it from the outside, to watch how the adult deals with it and to take it back modified.

Professionals too can become the recipient of aspects of clients which the client cannot for the time hold onto. Sometimes an ill person wants someone else to represent their own health and goodness, which they cannot for a while access, and a professional may stand for this. The client 'lights up' when they come into the room: the whole world has not been destroyed by their illness! These clients may enjoy hearing about the professional's holiday, their family, their children, vicariously for a while belonging to a different world.

The presence of a professional in the patient's mind, who represents power, understanding and control to be used for the patient's well-being, can be satisfying for both patient and professional, whether they are present or securely registered in a mobile phone, carried with the patient at all times. Representing such a figure, coloured by childhood phantasies, can boost the professional's own feelings of importance and value in the world; a small amount of exaggeration may not come amiss for a while – until it breaks down.

Feelings conveyed by projective identification are those which resonate for the professional themselves. They feel as if they belong to the professional, *not* the client. Conveyed wordlessly by clients, they can leave a professional feeling bewildered. Symptoms are sometimes evoked in professionals by clients; but other, uncomfortable, feelings can also be evoked.

I described at the beginning of this chapter how the feeling of *being overwhelmed and in need of support* can be picked up by a professional working with a client who desperately needed support in childhood and never received it. Feelings of a *despairing hopelessness*, and a feeling that *it would be better if this client were dead* (which shocked me), have both been evoked in me by clients who were coping with serious illnesses. They were both exaggerated, and the clients almost immediately owned them when I found the courage to ask. Despairing hopelessness was hidden by a bright smile and 'positive thinking'; and the feeling that it would be better if the client were dead was a feeling that the client felt they could never share with anyone. Once the client acknowledged it, I was no longer overwhelmed by it and we could discuss who would miss her, and how they would actually feel. (Typically, people who feel themselves to be a 'burden' have never thought how friends and relatives would *really* feel if they killed themselves, yet they know people who have never got over the suicide of a relative.)

If they do not recognise what is happening, picking up such feelings can contribute to professionals 'burning out'. If an illness evokes despair in patients, the professionals around them may constantly be faced with their own despair; they may react by cutting off their feelings and seeing patients as 'the liver in bed nine' (as Menzies-Lyth described in her 1960 paper). Some organisations deal with the problem by rotating staff on a regular basis so that they do not stay too long in unpopular specialities, of which 'neuro' may be one.

On the other hand, one client regularly made me feel very clever indeed, and I enjoyed this, although I did suspect it was a bit excessive: it turned out she had learnt early on that she had to hide her own intelligence. The return to more normal levels of shared cleverness was a relief, though

I was a bit ashamed of myself for letting an idealisation go on so long. Nurses and other professionals may also enjoy those interactions with patients which leave them feeling special, clever, admired, even if it is in a way which goes further than reality would warrant. Sadly, they may be vulnerable to feeling disappointed and upset if these idealisations break, perhaps for reasons which have little to do with the actual therapist.

Support from colleagues may help, particularly if they know the patients: an older colleague may alert a new member of the team to the likelihood of being 'dropped' by a particular client; though new working practices may reduce availability of such support. In particular, good support can enable professionals to 'take these projected feelings back' to the relationship with the client and use them as communication: 'Is it possible that you sometimes feel…?' Counsellors and psychotherapists have supervisors who may themselves pick up feelings which have been 'passed on' from the client, via the therapist. Supervisors can then help to distinguish whether a feeling which the therapist brings to supervision properly belongs to the client under discussion or simply to the therapist.

A rehabilitation team may provide something of the same containment when all the professionals working with a particular client have similar emotional reactions or similar thoughts about them. It can also happen that professionals find themselves with opposing feelings, and good team support can bring the opposing views together in a way which increases understanding of the client (and the team) rather than feeding conflicts which actually prevent or limit good work being done.

Team discussions and team support groups facilitated by a psychotherapist may provide important opportunities to observe and work with feelings evoked by clients, both positive and negative, for the benefit of all concerned.

PROFESSIONALS' THINKING ABOUT CLIENTS' CHILDREN

Professionals (health professionals; paid carers; teachers) sometimes meet parents who are worried about their children, or they observe children with ill parents who are showing signs of distress. Friends and neighbours (for example, parents of the children's friends) may be in a similar situation. Those who are brought face to face with distressed parents and children may find it very hard to know what, if anything, to do. They may be tempted to take sides with a child against their parents, or vice versa. They may be unclear what their own role could or should be. 'Interference' is generally frowned upon, but ignoring children in distress is not comfortable either. Parental illness, particularly the less visible mental, emotional or cognitive problems, can create moral and ethical conflicts outside the family as well as within it; illness can make everybody feel bad.

For many reasons, professionals generally feel that the problems of their patients' children are best ignored. There are real concerns about not wanting to undermine parents who are already undermined by their health problems. Some professionals are afraid of imposing their own culture-specific views; arguments about whether parents have the right to impose Female Genital Mutilation on their daughters are an extreme example of such conflicts. It is also quite realistically difficult to know at what point intervention would save a life and at what point it would simply make a bad situation worse. Knowledge of history, as well as revelations about current institutions which supposedly provide care, within or outside the home, may increase uncertainty.

> 'They took us from my dad because he was an alcoholic, but they put us into an orphanage which was run by an alcoholic matron. She made me beat my brother. It's more than 60 years ago now, but I've never forgiven her for that.'

Those whose job involves caring for sick or disabled adults may be explicitly told that their job does not include caring for those adults' children. Some even expect help from children, or become annoyed with children who do not offer what they consider sufficient help to a parent.

> 'She expects me to pick up after her kids; it's not right! My job is to look after her, not her great big sons. They leave their books lying on the floor and she wants me to put them away! They should do it themselves, we always had to when we were children.'

'Her daughters are terrible. They just quarrel all the time. It really gets her down. I don't know how they can do it. I'd bang their heads together if they were mine. And they sleep in her bed still. They're much too old for that. Can't they see she's not well, she needs to be left alone.'

Parents can (quite reasonably) get very angry if others try to tell them their business, and even a simple question about the children can be interpreted badly by a paranoid parent. Teachers, whose job does concern children directly, may hesitate to interfere in any way with an illness which is a family matter, and about which they know little or nothing, even if they do know that a parent is ill (which they might not).

However, professionals can sometimes be asked for help by parents; and they may be in a position to do something to help children with ill parents, either *through* the parents or (more problematically) *in spite of* the parents. They may be able to provide helpful literature, links to websites or other information about the parents' illness directed at children; or they may be able to refer to a young carer's scheme or a school counsellor. Any attention and emotional support which can be offered to parents and which they can use, either directed at their own anxieties about their or their partner's health, or aimed at facilitating thinking about the children, may indirectly help the children too.

Circumstances can make it very hard sometimes to see what action a professional could or should take, particularly if the parent is reluctant to call in help for an obviously distressed child. If a GP or other therapist insists on a referral to social services, their own relationship with the parent is under threat. Child Guidance clinics may only offer a service for children who show gross signs of disturbance, and may not be funded to provide any kind of preventative work, or to help with anxieties which children are currently hiding. Even referral to a school counsellor (if there is one) may require permission from a parent who is too afraid of what might be revealed. The reality is that children whose own parents cannot help them may be abandoned by others too.

Some of these issues are taken up in my co-authored book, *Helping Children with Ill or Disabled Parents* (Segal and Simkins 1996).

SUMMARY

Professional relations with people who have long-term chronic or deteriorating health conditions are complex; sometimes very satisfying, they may require a high level of tolerance for clients failing to get better. Conflicts can easily arise between management, professionals, family, carers and the person with the condition. Professionals can play a significant part in the internal world of the client, whatever their actual role in the external world. They may also have to cope with difficult feelings which the client cannot bear.

Illness makes people feel bad, and this applies to professionals too. In spite of their best efforts, there will be times when they feel bad about themselves and their work. With good support they may be able to translate this into understanding and support for their clients.

References

Atkinson, R. (2007) 'Do I want my sight back?' *Guardian*. Available at www.theguardian.
com/lifeandstyle/2007/jul/17/healthandwellbeing.health, accessed on 3 February
2017.

Barnes, J. (2008) *Nothing to Be Frightened Of.* London: Cape.

Barthes, R. (1981) *Camera Lucida: Reflections on Photography.* New York: Hill and Wang.

Bechara, A., Damasio, H., Tranel, D., and Damasio, A. (1997) 'Deciding advantageously
before knowing the advantageous strategy.' *Science* 275, 1293–1295.

Carroll, L. (1865) *Alice's Adventures in Wonderland.* London: Macmillan.

Dahl, R. (1960) *Kiss Kiss.* New York: Alfred A. Knopf.

Dahl, R. (1975) *Danny the Champion of the World.* London: Jonathan Cape.

Flatley, J. (2015) *Violent Crime and Sexual Offences – Intimate Personal Violence and
Serious Sexual Assault. Findings from the 2013/14 Crime Survey for England and
Wales and Police Recorded Crime over the Same Period on Violent Crime and Sexual
Offences.* London: Office for National Statistics. Available at www.ons.gov.uk/
peoplepopulationandcommunity/crimeandjustice/compendium/focusonviolent
crimeandsexualoffences/2015-02-12/chapter4violentcrimeandsexualoffencesin
timatepersonalviolenceandserioussexualassault, accessed on 3 February 2017.

Freud, S. (1917) 'Mourning and Melancholia.' In *The Standard Edition of the Complete
Psychological Works of Sigmund Freud, Vol. XIV.* Trans. James Strachey. London:
Hogarth Press and the Institute of Psychoanalysis, 1975.

Furman, E. (ed.) (1974) *A Child's Parent Dies: Studies in Childhood Bereavement.* New
Haven, CT: Yale University Press.

Guardian (2006, 22 November) 'The HIV nurse's tale: Julia.' Available at www.
theguardian.com/society/2006/nov/22/health.aids2, accessed on 3 February 2017.

Holt-Lunstad, J., Smith, T.B., Baker, M., Harris, T., and Stephenson, D. (2015) 'Loneliness and social isolation as risk factors for mortality: a meta-analytic review.'
Perspectives on Psychological Science 10, 2, 227–237.

Johnson, J. (2009) *Shrinking the Monster.* Republished 2014 as *Shrinking the Smirch: A Practical Approach to Living with Long Term Health Conditions.* Milton Keynes: Speechmark.

Klein, M. (1940) 'Mourning and its Relation to Manic-Depressive States.' In *The Writings of Melanie Klein: Love, Guilt and Reparation and Other Works 1921–45.* London: Hogarth Press and Institute of Psychoanalysis, 1975.

Klein, M. (1975) *Narrative of a Child Analysis. The Writings of Melanie Klein, Vol.IV.* London: Hogarth Press and Institute of Psychoanalysis.

Krahé, C., Drabek, M.M., Paloyelis, Y., and Fotopoulou, A. (2016) 'Affective touch and attachment style modulate pain: a laser-evoked potentials study.' *Philosophical Transactions of the Royal Society of London B: Biological Sciences 371.* Available at http://rstb.royalsocietypublishing.org/content/371/1708/20160009, accessed on 3 February 2017.

Lewis, C.S. (1955) *The Magician's Nephew.* London: The Bodley Head.

McEwen, E. (1985) *The 36 Hour Day.* London: Hodder & Stoughton with Age Concern.

Menzies-Lyth, I. (1960) 'Social systems as a defence against anxiety: an empirical study of the nursing service of a general hospital.' Republished in Menzies-Lyth, I. (1988) *Containing Anxieties in Institutions.* London: Free Association Books.

Milne, A.A. (1924) 'Disobedience.' In A.A. Milne, *When We Were Very Young.* London: Methuen.

Perreault, S. (2009) *Criminal Victimization and Health: A Profile of Victimization Among Persons with Activity Limitations or Other Health Problems.* Canadian Centre for Justice Statistics. Statistics Canada, Catalogue No. 85F0033M. Available at www.statcan.gc.ca/pub/85f0033m/85f0033m2009021-eng.pdf, accessed on 3 February 2017.

Rieff, D. (2008) *Swimming in a Sea of Death: A Son's Memoir.* New York: Simon & Schuster.

Rowling, J.K. (1997) *The Philosopher's Stone.* London: Bloomsbury.

Saxton, T.K., Little, A.C., Rowland, H.M., Gao, T., Roberts, S.C., and Craig, S. (2009) 'Trade-offs between markers of absolute and relative quality in human facial preferences.' *Behavioral Ecology 20,* 5, 1133–1137.

Segal, J.C. (1979) 'Mother, sex and envy in a children's story.' *International Review of Psychoanalysis 6,* 4, 483–497.

Segal, J.C. (1985) *Phantasy in Everyday Life.* London: Pelican. Reprinted 1995, 2005, London: Karnac Books.

Segal, J.C. (1998) 'The role of a parent's illness in the emotional experience of a child: evidence from Klein's *Narrative of a Child Analysis.*' Paper written for the 80th birthday of Hanna Segal. *Psychodynamic Counselling 4,* 487–504. Available at www.tandfonline.com/doi/abs/10.1080/13533339808402525, accessed on 3 February 2017.

Segal, J.C. (2009) 'Flirting with death: the effects on relationships of surviving a life-threatening illness.' *Psychodynamic Practice 15,* 1, 77–83. Available at www.tandfonline.com/doi/abs/10.1080/14753630802601546, accessed on 3 February 2017.

Segal, J.C. (2013) 'Lies about death.' *Psychodynamic Practice* 20, 1, 54–61. Available at www.tandfonline.com/doi/abs/10.1080/14753634.2013.771567, accessed on 3 February 2017.

Segal, J.C., and Simkins, J. (1993) *My Mum Needs Me: Helping Children with Ill or Disabled Parents.* London: Penguin.

Segal, J.C., and Simkins, J. (1996) *Helping Children with Ill or Disabled Parents: A Guide for Professionals.* London: Jessica Kingsley Publishers. Previously published as Segal, J.C., and Simkins, J. (1993) *My Mum Needs Me: Helping Children with Ill or Disabled Parents.* London: Penguin.

Skinner, B.F. (1948) '"Superstition" in the pigeon.' *Journal of Experimental Psychology* 38, 168–172.

Tolkien, J.R.R. (1954, 1955) *The Lord of the Rings Trilogy.* London: George Allen & Unwin.

United Nations (2006) *Convention on the Rights of Persons with Disabilities.* Available at www.un.org/disabilities/documents/convention/convoptprot-e.pdf, accessed on 3 February 2017.

Walby, S., and Allen, J. (2001) *Home Office Research Study 276. Domestic Violence, Sexual Assault and Stalking: Findings from the British Crime Survey.* Available at http://eige.europa.eu/gender-based-violence/resources/international/home-office-research-study-276-domestic-violence-sexual-assault-and-stalking-findings-british-crime-survey, accessed on 3 February 2017.

Waldstein, S.R., and Elias, M.R. (2015) *Neuropsychology of Cardiovascular Disease.* Hove: Psychology Press.

Yahav, R., Vosburgh, J., and Miller, A. (2005) 'Emotional responses of children and adolescents to parents with multiple sclerosis.' *Multiple Sclerosis* 11, 4, 464–468.

Index